Pauper Prisons, Pauper Palaces

The Victorian Poor Law in the East and West Midlands 1834-1871

Edited by Paul Carter and Kate Thompson

Matador
9 Priory Business Park,
Wistow Road, Kibworth Beauchamp,
Leicestershire. LE8 0RX
Tel: 0116 279 2299
Email: books@troubador.co.uk
Web: www.troubador.co.uk/matador
Twitter: @matadorbooks

ISBN PB: 978 1788032 605
HB: 978 1788033 046

British Library Cataloguing in Publication Data.
A catalogue record for this book is available from the British Library.

Printed and bound by CPI Group (UK) Ltd, Croydon, CR0 4YY
Typeset in 11pt Minion Pro by Troubador Publishing Ltd, Leicester, UK
First edition published 2016 by the British Association for Local History (BALH).

Matador is an imprint of Troubador Publishing Ltd

For Christine Hope Lawrence

Acknowledgements

BALH would like to thank The Friends of The National Archives for their assistance in helping to fund the *Pauper Prisons... Pauper Palaces (the Midlands)* project. We would also like to thank The National Archives for their kind permission to reproduce images from their collections (other permissions are referenced individually).

The *Pauper Prisons... Pauper Palaces (the Midlands)* project was primarily funded by the Heritage Lottery Fund (HLF). We would like to thank HLF for supporting us in all of the project activities. Without such funding the project research, project conferences and this project volume would not have been possible.

Lots of people did a great deal of work over the life of the *Pauper Prisons... Pauper Palaces (the Midlands)* project – and you know who you are. Special thanks go to Natalie Carter, project research and records officer (and much more), Christine Lawrence and Ruth Paley, BALH project managers, and Ann Morton, Friends of TNA committee member.

Contents

List of images and graphs

Front cover: 1836, extract from "The Glorious Working of the Whigs!". TNA: MH 32/60, Henry Walter Parker, correspondence and papers, 1834-1845.

1/1: Poor Rate Expenditure, England and Wales (£millions). Page 4.

1/2: Total Numbers on Relief in England and Wales by Indoor and Outdoor Relief, 1840-1870 (five year intervals). Page 11.

2/1: Bromsgrove Workhouse building. Page 22.

3/1: Letter from Thomas Marriott, Clerk to the Guardians of the Southwell Union, to the Poor Law Commission, 17 March 1841. TNA: MH 12/9526/182, f 331. Page 42.

3/2: Part of vagrant mill plan enclosed in letter from S Weightman, Southwell Poor Law Union Workhouse Master, to Robert Weale, Assistant Poor Law Commissioner. 4 November 1844. TNA: MH 12/9360/303, ff 430-433. Page 49.

3/3: Model of Southwell Union vagrants' mill (built by Derek Wileman). Page 51.

3/4: Part of vagrant mill plan enclosed in letter from S Weightman, Southwell Poor Law Union Workhouse Master, to Robert Weale, Assistant Poor Law Commissioner. 4 November 1844. TNA: MH 12/9360/303, ff 430-433. Page 51.

4/1: Example of one of the forms to be completed by the parish and passed to the central authority via the board of guardians. Letter from Henry Saunders, Clerk to the Guardians of the Kidderminster Poor Law Union, to the Poor Law Commission, enclosing copies from the vestry book concerning the emigration [of Lucy Webb and family]. 22 June 1844. TNA: MH 12/14018/130, ff 214-216. Page 59.

5/1: Map of the Bromsgrove Poor Law Union (giving names of parishes). Page 79.

5/2: Printed Vaccination Poster, 1845. TNA: MH 12/13907/8, f 13. Page 91.

5/3: Report from Alfred Austin, Assistant Poor Law Commissioner, to the Poor Law Commission. 28 October 1844. Ground Plan of Bromsgrove Poor Law Union Workhouse. A: Old Men's yard; B: Old Women's yard; C: Hospital; D: Ward containing old men's and children's day rooms; E: Ward containing old and young women's day rooms; 40: Well supplying pumps a and b; 41-44: Tanks. TNA: MH 12/13906/234, ff 395-399. Page 97.

6/1: The Hand family grave in St George's Churchyard Newcastle under Lyme. Page 119.

9.1: A portrait of Thomas Day, clerk to the guardians of the Bromsgrove Poor Law Union. Page 202.

9.2: Interior of a Broomsgrove nailmaker's shed. Page 212.

Abbreviations used in footnotes:

GRO:	General Registry Office
NA:	Nottinghamshire Archives
OLSA:	Oldham Local Studies and Archives
PP:	Parliamentary Papers
SRO:	Staffordshire Record Office
SSTAS:	Staffordshire and Stoke on Trent Archive Service
TNA:	The National Archives
WAAS:	Worcestershire Archives and Archaeology Service

Preface

This book is a product of the *Pauper Prisons... Pauper Palaces (Midlands)* (PPPPM) project which has been managed over the last few years by the British Association for Local History. The archival work was undertaken by a group of around 100 local historians across the Midlands who were interested in examining the lives of poor people in the nineteenth century.[1] The main source which the following accounts originate from is the huge poor law union correspondence series of records held at The National Archives (TNA) in Kew. The poor law union correspondence rivals, if not eclipses, the Victorian census as the domestic archival nineteenth century *tour de force* and provides some of the most detailed accounts of the lives of ordinary English and Welsh men, women and children.

Project members painstakingly read through each piece of correspondence for the various poor law unions of Basford, Bromsgrove, Kidderminster, Mansfield, Newcastle under Lyme and Wolstanton and Burslem (the Southwell correspondence had been listed earlier). A catalogue entry was then created, noting names, places and subject matters, and entered into the TNA online Discovery Catalogue. Once listed and made available via the TNA catalogue it seemed only fitting that the first fruit of this research should be undertaken and published by PPPPM project members.[2]

In Britain we are currently in the process of redefining welfare. The banking crisis which began in 2007 has been seen as the starting point for economic austerity, cuts to public services

---

1   Many project members also worked on the earlier *Living the Poor Life* project run by The National Archives between 2008 and 2010.
2   The correspondence for Basford, Bromsgrove, Kidderminster, Mansfield, Newcastle under Lyme and Wolstanton and Burslem have now been catalogued from 1834 to 1871. The correspondence for Southwell is catalogued from 1834 to 1900.

and a contraction of welfare. Notwithstanding the banking crisis, modern governments in Western Europe are regularly faced with questions about welfare; who should receive it, how much should they receive, when and how should they receive it, and who pays? The answers to these questions are as much political as economic decisions. The answers are as much about what kind of society a government believes is desirable as they are about what can be afforded. The questions we may pose about current welfare issues such as the levels of unemployment benefit, pensions for the elderly, medical services for those with mental or physical health problems; we may also ask of past societies as we enquire what their governments thought desirable.

The chapters that follow seek to throw a bright light on the sometimes dark sides of Victorian history by concentrating on specific aspects of the New Poor Law. In this volume project members engage with the archive in regard to such topics as working for welfare, the movement of 'excess' labour, the nature and limits of public health concerns, local government as an employer, and the fate of widowed welfare recipients. These issues, then and now, remind us of just how close we still are to the Victorian world. These accounts are far more than simple local accounts of towns, villages or individuals. For here we see national politics and government administration intersect with the lives of ordinary people.

Paul Carter, Nether Broughton
Kate Thompson, Letchworth Garden City
April 2017

1.

Reconstructing Welfare: The Management of Pauperism, 1834 to 1871

Paul Carter

In the late summer of 1834 the British parliament passed the Poor Law Amendment Act.[3] Over the next few years the 'New Poor Law' workhouse system spread across England and Wales. The changes were designed to be far reaching. Indeed, the New Poor Law was indicative of a change in the way government sought to govern. Under the legislation of 1834 poor relief moved from being a largely local concern, where discretion reigned supreme, to one in which government pursued policies to bring increasing centralisation and supervision to bear. David Eastwood sees this period in domestic history as one where a

> ...body of centralizing and proscriptive reforming statutes was being elaborated. The classic example was the 1834 Poor Law Amendment Act, which imposed new agencies at both central and local level, but similar principles were being applied to factory, education and prison reform.[4]

While undoubtedly the poor law after 1834 was a feature of government centralisation, the local experience of poverty could differ markedly, as this centralisation was unevenly secured.

---

3   4 & 5 Will. 4 c. 76. *An Act for the Amendment and better Administration of the Laws relating to the Poor in England and Wales*, 1834.
4   Eastwood, D. Government and Community in the English Provinces, 1700-1870, Macmillan Press Limited, 1997, p 160.

This partly explains the huge New Poor Law historiography which faces the student of nineteenth century welfare.

We should be clear from the outset that the history of the New Poor Law is not the history of the workhouse, although these are clearly intertwined. The history of the workhouse does not begin in 1834 as the workhouse as an institution was not a new feature in Victorian Britain. Workhouses had been built and used as part of the pre-1834 Old Poor Law. The Elizabethan poor laws stated that parishes should set the able bodied poor to work. Some towns did this through the provision of a building in which work activities could be organised. From the late seventeenth century Bristol, Exeter, Hereford, Colchester, King's Lynn, Gloucester and Plymouth built workhouses. An act of 1723, aimed at several areas of poor law provision, encouraged parishes to build workhouses. This act, foreshadowing the legislation of 1834, allowed local poor law authorities to apply the workhouse test, where those refusing an offer of 'the house' could be denied any further assistance.[5] In 1725 it was reckoned that there were 126 such workhouse establishments and in 1732 this had risen to 181; it was likely most of these were built prior to the act of 1723.[6] These figures have been regarded as an under-estimation of the scale of workhouse provision and Paul Slack has put the figure of workhouses at this time to be nearer 700.[7] By 1777 a parliamentary inquiry declared there were 1,916 workhouses housing over 90,000 paupers.[8] In 1782 Thomas Gilbert introduced an act that allowed parishes to combine into 'unions' for building and maintaining workhouses. Although

---

5   9 Geo. I, c 7. *For Amending the Laws relating to the Settlement, Imployment and Relief of the Poor*, 1723. The act gave parish authorities the right to refuse further relief to those who were offered a place in the workhouse.
6   An Account of Several Work-Houses for Employing and Maintaining the Poor, 1st ed., 1725, 2nd ed., 1732. See Hitchcock, T. 'Paupers and Preachers: The SPCK and the Parochial Workhouse Movement', in Lee Davison et al (eds), Stilling the Grumbling Hive: The Response to Social and Economic Problems, 1688-1750, Alan Sutton, 1992, pp 145-166.
7   Slack, P. The English Poor Law, 1531-1782, 1990, p 42.
8   Hitchcock, 'Paupers and Preachers', p 145.

not mandatory, some 1,000 parishes had formed into 68 Gilbert Unions by 1834 and we can therefore see that workhouses had a considerable history under the Old Poor Law.[9]

The Old Poor Law provided a largely mandatory system of publicly financed poor relief across England and Wales. The local unit of government responsible for the supervision and management of poverty was the parish.[10] Funds for the poor were raised through a local land tax, the poor rate, and this was paid by the occupiers of parish lands. Recipients were also local, and paupers were relieved by the parish in which they had a legal settlement determined by several criteria such as by birth, marriage or how long they had resided in a particular place. Most relief under the Old Poor Law was provided outside the workhouse, either as regular pensions or as irregular casual payments in money or in kind. The day to day administration of the system fell to the unpaid parish overseers of the poor and churchwardens, under the broader control of local magistrates. Although poor law expenditure increased in the seventeenth and eighteenth centuries, the simple land tax revenue raising and mixture of pensionable or casual and indoor and outdoor relief parish model, remained relevant until the crisis of the 1790s when poor harvests, high food prices, a rising population and war with France, combined to push poor rates ever higher.[11] Poor relief expenditure, which had been below £1 million annually in the mid-eighteenth century increased to £1.5 million by 1776, £2 million in the first half of the 1780s and £4.3 million by 1803. By the middle of the 1790s the political upheavals abroad and war with France combined to create a strong sense of crisis within the poor law system. Increases in the price of foodstuffs went hand

---

9   22 Geo. III c 83, For the Better Relief and Employment of the Poor, 1782. See also Driver, F. Power and Pauperism: The Workhouse System, 1834-1884, Cambridge University Press, pp 42-44.
10   In the northern counties many parishes were large and were divided into townships for poor law purposes.
11   Lees, L. H. The Solidarities of Strangers: The English Poor Laws and the People, 1700-1948, 1998, Cambridge University Press, p 25.

in hand with both unemployment and underemployment. Fear of radical politics and the social disorder of the time provided an atmosphere in which magistrates and parish officials could agree on increased levels of poor relief. Some parishes began to give some of their labourers, who were in full employment but unable to provide for their family's needs, an allowance from parish funds to top up their wages. The most well-known instance of this was when magistrates met at Speenhamland near Newbury in Berkshire in May 1795 to establish a sliding scale of poor relief benefit dependent upon the price of bread and the size of the labourer's family. Although not all allowance systems were strict in linking amounts of money with the costs of foodstuffs and family size, they became an indispensable and widespread (but by no means universal) mechanism which saw monies collected through the poor rates used to supplement inadequate wages.[12] By the end of the Napoleonic Wars the annual poor relief bill stood at £6.9 million and peaked in 1818 at £7.9 million. It remained stubbornly high in the 1820s and 1830s, constantly around the £6 million to £6.5 million mark.[13]

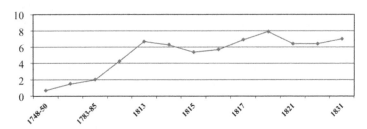

Figure 1/1: Poor Rate Expenditure, England and Wales (£millions).

Such increases in expenditure did not go unnoticed or uncommented upon and the debates ranged between the

12   Eastwood, Government and Community, pp 130-131; Poynter, J.R. Society and Pauperism, English Ideas on Poor Relief, 1795-1834, Routledge and Kegan Paul, 1969, pp 76-85.
13   Mitchell, R. B. and Deane, P. Abstract of British Historical Statistics, Cambridge University Press, 1962, p 410.

abolition or reform of the poor laws.[14] In the late 1790s the Reverend Thomas Malthus argued that the increase in population was outstripping food production. He criticised the poor laws for making more paupers by seeking to guarantee subsistence for all, thus making a bad situation worse.[15] Social commentators such as Jeremy Bentham, Patrick Colquhoun and William Cobbett all had much to say about the pros and cons of the poor laws and in the first three decades of the nineteenth century parliament investigated, collated data and reported on the various parts of poor law legislation on several occasions, but there was little central government activity. In 1818 and 1819 parliament passed legislation which amongst other things gave more power to the larger landowners in the elections of select vestries and also reduced the power of magistrates to overturn select vestries' decisions.[16] The 1820s saw experimentation in poor relief practices particularly around Upton, Southwell and Bingham in Nottinghamshire. Here the able bodied were to be forced to '…provide for themselves through the terror of a well-disciplined workhouse'. The local poor law authorities were to act as the '…most harsh and unkind friend' and the poor were to lose their '…independence and self-respect…' in applying for relief. Similar instances of the deterrent workhouse were also promoted in Berkshire, Hertfordshire, Gloucestershire, Cornwall and Derbyshire.[17]

Legislative intervention on a national scale was precipitated by the Swing riots of 1830-31. The thousands of 'Swing' activities such as sending threatening letters, incendiarism and the destruction of agricultural (and other) machinery, primarily

---

14   See Poynter, Society and Pauperism.
15   Englander, D. Poverty and Poor Law Reform in 19th Century Britain, 1834-1914, Longman, pp 7-9 .
16   Poynter, Society and Pauperism, pp 285-286; 58 Geo. III c. 69. Act for the Regulation of Parish Vestries (Vestries Act 1818), and 59 Geo. III c.12. Act to Amend the Law for the Relief of the Poor (Poor Relief Act 1819).
17   Lees, Solidarities of Strangers, pp 109-110; Brundage, A. The English Poor Laws, 1700-1930, Palgrave, pp 52-57.

in the south-east and East Anglia, but also scattered across the West Country and the midlands, illustrated in the clearest way possible the detrimental effect of enclosure, the restriction of boarding farm servants, and the devastating mixture of unemployment and underemployment which had reduced the living standards of rural labour in preceding generations. The contentious subject of the poor laws were not overlooked by those involved in the disturbances and historians have found properties of overseers and assistant overseers targeted by incendiaries and some workhouses damaged or destroyed during the riots.[18] Most historians agree that Swing did not constitute a radical political movement but it is possible to see that the disturbances led to a political climate in which a root and branch reform of the poor laws was possible. The 1834 Poor Law Amendment Act was possible after the disturbances of 1830-31 in a way in which such reform was not possible before. The sheer number of arson attacks, threatening letters, wage riots and attacks on machinery 'were seared into the memory of many M.P.s who consequently felt the need to restore the social fabric of the countryside'.[19]

In the aftermath of Swing, 19 people were executed, around 500 transported to Australia and more than 600 imprisoned.[20] The perceived maladministration of the poor laws, seen as a prelude to the disturbances, ensured the government would act over the issue of poor law reform. In 1832 a *Royal Commission into the Operation of the Poor Laws* was established, ostensibly to investigate and report on poor law practices in order that the government could consider what legislative changes might be made, but more likely to provide evidence to support proposed measures which were already being developed.[21] The *Royal*

---

18   Brundage, English Poor Laws, pp 58-59.
19   Brundage, A. The Making of the New Poor Law, 1832-39, Hutchinson University Library, 1978, p 15.
20   Hobsbawn E.J. and Rude, G. Captain Swing, Lawrence and Wishart, 1969, p 262.
21   Blaug, M. (1963). 'The Myth of the Old Poor Law and the Making of

Commission reported in 1834 and recommended a series of measures. The most important of these was that individual parishes were to be joined together into new local government units, styled poor law unions.[22] These unions would share workhouses designed and built for different categories of paupers. The unions would be governed by elected guardians and poverty managed by a professional staff of workhouse masters and mistresses, clerks, and a plethora of rate collecting, relieving and medical officers. Outdoor relief was to continue for the aged and infirm but was to be abolished for the able bodied labourer who would be offered the house. Conditions in the workhouse were to be 'less eligible' than that of the lowest paid labourer in order to make the workhouse a feared institution of last resort. The *Royal Commission*, in a now well-known passage from their report, proclaimed that

> The first and most essential of all conditions, a principle which we find universally admitted, even by those whose practice is at variance with it, is, that his [the able bodied pauper] situation on the whole shall not be made really or apparently so eligible as the situation of the independent labourer of the lowest class.[23]

In London a new central bureaucracy, the Poor Law Commission, was to be created to oversee the New Poor Law and to force, encourage and cajole the newly created unions into delivering a national and uniform system of relief.[24] The *Royal Commission's*

---

the New', Journal of Economic History, 23, pp 176-177.

22   Although parishes were brought together for poor law purposes under the Poor Law Amendment Act individuals parishes still paid for their paupers proportionally until 28 & 29, Vict., c 79. Union Chargeability Act, 1865. Until then common charges related to items such as the building and the upkeep of the workhouse and union officers' salaries.

23   Report from *His Majesty's Commissioners for Inquiring into the Administration and Practical Operation of the Poor Laws*, p 127. PP., 1834.

24   From 1834 this was the Poor Law Commission, from 1848 the Poor Law Board, and from mid-1871 the Local Government Board. For ease of use we will all use the generic 'central authority' as necessary.

report was published in February 1834 and this was followed quickly by the Poor Law Amendment Act which received its assent on 14 August 1834. On 23 August Thomas Frankland Lewis, John George Shaw Lefevre and George Nicholls, the first three poor law commissioners, sat down with Edwin Chadwick, their secretary, at the first board meeting and began constructing a new world for the poor. Thus began the work of the legislation that was not only the most important piece of nineteenth century social legislation enacted, but has also been one of the most controversial areas of later historical study.[25]

The early meetings of the Poor Law Commission were spent appointing their administrative staff, answering queries from parish officers and magistrates and sending out circulars setting out the business of the Commission itself. Slowly but surely, the Commission appointed the assistant commissioners whose role would include travelling through the districts to which they were appointed to meet local landowners and decide/negotiate union boundaries. Such work was necessarily slow and the resulting unions were often dependent on the desires of landowning elites who wished to shape the unions in which their lands were situated, which in turn would help to maintain their local and regional influence. Furthermore, existing Gilbert Unions had to be physically worked around if they were unwilling to dissolve themselves, as the Commission had no power to break them up.[26]

As well as setting the new boundaries for poor relief management the New Poor Law experimented in moving paupers into areas where better employment prospects were thought to be available. If the poor were pauperised in their own locality then why not move them to a place where jobs were

25   Englander, Poverty and Poor Law Reform, p 1; Laybourn, K. The Evolution of British Social Policy and the Welfare State, 1800-1993, 1995, Keele University Press, p 15.
26   Crowther, M.A. The Workhouse System, 1834-1929: The History of an English Social Institution, University of Georgia Press, 1981, p 45; Brundage, English Poor Laws, pp 71-72.

more abundant? The New Poor Law allowed for both migration and emigration schemes. Chadwick maintained there was no surplus population, only pockets of idle rural labour which needed moving to urban and industrial towns and cities. The unpopular and short-lived Migration Agency was abolished in 1838. Emigration was used in greater but not huge numbers. In 1834-35 there were only 320 assisted emigrants through the poor law system although this increased in 1835-36 when there were as many as 5,241.[27] The majority of these came from Norfolk which experienced what one historian has styled an 'emigration fever' in that year. Nevertheless, emigration through the poor law was a minor activity with an average of around 1,000 per annum between 1836 and 1860.[28]

Notwithstanding this busy administrative work, Anne Crowther has commented that 'The early years of the New Poor Law arouse that peculiar fascination which comes with watching an elaborately devised machine fail to start'.[29] It is certainly the case that the new arrangements for managing pauperism found themselves opposed and unionisation a slow process. In the north the anti-poor law movement resisted the New Poor Law in places such as Bolton, Bradford, Bury, Huddersfield, Keighley, Oldham, Preston and Todmorden. Here the workers' short time committees, which had campaigned over factory reform, took up the issue of the 'New Bastilles' as the workhouses came to be called. Speaking for many, Bronterre O'Brien claimed the new law was passed to position '… the whole of the labouring population at the utter mercy and disposal of the monied or property owning classes'.[30] The anti-poor law movement itself

---

27   Brundage, English Poor Laws, pp 100-101.
28   Howells, G. 'Emigration and the New Poor Law: The Norfolk Emigration Fever of 1836', Rural History: Economy, Society, Culture, 11 (2), 2000, p 146.
29   Crowther, Workhouse System, p 30.
30   Rose, M. E. 'The Anti-Poor Law Agitation', in Ward, J.T. ed., Popular Movements c. 1830-1850, MacMillan Press, 1970, p 81.

was an important part of forging late 1830s Chartism.[31] Indeed, Edward Royle points to 1838-39 as the period in which the anti-poor law movement moved to Chartism, '...taking with it a legacy of organisation, leadership, experience, and hatred'.[32] However, the Poor Law Commission was dealing with the politics of the possible and as an administrative body had, as we have seen, been putting the administrative pieces into place. The Poor Law Commission was given an initial life of five years when it commenced in 1834. In 1839 this was renewed annually and then in 1844 it was extended for an additional three years. During this time a host of workhouse scandals were reported through the Chartist and radical press, provincial newspapers and *The Times*.[33] The most well-known of these was the Andover scandal. News in 1845 of inmates gnawing on rotten bones, which they had been given to crush for the production of fertiliser, was reported in the press, raised in parliament and was the subject of a select committee. In 1846 the damning parliamentary report found that diets were lower than even the 'less eligible' dietaries laid down by the Poor Law Commission. Paupers were thus forced to seek what marrow and gristle might be afforded from the rotting bones allocated to them as part of their work. [34] The scandal brought the Poor Law Commission to an end. However, it did not bring the New Poor Law to an end. In 1847 the Poor Law Board, which consisted of four senior ministers, was created, thus giving a more direct link to government and parliament.[35] By the early 1850s the New Poor Law was in place, established and fully functioning.

---

31   See Edsall, N.C. The Anti-Poor Law Movement, 1834-44, Manchester University Press, 1971, pp 167-186; Knott, J. Popular Opposition to the 1834 Poor Law, Croom Helm, 1986, pp 129-144. Wright, D.G. Popular Radicalism: The Working-Class Experience, 1780-1880, Longman Group, 1988, pp 106-111.

32   Royle, E. Chartism, Longman Group, 1986, 2nd ed., 1986, p 16.

33   Brundage, English Poor Laws, p 87.

34   Anstruther, I. The Scandal of the Andover Workhouse, Geoffrey Bles, 1973.

35   Brundage, English Poor Laws, pp 88-89.

Although the workhouse looms large in the historiography of the New Poor Law we should understand that only a small proportion of English and Welsh paupers, were relieved in such institutions. Centrally collected figures suggest one in seven paupers in the mid-1840s was a workhouse inmate and in the early 1860s this had fallen to around one in eight.[36] However, these figures do not diminish the significance of the Victorian workhouse. The workhouse, and in particular its ability to deter applicants, was always a central feature of the New Poor Law which was aimed at able bodied labourers and their families. The act sought to repel applications for relief, not encourage them.

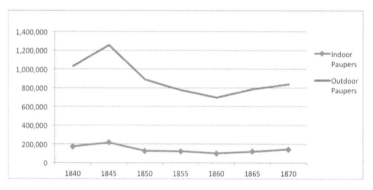

Figure 1/2: Total Numbers on Relief in England and Wales by Indoor and Outdoor Relief, 1840-1870 (five year intervals).

Historians have pointed out that the workhouse test set up unresolvable tensions. How was an 'institution simultaneously [to] deter the able-bodied poor while acting as a humane refuge for the ailing and helpless?'.[37] Deterrence was a key aspect of the new system and was regarded as being as important as settlement and entitlement, rating procedures and the auditing of union funds. As the Commission made plain in its recorded minutes of meetings, the only remedy for the '...ultimate

---

36   Figures taken from Williams, K. From Pauperism to Poverty, Routledge and Kegan Paul, 1981, pp 157-158.
37   Crowther, Workhouse System, p 3.

extinction of the various evils which have been generated by the faulty administration of the poor laws is The Workhouse System'.[38]

The Poor Law Commission had called for the continued use of some of the pre-existing parish workhouses, which would allow for different categories of paupers within the same union to be contained separately.[39] This idea was abandoned and the Commission urged boards of guardians to construct new large union workhouses which would be more than functional institution buildings. Sir Francis Head, an early assistant poor law commissioner, proclaimed that

> The very sight of a well-built efficient establishment would give confidence to the Board of Guardians; the sight and weekly assemblage of all servants of their Union would make them proud of their office; the appointment of a chaplain would give dignity to the whole arrangement, while the pauper would feel it was utterly impossible to contend against it.[40]

E C Tufnell, another early assistant poor law commissioner, proclaimed his support for the deterrent workhouse. He praised the workhouses' similar appearance to the prison 'and the notion that they are intended to torment the poor, [which] inspires a salutary dread of them'.[41] Inside the workhouse walls paupers were to be classified, separated from family, fed a boring and unimaginative diet, uniformed, set to work breaking stones, picking oakum or undertaking domestic work, and live under the command of the union officials.

---

38   TNA: MH 1/1, Poor Law Commission, Minute Book, 4 November 1834.

39   Report from *His Majesty's Commissioners for Inquiring into the Poor Laws*, p 314. PP., 1834; Brundage, Making, pp 94-95.

40   Among the first four appointed assistant poor law commissioners on 28 October 1834 he served for a year before resigning. Brundage, Making, p 82. Webb, S. and Webb, B. English Poor Law History: Part II: The Last Hundred Years, Vol I, with an introduction by W A Robson (1929/1963), pp 122-127.

41   Lees, Solidarities of Strangers, p 148.

Although the administration for the New Poor Law was carefully being put into place, the very early years saw the Poor Law Commission having to balance its principles with those of local administrators. The wording around 'able-bodied' in the legislation allowed many boards of guardians to retain traditional local authority and in this sense there was significant continuity between the old and new poor laws. As the central administration established its authority and found considerable diversity in relief practice it sought to be more precise in its definition of 'abled-bodied' through issuing three outdoor relief directives: the 1842 Outdoor Labour Test, the 1844 Outdoor Relief Prohibitory Order and the 1852 Outdoor Relief Regulation Order. The 1842 Test allowed boards of guardians the option of employing relief claimants in the workhouse through the day for a small amount of out relief. The 1844 Order sought to tighten out relief in rural unions by insisting that all able bodied applicants and their families either supported themselves or entered the workhouse. However, the order allowed a continuation of out relief by including clauses around cases of sudden and urgent necessity, or sickness, accident or infirmity, or a death in the family. Such clauses allowed for discussion, digression and interpretation rather than setting out clear and specific rules. In effect, the order may have increased diverse poor law practice in rural unions rather than diminished it.[42] The urban 1852 Outdoor Relief Regulation Order sought to standardise regulations relating to out relief. In August the issued order included restrictions relating to the sick, aged and widows; this was new. However, following protests from boards of guardians a revised order was issued in December which reverted to dealing with able-bodied males.

Lyn Holland Lees considers the change from the 'Old' to the 'New' Poor Law to be one where 'Work became a punishment,

---

42   Lees, Solidarities of Strangers, p 201. Further exceptions were made in regard to widowhood or where a person was married to, or a child of, a soldier, sailor or marine.

rather than a means of support' and that from 1834 to the 1860s '...a much more strongly disciplinary style of welfare was widely adopted in England and Wales.[43] By 1871, in around half of the unions, men could only get outdoor relief by undertaking tasks which were '...difficult and nasty' by design. Breaking stones, digging ditches, grinding corn by hand, clearing rubbish from canals; the idea that work brought discipline crystallised and passed into practice. Even at times when it was clear that there were no jobs and thousands were unemployed the guardians feared a subsidy on idleness and thus imposed labour tests.[44]

By the 1850s the New Poor Law was solidly in place but did not remain a static system. Provisions for the expansion of poor law education and medical services were secured, although these were uneven in practice. Old Poor Law parish workhouses had done little if anything in terms of pauper education although some cities had schools of industry which provided rudimentary reading, writing and arithmetic. The 1832 *Royal Commission* had thought separate buildings would be provided for schooling but the general mixed workhouse, which quickly came into being after 1834, meant that education for pauper children struggled. Many boards were reluctant to allow funds, workhouse teacher salaries were low, added to which they often had to live in and to undertake additional duties. Part of the reticence of the boards can be explained by objections to pauper children having a better education than the children of labouring families. This appeared to benefit pauper families and invert the principle of less eligibility.[45] The pay and conditions of the workhouse teachers were not conducive to attracting and keeping dedicated and knowledgeable individuals. In the early years after 1834 teachers were usually unqualified, but from 1848 the situation improved when the Treasury started to make grants to union schools based on a teacher's qualifications

---

43   Lees, Solidarities of Strangers, p 114.
44   Ibid, p 146.
45   Brundage, English Poor Laws, pp 92-94.

and competence.[46] Workhouse schools were mainly relatively small and some of the assistant commissioners had preferred the idea of larger schools where the pauper pupils from across several unions would be graded, classified and taught in classes according to their ability. Early plans for the creation of large district schools to accommodate these ideas came to nothing and it was only in early 1848 that the Poor law Board secured the District Schools Act which, after some activity in the southeast, quickly ran out of steam as a national initiative. Some improvements overall may be charted; so in 1847 37% of male workhouse teachers received the higher certificates and by 1857 the figure had increased to 64%.[47] Whatever improvements were made the transient lives of workhouse children meant their education stopped and started when they entered or left the workhouse. Because of this real improvement came only with Forster's Education Act in 1870, at which time pauper children could attend local board of education schools.[48]

In the Poor Law Amendment Act 1834 medical services were originally envisaged only to apply to workhouse inmates. However, local guardians were used to contracting for medical men to provide medical care for all of those claiming relief to ensure sick individuals could re-enter the workforce and be removed from the rates. Initially local boards of guardians would contract annually for the lowest amount possible. Medical officers were contracted to serve both inmates and outdoor relief claimants. Following the General Medical Order 1842 contracts gave way to salaried appointments.[49] The reputations of workhouse medical officers were mixed. They were not the most senior of the union officers and their recommendations for sickly paupers to receive wine, brandy, better food, clothes etc. were resisted by workhouse masters, guardians and the

46   Crowther, Workhouse System, p 131.
47   Brundage, English Poor Laws, p 95.
48   33 & 34 Vict., c 75. *Elementary Education Act*, 1870.
49   Brundage, English Poor Laws, p 96.

central authority.[50] In such cases medical officers battled for their patients against individuals and bodies who measured healthcare against strict ideas of budgets and rate levels.[51] Other medical officers were poorly qualified and incompetent, but such inadequacies in care were overshadowed by the standards in nursing.[52] Although some unions appointed paid nurses the profession itself was hardly in existence in 1834. The result was that most unions used pauper inmates as nurses, a practice which continued until prohibited by the Local Government Board in 1897.[53] A further important area of medical history also linked to the New Poor Law is that of the care of people with mental health problems. Indeed, Peter Bartlett has recently considered that 'the nineteenth century asylum is to be understood in the context of the nineteenth century Poor Law'.[54] Throughout the middle decades of the nineteenth century workhouses were a major institutional resource for the accommodation of the insane. The report of the 1832 *Royal Commission* said little on the subject of county asylums although some assistant commissioners did refer to the desirability of such institutions for insane paupers. Dangerously insane paupers were to be sent to asylums, but those seen as non-dangerous were allowed to be held in union workhouses. Many boards of guardians kept insane paupers in the workhouse as costs were thought to be lower than in an asylum. County asylums were made mandatory in 1845 although this did not mean workhouses lost their role in

---

50   Brundage, English Poor Laws, pp 97.
The Poor Law Commission had considered giving guardians the powers to ignore the medical officers' recommendations but then rejected the notion. See Crowther, Workhouse System, p 159.
51   Brundage, English Poor Laws, pp 96-97; Crowther, Workhouse System, p 159.
52   Wood, P. Poverty and the Workhouse in Victorian Britain, Allan Sutton, 1991, p 111.
53   Brundage, English Poor Laws, p 97; Crowther, Workhouse System, pp 165-167.
54   Bartlett, P. The Poor Law of Lunacy: The Administration of Pauper Lunatics in Nineteenth-Century England Leicester University Press, 1999. p 32.

providing accommodation for insane paupers. In the late 1840s and early 1850s the numbers of workhouse inmates regarded as insane fell but then rose again as the asylums filled up. Some unions remained ill-equipped to house pauper lunatics while others began to provide lunatic wards. [55]

The development of education and health services may give us a false sense of an ever improving Victorian welfare system. Undoubtedly, along with the scandals and cases of neglect and cruelty, many guardians and union officers sought to improve the material lives of individual paupers. However, the 1860s saw an increase in outdoor relief which brought a terrible hostile response and re-assertion of the principles of 1834. Towards the very end of the 1860s the Poor Law Board began to frame a new chilling poor law regime known as the 'Crusade Against Outdoor Relief'. This would be to create what one historian has styled '...a world without welfare'. The policy, which was to cut outdoor relief payments, was taken forward as the Poor Law Board's responsibilities were merged in a new government department. The Local Government Board saw the Poor Law Board, the Medical Departments of the Privy Council, Local Government Act Office and the General Register Office come together. The 'crusade' launched by the Local Government Board takes us past the chronological span of this volume but reminds us that welfare policy is a political beast. [56] The 'crusade' was a most dramatic policy and reminds us that welfare policies have historically been fickle, short lived and prone to dramatic changes. The following chapters take us beyond the purview of an overarching synopsis to examples of individual case histories.

---

55   Bartlett, The Poor Law of Lunacy, pp 41-42; Brundage, English Poor Laws, pp 99-100.
56   For a recent account of the crusade against outdoor relief see Hurren, E.T. Protesting about Pauperism: Poverty, Politics and Poor Relief in Late-Victorian England, c. 1870-1914, Boydell and Brewer, 2007.

2

Staffing Issues in a Closed Institution: The Bromsgrove Union Case of 1863

David Finlow

Historians have often commented upon the difficulty faced by workhouse staff in the post 1834 period. We can see that the routine imposed on pauper inmates meant that a routine was thus also imposed on staff. We can also see that the workhouse was to a relatively high degree a closed institution with little contact with the world outside. This forced seclusion was a deliberate move on the part of the Poor Law Commissioners in regard to the pauper inmates but it also had the less intended effect of throwing together the small number of workhouse staff with few breaks and little opportunity for mixing with other (non-pauper) people.[57] Not only could the relationships of the few indoor staff lead to a claustrophobic atmosphere but the strict hierarchy meant the establishment of a pecking order, with the post of workhouse master dominating the other officers whose continued employment could be jeopardised by a complaint from him.[58]

There was therefore a structural element built into the way in which workhouse staff were bound together for long periods, during which time the hierarchical structure could lead to disagreements or personality clashes which in turn could lead to low level bickering or squabbling, violent arguments or forceful confrontations which made continued employment of all parties impossible. Undoubtedly there were many occasions

---

57   Crowther, Workhouse System, p 114.
58   Ibid, p 130.

when disputes were managed locally and with little fuss. At other times these antagonisms spilled over and became known in the wider locality and needed the intervention of the central authority.

One such example of this can be found in the Bromsgrove Poor Law Union in Worcestershire. Towards the end of 1863, the workhouse was, in the words of the guardians

> ... in a disturbed and unsatisfactory state......(with)....an increased amount of insubordination growing up among the inmates.[59]

The deterioration of standards in the workhouse began in the early part of 1863 when a series of events occurred which, although seemingly trivial, took up a good deal of the guardians' time as well as that of the Poor Law Board. The incidents centre on the disagreements which arose between the schoolmistress and a newly appointed matron.

Despite the somewhat trivial nature of the disagreements they are of real interest to the welfare historian and raise questions for further investigation at a number of levels and for a number of reasons. Firstly, the case provokes general questions concerning conditions of employment and what, if any, legal protection of employment was enjoyed by workhouse staff. Secondly, the case raises specific questions as to why the guardians did not foresee problems arising at the stage of appointing the matron. Thirdly, the case illustrates the way in which the official poor law correspondence gives a clear insight into life in the workhouse. The correspondence between the Bromsgrove guardians and the Poor Law Board in London gives one perspective on the situation, and comments from the Board's inspector enhances these more official insights. In

---

59   WAAS: b251/BA 400/6, Bromsgrove Guardians Minute Book, 1856-1865, 10 November 1863.

addition, the letters from both the matron and the schoolmistress give an unusually clear narrative and first-hand account of the day to day happenings from the workhouse officers themselves.

Let us then turn to the events at mid-century Bromsgrove. Until 1862 the workhouse master was John Aurelius Rose while the matron was Mary Ann Kings. In fact Kings had been matron since late 1844 prior to which she had been a dress-maker and, during her late husband's life, had kept an inn at Stourbridge. She was, unusually for the time, never employed as one of a married couple, and her time as matron saw her paired with four separate masters: William Owen, Henry Horton, Samuel Clarke and finally Rose. With the resignations of both Rose and Kings in 1862 the guardians took the opportunity to employ a married couple as master and matron; the first time the posts were joined in such a way since 1844. The appointments of Joseph and Anne Pope were confirmed in December 1862. The Popes had been previously employed as master and matron at the Penkridge Poor Law Union, in Staffordshire, at its workhouse in Brewood. Before that Anne had been a schoolmistress, also at the workhouse at Penkridge.[60] So much then for the matron; we now turn to the Bromsgrove schoolmistress in this case. Elizabeth Dance had been the schoolmistress since her appointment in July 1859 when she moved to Bromsgrove from the Droitwich Poor Law Union where she had held a similar post.[61]

The potential for tensions which the guardians might have foreseen lay in two additional employment details. We have already seen that prior to her appointment as workhouse matron, Mrs Pope's employment at the Brewood Workhouse had been as the schoolmistress. In addition, prior to the

---

60   TNA: MH 12/13912/78, ff 101-104. Letter from Thomas Day, Clerk to the Guardians of the Bromsgrove Poor Law Union, to the Poor Law Board. 27 December 1862.
61   TNA: MH 12/13911/385, ff 553-554. Appointment form for Elizabeth Dance. 29 September 1859.

appointment of Mrs Pope, the then matron at Bromsgrove had been quite seriously ill and the guardians had asked Miss Dance to undertake a significant number of her duties. This meant that a situation had evolved in the Bromsgrove workhouse where, with the appointment of Anne Pope, the matron had recently been a schoolmistress and the schoolmistress had been virtually an acting-matron.

This may have been enough to initiate problems, but the roles of the two posts, schoolmistress and workhouse matron, involved a good deal of overlap and role ambiguity. Whilst each union could undoubtedly instruct its officers as to the work needed to be done we can see the official roles intermixed tasks of both matrons and schoolmistresses and thus areas of potential conflict were inbuilt. For example the matron was to oversee the employment and occupation of female paupers, to assist the schoolmistress in training up the children so as best to fit them for service, to see they were clean and decent in their dress and persons, to pay particular attention to the moral conduct and orderly behaviour of the females and children, see they were clean and decent in their dress and persons, to take proper care of the children and sick paupers, and to provide the proper diet for the same. The role of the school-teacher, male and female, included the regulation of discipline and arrangements of the school, the industrial and moral training of the children, to keep the children clean in their persons and orderly in their conduct, and to assist the master and matron in maintaining subordination in the workhouse.[62]

The working environment for these two officers was that of a closed and crowded community. In 1861 the census reported 92 inmates and that only five officers, the master, matron, schoolteacher, nurse and porter, were onsite.[63] However, the number of inmates could fluctuate wildly and in October 1861

---

62   *Consolidated General Order of the Poor Law Commission*, 1847.
63   TNA: RG 9/2113, f 27, p 46–f 29, p 49. Census. 1861.

John Thomas Graves, Poor Law Inspector, reported, via his inspection report, that the workhouse capacity was 320 and the number of inmates was 217. The following June workhouse numbers had fallen to 144, although this might reflect seasonal changes to work patterns.[64]

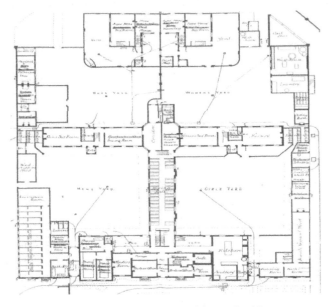

Figure 2/1: Bromsgrove Workhouse building.

The workhouse building in Bromsgrove, although having a quite large overall footprint was designed in the typical cruciform shape (see plan).[65] It had four segregated yards for the inmates, an octagonal centre to the building which gave sight to all of the courtyards and a relatively small proportion of the site was given to sleeping accommodation, school room, dining room and so

64   TNA: MH 12/13911/551, ff 755-758. Workhouse Inspection Report from John Thomas Graves, Poor Law Inspector, to the Poor Law Board. 29 October 1861; and MH 12/13912/29, ff 35-36. Workhouse Inspection Report from John Thomas Graves, Poor Law Inspector, to the Poor Law Board. 10 June 1862.
65   http://www.workhouses.org.uk/Bromsgrove/ accessed 15 January 2016.

forth. In summary then we have two officers, each having had recent experience of the other's job, duties that seem to show significant and ambiguous areas of overlap and an environment that necessitated working in close proximity within a closed, quite cramped community.

Given the inevitable tensions these factors must have created, were the guardians somewhat insensitive in appointing a matron who had been a schoolteacher? There seemed to be no shortage of suitable applicants to choose from. The minute book for 23 December 1862 shows that seven couples were in attendance and that four proposals were made for the posts of master and matron. At the first vote the guardians were split 5-5-4-1 so clearly three of the four seemed appointable. At the second vote nine guardians voted for the Popes which made them the successful applicants. Not a 'landslide victory' by any means, which might make us wonder if the guardians, or some of them at least, had foreseen the potential for conflict between these two employees. Certainly in terms of role conflict, the guardians seem to have had cause to clarify the job descriptions of the staff as early as March 1863 for the minute book for 3 March 1863 states

> The Master, Matron, Schoolmistress and Nurse severally appeared before the Board and were instructed in their several duties.[66]

Only five and a half months from the matron's appointment had passed before problems had reached the point of appearing more explicitly in the guardians' minute book.

> The Master brought unto the notice of the Board the unbecoming and insolent conduct of the Nurse. The Nurse complained of the Matron for taking charge of a sick child and

66   WAAS: b251/BA 400/6, Bromsgrove Guardians' Minute Book, 1856-1865, 3 March 1863.

for calling her a liar. The Board, after a patient investigation, deemed it proper to support the authority of the Matron and admonished the Nurse.[67]

The phrase '…after a patient investigation…' suggests both a protracted dialogue between the guardians and the complainants and also a certain weariness which, along with the earlier entry quoted above, might indicate that this was not the first instance of tension but maybe the first to be explicitly recorded. The guardians may well have come to regret their decision to deem it proper to support the matron. By the next meeting of the guardians matters had clearly not improved.

> The Master complained of the interference of the Schoolmistress in the management of the Workhouse. The Schoolteacher made a statement to the Board, so did the Master and they were ordered to conform to the rules of the workhouse and to attend to their respective duties.[68]

It is interesting that the guardians no longer felt it necessary to pick a side to support and ordered both to conform. By the next month the guardians were asking the Poor Law Board for an inspector to be sent to enquire into the problems and dissent within the staff.

> Resolved that the Poor Law Board be informed that the Matron Schoolmistress and Nurse are frequently complaining to the Board of each other and taking up the time of the Guardians unnecessarily and that the Poor Law Board be requested to send down an Inspector to investigate the differences which exist between them, the Guardians believing that these dissentions interfere with the discipline and proper conduct of the House.[69]

---

67   Ibid, 12 May 1863.
68   Ibid, 6 May 1863.
69   TNA: MH 12/13912/144, f 188. Letter from Thomas Day, Clerk to

After further correspondence, additional delays and more time spent gathering evidence from the various officers, Graves arrived in Bromsgrove to conduct his enquiry. Graves was a veteran inspector, having been appointed as an assistant poor-law commissioner in 1846, and so by the time of his investigation in Bromsgrove he would have had some 17 years' experience. The guardians' minutes records a lengthy examination and a late night for Graves.

> The Poor Law Inspector read the correspondence between this Board and the Poor Law Board and the respective statements of the Matron and the Schoolmistress and stated that this was the first opportunity he had of holding the inquiry and explained the mode of investigation he intended to pursue. Miss Dance and Mrs. Pope were examined at great length and several witnesses were called on both sides and Mr. Graves was engaged taking down the evidence until after 11 o'clock at night.[70]

While waiting for the inspector's response, further examples of disorder appear in the minutes. The master reported that two of the female inmates, Harriet Dipper and Sarah Stevens, had insulted the schoolmistress and following a board meeting it was ordered that both were to be confined in the refractory ward for 12 hours with bread and water only. The master also reported Sarah Anne Guest, a third female inmate, for refusing to work while Joseph Dipper was reported for misconduct in the school. Guest was locked up for six hours while young Dipper was 'slightly corrected' with the rod. At this stage the guardians eventually concluded that someone would have to go.

---

the Guardians of the Bromsgrove Poor Law Union, to the Poor Law Board. 7 July 1863.
70   WAAS: b251/BA 400/6, Bromsgrove Guardians Minute Book, 1856-1865, 1 September 1863.

Resolved. That the Poor Law Board be informed that the workhouse continues in a disturbed and unsatisfactory state, that there is an increased amount of insubordination growing up among the inmates occasioned as the Guardians believe from the hatred and ill-feeling existing between the Matron and the Schoolmistress and the Guardians are of the opinion that good order and regularity will not be brought about until one or both of these officers be removed by resignation or dismissal.[71]

The Poor Law Board were uneasy at this stage as to whether there was enough evidence to ask for any resignations or issue any dismissals. Graves revisited Bromsgrove but, by December 1863, the guardians were still awaiting a response to this second visit.

The Board of Guardians was disappointed today at finding that no definite decision was come to by your Board in relation to the Matron and Schoolmistress. The time of the Guardians was again this day occupied in hearing complaints made by the Master against the schoolmistress and Nurse and much irregularity and increased ill-feeling prevails amongst the Officers of the Establishment which necessarily interferes with the general management of the House.

The letter continued by emphasising the increasing ill feeling and the amount of time that the guardians had needed to devote to hearing sundry complaints. They asked that the Poor Law Board come to a decision on the matter before the next guardians' meeting.[72]

The annotated draft reply to this letter, initialled by Graves, indicates that a significant amount of unrecorded action must

---

71   Ibid, 10 November 1863.
72   TNA: MH 12/13912/222, ff 371-372. Letter from Thomas Day, Clerk to the Guardians of the Bromsgrove Poor Law Union, to the Poor Law Board. 6 December 1863.

have been taking place behind the scenes between Graves himself and Lord Lyttelton, the chairman of the Bromsgrove Union. Graves states that he has been in touch with Lyttelton on the subject of Anne Pope and Elizabeth Dance but did not feel justified in recommending any step before he met the guardians again. Fudging the matter somewhat, Graves suggested that the guardians be informed that '…the subject of these papers [concerning the two officers] is under the consideration of the Board' and that before they decide as to the suitability of asking for the resignation of any officer, they wish their inspector to visit the union once more to confer with the guardians.[73]

On 22 December 1863, close to one year from the appointment of Anne Pope as matron, Graves returned to Bromsgrove for a further investigation. At the meeting that day a series of resolutions were passed by the Bromsgrove guardians. Firstly, that the workhouse was in a state of insubordination and that the required level of discipline needed was unlikely to be put in place as long as the present matron remained in office. Secondly, that the matron was unfit to hold office in the Bromsgrove workhouse and they came to that conclusion from her general conduct founded on their general observations on her manner, demeanour and disposition. Thirdly, they believed that there was no other officer at present employed by the union who ought to be removed. They believed that the schoolmistress should have an opportunity to regain 'that moral influence over the children which she has lately lost'.[74]

Were these resolutions an attempt by the guardians to move the Poor Law Board into faster action than after the previous visit and with a view of clearing the matter up before Christmas, or were they designed to prompt the Poor Law Board into coming to a decision favoured by the Bromsgrove guardians? Whatever the reason for these resolutions they had to wait until the early

---

73   Ibid.
74   WAAS: b251/BA 400/6, Bromsgrove Guardians Minute Book, 1856-1865. 22 December 1863.

1864 to get a response and the response initially seemed to meet the guardians' wishes. The Poor Law Board wrote that Mrs Pope has shown that 'owing to her temper and demeanour is unable to enforce and preserve due subordination and discipline among the officers and inmates of the Workhouse and that she has in consequence forfeited the confidence of the Guardians'. They therefore decided that they could not agree to Pope's continuation as workhouse matron and asked the guardians to request her resignation.

Although the guardians may have been content with this part of the response the Poor Law Board continued to say that they were

> ...satisfied that Miss Dance had not endeavoured to improve the feeling existing between herself and Mrs. Pope but had adopted a course of conduct which could not fail to perpetuate the discord and insubordination which now prevail.

This was surely an unexpected turn of events especially as the letter ended with a request for the guardians to ask Miss Dance for her resignation also.[75] Even with such an unintended outcome the guardians acted without delay. They met on the following evening and in a letter to the Poor Law Board they reported

> ...that at the Guardians' meeting of 5 January Mrs Pope, Matron, and Miss Dance, Schoolmistress, had been asked to resign and had both done so with effect from the end of the month.[76]

---

75   TNA: MH 12/13912/231, ff. 388-389. Draft letter from the Poor Law Board, to Thomas Day, Clerk to the Guardians of the Bromsgrove Poor Law Union. 4 January 1864.
76   TNA: MH 12/13912/233, ff 393-394. Letter from Thomas Day, Clerk to the Guardians of the Bromsgrove Poor Law Union, to the Poor Law Board. 5 January 1864

So far then we have seen the more formal accounts of the situation and its resolution. The formal accounts do little to give us any detail of the incidents which generated so much 'hatred and ill-feeling' between Pope and Dance. Lengthy letters, however, were written by Pope and Dance to the Poor Law Board regarding their complaints about each other and these survive in the pages of the poor law correspondence.[77] The letters give us additional perspectives on the situation and a glimpse into what life in the cramped and insular workhouse on a day to day basis might have been like. In each letter the protagonist not only made accusations, but also countered the accusations made by the other officer. Presumably then, they had had the opportunity to voice their complaints to the guardians and to hear the complaints each had of the other. In order to more easily understand these complaints, the following extracts from the letters of Pope and Dance are put sequentially, matching claim and counter claim, as if in a conversational argument.

Matron: 'The Schoolmistress has behaved herself with rudeness and violence towards me in the dining hall in the presence of all the inmates who were assembled for breakfast'.

Schoolmistress: 'The rudeness she refers to is as follows: I told a schoolgirl when at breakfast to sit down. She replied I shan't for you, I'll tell the Matron of you. I took her to the Matron and told her what the girl had said and asked her if she would please to speak to her on this subject. The Matron ordered the girl to her place. Nothing else passed'.

Matron: 'With reference to the charge that I said to one of the inmates "Did you see old Dame Dance come in this morning?

77   TNA: MH 12/13912/209, ff 343-344, Letter from Anne Pope, Workhouse Matron of the Bromsgrove Poor Law Union, to the Poor Law Board, 23 November 1863; and in MH 12/13912/147, ff 191-196, Letter from Thomas Day, Clerk to the Guardians of the Bromsgrove Poor Law Union, to the Poor Law Board. 21 July 1863.

She has been out all night", I beg to deny that I ever said anything of the kind, or have heard it said by no-one, but I am informed by the woman employed as Cook that the inmate who said I made the remark, said it herself in my presence in the kitchen, but being busy I did not notice it. The Cook is prepared to swear to this. I can also produce evidence that this woman is one of the worst characters in the House, and not to be believed in anything she may say'.

Schoolmistress: 'On 3 Nov I returned home at 9.30pm. The outer gate being locked and the bell since out of repair I could make no one hear and remained (with a female witness) outside till 10pm (the night being cold and windy). I then went back into the town and obtained leave to stop with Mrs Sling (the late Matron). I returned the next morning a little after 7 o'clock and at once acquainted Mr Pope of the circumstances. I told him that I did not think the Porter would lock me out intentionally. He replied 'that would depend on what sort of temper he was in at the time; he was drunk last night and insulted me'.

It is interesting in the last example of exchanges that the schoolmistress was at pains to show that she was with a female friend, a sign of the social pressures on females at that time. Also interesting is that she should look to a previous workhouse matron for accommodation overnight. This can be taken as a further sign that the insular and closed nature of workhouse life meant one's social circle was limited to colleagues and ex-colleagues. The porter too was clearly an added complication in this mix of interpersonal relationships. The written conversation continues.

Matron: '... the Schoolmistress has for some time past discontinued sleeping in her own apartments and taken to sleeping with the Nurse so she is quite away from the children and they have no means of access to her should there be anything amiss in the children's bedroom during the night. She has continued to do so since the Guardians told her to choose a child to sleep with'.

Schoolmistress: 'Some person attempted to get into my sleeping apartment during the night. I felt much alarmed and in danger which led to my sleeping with the Nurse. I now feel that I have reason to be glad that I have done so since it is the evident intention on the part of the Matron to exaggerate my every act. Had I remained in my room I know not what scandal might have been raised against me. I am not aware that I have disobeyed the orders of the Board. The Chairman certainly told me that I might have one of the girls to sleep with me but when it was known that the children had a skin disease I was allowed to continue (for the present) with the Nurse'.

This indicates very clearly that the tensions in the workhouse extended even to include the sleeping quarters of the staff and these were clearly not private nor even felt to be secure.

Matron: 'It is well known in the House that previous to my appointment as Matron, Miss Dance has been repeatedly guilty of inflicting severe corporal punishment upon children of both sexes. She has had girls locked up for many hours and kept them upon bread and water without it being reported in the punishment book…'.

Schoolmistress: 'I solemnly affirm that I have not beaten any child in any way since the receipt of the letter of the Poor Law Board dated 5 Oct 63 but have taken them to the Master to punish. Mrs Pope is well aware that the man when called upon denied in the presence of herself and Mr Pope that I had boxed the ears of any child or that I had allowed him to do so'.

In this exchange the matron appears to be struggling for clear evidence and relies on hearsay. The phrase, 'since the receipt of the letter of the Poor Law Board dated 5 Oct 63' is an interesting one which suggests that the matron's accusations were correct prior to that date.

> Matron: 'The conversation between myself and the Nurse was intended to be a private one...(she)...was talking to me ......and I did say, have you heard that two of the girls are to be taken before the Board for misconduct towards the Schoolmistress and in the course of conversation I told her that when I was first appointed to the office of Schoolmistress of the Brewood Workhouse the school there was in a state of great disorder that some of the women used to kick at the schoolroom door and curse me and call me bad names for correcting their children in school, that if I had taken them all before the Board for being so rude there would have been no end to it, and that after I had been there two years I had the praise of the Guardians for getting the school in a satisfactory state. The conversation between myself and the Nurse was not intended as any slur upon the character of the Schoolmistress of this Union, nor did I think the Nurse would mention it to anyone'.

The assertion that the conversation between Pope and the nurse was intended to be a private one demonstrates again the lack of privacy in the union workhouse environment.

> Schoolmistress: 'She has allowed children to carry cans of soup to and from the dining hall after meals when I have forbidden them. On remonstrating with her I was told it was nothing to do with me... I have been refused bed linen for a child after making two applications. The result was the child had no change for at least a fortnight ...several of the paupers have been allowed extras from the officers' tables without any recommendations from the Guardians or the Medical Officer'.

Again, we have an insight into the procedural tensions in the workhouse with the schoolmistress clearly having some responsibility for the health, cleanliness and good hygiene habits of the children, but being hampered by the matron in fulfilling this role. We also get a glimpse of the hierarchical structures with the officers eating at their own table, with enough food for some to be given away, in front of the inmates who had a diet restricted by the rules and close monitoring of the Poor Law Board.[78] This might be described as a recipe for resentment among the inmates, particularly if some were receiving 'extras' and others not which then added to the difficulties of managing inmates' behaviour; although it might also be a form of reward, a positive behaviour management strategy.

> Matron: 'The Gentleman who occupied the chair in Lord Lyttelton's absence is a staunch friend of Miss Dance's. I believe she constantly visits some of the Guardians and states everything she can to them, true and not true. She also waylays them in the chapel as they go from the Boardroom to their lunch. She follows them out when they leave the house and to my knowledge has called a Guardian out to confer privately with him'.

This appears as a last ditch attempt by the matron to discredit the decisions of the guardians and prevent her dismissal. If so, it did not work, for, as we already know from the formal records of this period, the letters from the matron and the schoolmistress did not prevent either of them both from being asked to resign.

What effect did the resignations of these two women have upon them? We would need to follow their careers further to get a full answer to that question but we know that Dance was allowed to apply for further posts within the poor law system as schoolmistress, as she wrote to the Poor Law Board asking

---

78   Union guardians were required to submit, for approval, detailed accounts of weekly menus and ingredients.

for clarification of her position. She was told that she was not legally disqualified by her resignation for holding the office of schoolmistress in any other workhouse and that as long as a board of guardians, with knowledge of the circumstances under which she left the Bromsgrove Union, thought it proper to elect her then the Poor Law Board would not withhold their consent to her appointment.[79]

With the resignation of Anne Pope, matron, there remained the problem of what to do with Joseph Pope, master. The master and matron usually came as a married couple (yet we have already seen that Bromsgrove had earlier defied that particular convention) and although the guardians had had no issue with the master, they wrote to the Poor Law Board requesting that the master be asked to leave at the end of the month, along with his wife, with the suggestion that he be paid until the next quarter day. Annotations on their letter suggest that some members of the Poor Law Board were wary of terminating contracts in this manner but in conclusion both Mr and Mrs Pope were allowed to leave at the end of the month but paid to the end of the quarter. Reference was made to a previous instance when an officer had claimed for lost accommodation and board under similar circumstances and the matter was obviously passed around a number of the Poor Law Board members and legal advisors for comment before a decision was confirmed.

J T Lea, one of the clerks at the Poor Law Board, understood that the master may claim his salary to the end of the present quarter and he knew that in a similar case an additional claim was made for loss of board and lodging when the officer was requested to leave before the time when his office would expire. Lea thought it best that the master and matron should go immediately. He also thought that if there was no legal objection, then the guardians should receive the sanction of

79   TNA MH 12/13912/235, ff 396-398. Letter from Elizabeth Dance, Schoolmistress of the Workhouse in the Bromsgrove Poor Law Union, to the Poor Law Board (see annotations), 19 January 1864.

the Poor Law Board for the end of the quarter as proposed by the guardians. This he considered could be done under article 172 of the General Consolidated Order 1847. William Golden Lumley, Assistant Secretary to the Poor Law Board, disagreed, stating that the Popes could only be paid their salary up until the time when they ceased to hold their offices and, as he pointed out, at present there was only a promise to resign at the end of the month. Payment, claimed Lumley, would be due up to that time but not after. Henry Fleming, Secretary of the Poor Law Board, was less legally precise but perhaps more pragmatic. Agreeing that Lumley was quite right as to the actual legal claim he believed that under the circumstances the proposal of the guardians should be sanctioned.[80]

The manner in which the guardians constantly involved the Poor Law Board in deciding the future of the master, matron and schoolmistress, the Board's delays and repeated inspections before removing them from their posts and the fact that they were not dismissed but asked to resign, all raise questions about employment rights of the time. However, these officers were not dismissed and in the process leading to their resignation each had opportunities to access the guardians in order to complain about each other and equally had their correspondence investigated by senior officers within the Poor Law Board. Although the extracts used above were from letters requested by the Poor Law Board, they each wrote to the Board at other times asking, for example, that previous testimonials be taken into account in the decision making. The Poor Law Board's quoting of previous dismissals with reference to the master's continuing employment would seem to suggest that employment rights and the right to be treated fairly for these senior union officers were considered, but not, as we have seen, overgenerous.

This is a short account of a brief period in a single mid-

---

80   TNA: MH 12/13912/233, ff 392-394. Letter from Thomas Day, Clerk to the Guardians of the Bromsgrove Poor Law Union, to the Poor Law Board (see annotations). 5 January 1864.

Victorian workhouse in the midlands. We could characterise the antics of and accusations thrown around by Anne Pope and Elizabeth Dance, the two women workhouse officers who, to put it very mildly, did not get on with each other, as trivial. However, this would belie the fact that thousands of employed union officers in hundreds of workhouses in England and Wales shared the similar circumstances of living in a closed institution in enforced close proximity, working in hierarchical employment and undertaking overlapping duties. The letters of the main protagonists present us with a relatively rare glimpse into a situation perhaps far more common than we might initially think. The workhouse, then, was home for staff as well as inmates and the multiple roles of the workhouse of asylum, schoolhouse, general hospital etc. '…made for tense and stressful relations between inmates and staff alike'.[81]

---

81   Englander, Poverty and Poor Law Reform, p 35.

3.

Managing Useless Work: The Southwell and Mansfield Hand-crank of the 1840s

Paul Carter and Derek Wileman

…most of them [tramps and vagrants] are idle profligates, a worthless set of vagabonds who never work, but tramp from one place to another, stealing or begging in the day, and applying for lodging in the workhouse at night.[82]

One of the most obvious, but perhaps less investigated aspects of the Victorian poor law, is that the name of the building, which more than anything characterizes the New Poor Law, was the workhouse; a house in which work was expected to be undertaken. Of course work itself had been interwoven into the notion of welfare from the second half of the sixteenth century. Relief was something due to people because of past or impending work and thus connected current pauperism to previous or future productive labour. Welfare authorities therefore struggled to combine welfare and work in an effort to create an industrious pauper population. The Old Poor Law itself specified for the

…setting to work all such Persons, married or unmarried, having no Means to maintain them, and use no ordinary and daily Trade of Life to get their Living by: And also to raise weekly or otherwise (by Taxation of every Inhabitant, Parson,

---

82   *Nottinghamshire Guardian,* 24 August 1866, 1071, p 6. The piece was titled 'Our Vagrants'.

Vicar and other, and of every Occupier of Lands, Houses, Tithes impropriate, Propriations of Tithes, Coal-Mines, or saleable Underwoods in the said Parish, in such competent Sum and Sums of Money as they shall think fit) a convenient Stock of Flax, Hemp, Wool, Thread, Iron, and other necessary Ware and Stuff, to set the Poor on Work.[83]

Examples abound of local authorities under the Old Poor Law attempting to provide paupers with useful labour from which an extraction of profits was possible. Although pre-1630 sources are fragmentary, Steve Hindle has found that evidence of hemp-spinning, flax-winding and lace making exists in some of the early parish accounts which have survived. Thus at Eaton Socon in Bedfordshire there is evidence of poor children being taught how to work bone lace, while at Cowden in Kent the parish sold woven, washed and whitened canvas which the poor had produced. In 1606 it was reported that only four of the 86 Warwickshire parishes made any explicit reference to the poor being set to work. However, he found more fulsome accounts in Essex and Norfolk. From the latter county the parish accounts for Holt Market and Houghton-next-Harpley in 1601 show wool and hemp was purchased for setting the poor to work and at Cawston in Norfolk in 1606 the parish officers stated that the aged poor had as much 'works' as were needed. It is unclear how long some of the schemes of this period lasted for but it appears that many were 'short-lived and often ill-managed experiments'.[84] This being the case it did not stop other commentators or local authorities advocating or attempting to make the workhouse an institution where unemployed labour could be harnessed and a profit for the parish made. In the late seventeenth century Matthew Hale and Josiah Child argued that the workhouse could indeed make a profit and advocated

---

83   43 Eliz I, c 2. *An Act for the Relief of the Poor*, 1601.
84   Hindle, S. On the Parish? The Micro-Politics of Poor Relief in Rural England c.1550-1750, Clarendon Press, 2004, pp 177-178.

the role of the unemployed poor as a resource which needed to be tapped.[85] In the early eighteenth century Sir Humphrey Mackworth introduced bills to establish factories in every parish in which the poor would be set to work. The failure of the bills, at least in part, was because such pauper labour would create no new jobs as such but would compete with those workers already employed in that sector of the economy the new 'factories' were aimed toward.[86]

This desire to have the unemployed pay for their own benefits through a scheme of work still exists. Indeed, we can hear the echoes of earlier policies in the statement from the Prime Minister's Office, published in November 2011, in regard to the then new proposals for those claiming jobseeker's allowance.

> Speaking at a Parliamentary Liaison Committee today, the Prime Minister said: Today we are announcing that if you go through the work programme but still don't find work, then we are actually going to be asking people to go through a community work programme where they work 30 hours a week for 26 weeks to contribute to their community.[87]

Under this scheme jobseekers were to work in placements which were organised by Jobcentre managers. The arrangements could be up to eight weeks for 30 hours a week. The placements, which had previously been limited to just two weeks and were designed for only charities and public bodies, were now planned to take place in private businesses. The scheme attracted odium and protest with several firms such as Waterstones, Tesco's, Sainsbury's and TK Maxx distancing themselves from it following protests and condemnations in the press. Polly

---

85   Brundage, English Poor Laws, p 13.
86   Slack, P. *The English Poor Law, 1531-1782*, Macmillan, 1990, p 41.
87   https://www.gov.uk/government/news/community-work-for-job-seekers. Accessed 26 October 2015.

Toynbee, social policy commentator for *The Guardian* wrote that workfare was unfair to most as it gave free slave labour to big companies. She claimed that:

> Michael Heseltine's scheme that was dubbed workfare had three vitally different ingredients. He paid jobseeker's allowance recipients extra for working, he ensured the work was for charities or community projects – no risk of job substitution – and the job market was rising. Iain Duncan Smith and Chris Grayling breached all those, absurdly calling objectors 'job snobs'. The protesters gave them the bloody nose they deserve.[88]

The point we are making here is that the entanglement of work and welfare has a long history as well as being a modern aspirational political goal. Squaring this particular circle had appealed to some politicians and social commentators for several hundred years. Our object now, in this chapter, is to examine work in the context of the nineteenth century workhouse and nineteenth century welfare.

The New Poor Law was built around classification: what age or gender was the applicant for relief, were they able-bodied or impotent and unable to work. This chapter focuses on those classed as vagrants. Indeed we will focus tightly on a particular, but short term work experiment, carried on in the Southwell Union workhouse in the 1840s, to provide disagreeable employment to those vagrants who passed through the union and who sought relief overnight in the workhouse. The Southwell guardians sanctioned the building of a hand crank and insisted all able bodied vagrants were to spend four hours each morning turning the handles.

Before we look to the specifics at Southwell it would be useful to review the immediate general history of the vagrant.

---

88   http://www.theguardian.com/politics/2012/feb/23/chris-grayling-work-experience-critics. Accessed 26 October 2015.

The 1834 Poor Law Amendment Act does not make any specific reference to vagrants or vagrancy and little appears to be prepared for the guidance of unions on the matter. Some unions believed that since vagrants, or casuals as they were sometimes referred to, were not mentioned in the legislation, they were not obliged to provide relief for them.[89] Some unions believed that as the vagrant was ignored by the *Royal Commission's* report of 1834 then this class of person would be dealt with under the Vagrancy Act of 1824 making them the concern of the police rather than the new local poor law authorities.[90] The result of all this was to have the vagrant considered as the least deserving of the undeserving poor.

However, the lack of reference to vagrancy in the initial legislation did not bring vagrancy to an end and the lack of advice to unions did not remove vagrancy as a social problem. In August 1837 Richard Mayne, Commissioner of the Metropolitan Police, complained to Edwin Chadwick

> ...that difficulties still occur in obtaining that immediate relief which the extreme urgency of some of the cases demands, and all plea and claim for any relief is resisted in others on the ground that the party should seek it elsewhere, perhaps in a distant parish...[91].

The Poor Law Commission responded by setting out in their letter back to Mayne the requirements for unions regarding claims by vagrants. They referred him to the Poor Law Amendment Act which provided for the right of any destitute person in case of 'sudden or urgent necessity' to relief.[92] Unwillingness to mix local pauper inmates with outside, alien 'idle profligates', led unions

---

89   Crowther, Workhouse System, p 247.
90   Wood, *Poverty and the Workhouse*, p 117.
91   *Fourth Annual Report of the Poor Law Commissioners for England and Wales,* with appendices, letter from Mayne to Chadwick, p 96. PP., 1837-38.
92   Ibid, letter from Chadwick to Mayne, pp 96-97.

to provide specific vagrant accommodation with the 'Casual Ward' being a standard feature of the Victorian workhouse. However, in the late 1830s and early 1840s the treatment of casuals varied enormously with many unions providing only the most basic bedding in an outhouse unattached to the main building, with perhaps bread and water for supper and no meal in the morning. The system was one of utter simplicity; get rid of such people as quickly as possible.

In the early years of the Southwell Union there appear to have been few issues concerning vagrancy. Indeed, in responding to a letter from the Poor Law Commission the guardians state that they 'have had little experience on the subject of vagrants'. Nevertheless, they believed that '…able bodied vagrants should be set to work in the workhouse until the expiration of 6 hours instead of the usual notice of 3 hours… [this] would be effectual in preventing the abuse of workhouse

Figure 3/1: TNA: MH 12/9526/182, f 331. Letter from Thomas Marriott, Clerk to the Guardians of the Southwell Union, to the Poor Law Commission, 17 March 1841.

relief'.[93] This letter was actually a result of a consultative exercise by the Poor Law Commission and similar responses can be found for the same time from other unions across the country.[94]

---

93   TNA: MH 12/9526/182, f 331. Letter from Thomas Marriott, Clerk to the Guardians of the Southwell Union, to the Poor Law Commission, 17 March 1841.
94   *Copy of Circular Letter of the Commissioners to Boards of Guardians,*

For example, the neighbouring Basford Union stated that the guardians were unable to respond as no vagrants had been received at the union workhouse and they attributed this state of affairs to their proximity to Nottingham. The Wolstanton and Burslem Union believed that the period of labour could be reasonably increased from four to six hours as this would pay for supper, overnight accommodation and breakfast. In the Bromsgrove Union the guardians thought it desirable that they should have the power of detaining an able-bodied vagrant for six hours during working time on the day following his or her admission to the workhouse. They also suggested the county constabulary might be instructed to apprehend the idle and dissolute and lodge them at the station for the night with the view of inflicting further punishment.[95] The following year saw the passage of the Poor Law Amendment Act 1842.[96] In section five of the 1842 Act it stated

> That it shall be lawful for the Guardians, subject always to the Powers of the Poor Law Commissioners .... to prescribe a Task of Work to be done by any Person relieved in any Workhouse, in return for the Food and Lodging afforded to such Person; but it shall not be lawful to detain any Person for any Time exceeding Four Hours from the Hour of Breakfast in the Morning succeeding the Admission of such Person into the Workhouse...

dated 15th February 1841, Respecting Relief of Vagrants, with Tabular Abstract of Answers, and Selected Answers. PP., 1841.
95   TNA: MH 12/9231/89, f 201. Letter from William Ashton, Clerk to the Guardians of the Basford Poor Law Union, to the Poor Law Commission. 25 February 1841; MH 12/11196/170, ff 318-319. Letter from Joseph Lowndes, Clerk to the Guardians of the Wolstanton and Burslem Poor Law Union, to the Poor Law Commission, 27 February 1841, and MH 12/13905/22, ff 38-46. Letter from Thomas Day, Clerk to the Guardians of Bromsgrove Poor Law Union, to the Poor Law Commission. 26 February 1841.
96   5 & 6 Vict., c 57. An Act to Continue Until the Thirty-first Day of July One Thousand Eight Hundred and Forty-Seven, and to the End of the then next Sessions of Parliament, the Poor Law Commission; and for the Further Amendment of the laws Relating to the Poor in England, 1842.

Furthermore, this section referred to the Vagrancy Act 1824 and specified that anyone refusing or neglecting to undertake such tasks of work would be deemed '...an idle and disorderly Person' within that Act.[97] The New Poor Law then acknowledged that the 'occasional poor' existed and stipulated that they were to be dealt with in the workhouse.

The type of work set by local boards of guardians varied across the country. In 1841 casual paupers at Newport Pagnall in Buckinghamshire were offered relief and instructed to pick apart two pounds of oakum.[98] In the Mitford and Launditch Union in Norfolk a letter the guardians wrote to the Commission on 17 January 1844 stated the workhouse master was to

> set to work all the able bodied men (vagrants & tramps) ...
> to cart manure, gravel, or other employment, suited to their
> respective ages, strength and competence. ... If they refuse
> or neglect to perform such task work ... the master ...to take
> such persons before the magistrates.[99]

In May 1844 the clerk of the Axminster Union in Devon confirmed that 'pounding or crushing bones... is almost wholly confined to the vagrant Class of Pauper'.[100] Other unions, such as that at Clutton in Somerset, simply observed that wayfarers and vagrants were so rare that the guardians had not found it necessary to pass a resolution on the matter.[101] In 1847 in was

---

97   Referring to 5 Geo IV, c 85, c 3. *An Act for the Punishment of Idle and Disorderly Persons, and Rogues and Vagabonds, in that part of Great Britain called England*, 1824.

98   TNA: MH 12/488/237, ff 348-349. Letter from Thomas Paine for William Powell, Clerk to the Guardians of the Newport Pagnell Poor Law Union, to the Poor Law Commission. 29 July 1841.

99   TNA: MH 12/8477/90, ff 140-141. Letter from Samuel King, Clerk to Guardians of the Mitford and Launditch Poor Law Union to the Poor Law Commission. 17 January 1844.

100   TNA: MH 12/2097/180, ff 309-310. Letter from Charles Bond, Clerk to the Guardians of the Axminster Poor Law Union, to the Poor Law Commission. 4 May 1844.

101   TNA: MH 12/10322/36, f 68A. Letter from J and W Rees Mogg, Clerks to the Guardians of the Clutton Poor Law Union, to the Poor Law

reported by W H T Hawley, Assistant Poor Law Commissioner, that in the Tynemouth Union workhouse the male vagrants were employed in picking oakum as the guardians are not able to procure a supply of stones for stone breaking.[102] Looking at a number of Midland examples we find that at the Wolstanton and Burslem Union in Staffordshire, the guardians reported to the Poor Law Commission on 28 February 1844 that the casual poor and vagrants were to pick one pound of oakum in return for their supper, lodging and breakfast.[103] At neighbouring Newcastle Under Lyme, the clerk reported that vagrants who were relieved in the workhouse were to pick oakum and not to be detained above four hours after breakfast, while exempting those whose age and strength appeared insufficient.[104] At the Kidderminster Union it was reported that able bodied vagrants or wayfarers were to receive supper and breakfast upon application provided they break two cartloads of stone first. Old people, women and children being vagrants or wayfarers were to receive supper and breakfast, however able bodied women would only receive the same on application. The latter rule was regarded as lax by the Poor Law Commission and the Kidderminster guardians were instructed that the giving of food should be based on need not just application.[105] Vagrancy at Bromsgrove was more complicated. In December 1843, vagrants there were only housed in the workhouse when they were ill, and the guardians had therefore not passed any resolutions in respect of their

Commission. 8 January 1844.

102   TNA: MH 12/9158/30, ff 48-49. Workhouse Inspection Report Form from W H T Hawley, Assistant Poor Law Commissioner, to the Poor Law Commission. 9 August 1847.

103   TNA: MH 12/11197/39, ff 1-3. Letter from Joseph Lowndes, Clerk to the Guardians of the Wolstanton and Burslem Poor Law Union, to the Poor Law Commission, 28 February 1844.

104   TNA: MH 12/11364/33, f 44. Letter from Samuel Harding, Clerk to the Guardians of Newcastle under Lyme Poor Law Union, to the Poor Law Commission. 13 February 1844.

105   TNA: MH 12/14018/81, ff 129-131. Letter from Henry Saunders, Clerk to the Guardians of the Kidderminster Poor Law Union, to the Poor Law Commission. 16 January 1844.

working in return for food and lodging. Previously vagrants were housed at lodging houses in Bromsgrove but a year earlier the guardians hired two tenements, one for males and one for females, where vagrants were overseen by a man and his wife, who lived there rent free. The houses were superintended by the assistant overseer of Bromsgrove and were reported to be kept better ventilated and cleaner than ordinary lodging houses.[106] In 1841, as we have seen, the Basford Union responded to the Poor Law Commission's enquiry concerning vagrancy by stating that the guardians cannot answer their question as no vagrants have been received at the union workhouse and that they attribute this to their proximity to Nottingham.[107] In 1846 a return giving the numbers of vagrants received into the workhouse between 1841 and 1845 showed that none were received in each of the years.[108] In the mid-1840s the Mansfield Union adopted a scheme similar to that we will see at Southwell, the use of a hand-crank as a task of work. By the early 1850s it was complained that vagrants at Mansfield were relieved by tickets to stay at lodging houses and by allowing one pound of bread in cases where the police superintendent deemed it necessary.[109] The Mansfield Union appears to have followed a particularly hard line with vagrants and resolved in 1856 that able bodied vagrants, those who would need to undertake a task of work, would only be admitted in cases of extreme destitution.[110] By

---

106   TNA: MH 12/13906/141, ff 262-263. Letter from Thomas Day, Clerk to the Guardians of the Bromsgrove Poor Law Union, to the Poor Law Commission. 22 December 1843.

107   TNA: MH 12/9231/89, f 201. Letter from William Ashton, Clerk to the Guardians of the Basford Poor Law Union, to the Poor Law Commission. 25 February 1841.

108   TNA: MH 12/9236/36, ff 43-44. Letter from R B Spencer, Clerk to the Guardians of the Basford Poor Law Union, to the Poor Law Commission. 4 March 1846.

109   TNA: MH 12/9363/6, f 7. Letter from W E Goodacre, Clerk to the Guardians of the Mansfield Poor Law Union, to the Poor Law Board. 16 January 1850.

110   TNA: MH 12/9365/329, ff 447-450. Workhouse Inspection Report Form from Robert Weale, Poor Law Inspector, to the Poor Law Board. 1 January 1856.

the late 1860s at least, the Mansfield guardians had resolved that in exchange for receiving food and lodging in the workhouse each male vagrant was to break 300 weight of boulders to pass through a one and a half inch mesh riddle or to pick one and a half pounds of oakum. The female vagrant was to pick half a pound of oakum or to work three and three-quarters of an hour cleaning the vagrant wards or doing washing.[111]

At the Southwell Poor Law Union we know a little more detail about the treatment of local vagrancy. During the early 1840s the guardians' minutes are punctuated with references to small (and sometimes larger) payments for vagrants. Examples from the first half of 1841 include 10d allowed for two vagrants at Oxton, £1 8s 6d towards the funeral expenses of Thomas Morgan, vagrant at Southwell, 2s allowed for John Dring, a vagrant casual at North Muskham and 1s 11d allowed for John Oakes, a sick vagrant at Southwell.[112] Concerns appeared to grow concerning relief expenditure on vagrancy and in June 1843 the guardians called for a special meeting to be held in the following month which would continue current discussions for a school house but also '...the necessity of Erecting further buildings for the Vagrants + Sick...'.[113] This is the first surviving reference to a vagrant building at Southwell. The special meeting was held in July 1843 and the erection of new vagrant buildings was discussed. It was resolved '...that the plan for the Vagrant Ward be revised by Mr Nicholson particularly as to the Mill-room and submitted at another Meeting – That it should be sent to the Commissioners for their approval'.[114] Much of the internal correspondence on the matter does not survive. However, it seems that a letter was read at a later

111   TNA: MH 12/9371/99, ff 146-150. Letter from W E Goodacre, Clerk to the Guardians of the Mansfield Poor Law Union, to the Poor Law Board, 11 September 1869.
112   NA: PUS 1/1/3, f 34v. Southwell Poor Law Union, Guardians' Minute Book, 1841-1845. 22 February 1842; f 40, 22 March 1842; f 40v, 22 March 1842; f 43v, 5 April 1842.
113   NA: PUS 1/1/3, f 131r. Southwell Poor Law Union, Guardians' Minute Book, 1841-1845. 13 June 1843.
114   Ibid, f 125r, 4 July 1843.

meeting and the clerk was asked to inform a Mr Nicholson to prepare 'the plan and specifications of the Intended vagrant Ward + Mill room' for the following meeting. This was presumably done and the clerk was directed to forward the same to the Poor Law Commission in late August 1843.[115] The correspondence with the Poor Law Commission included a plan of the new buildings and was sanctioned the following month.[116] In September the clerk was to advertise for contracts for the building of the vagrant ward and the mill room. These were advertised and the tenders of Messrs Parr and Parkin were accepted at a cost of just under £85.[117] Until the new vagrant buildings were complete the guardians ordered that the workhouse master 'be directed to cause the ablebodied Vagrants to work for two hours in the Morning at all periods of the year before they have their breakfast, and for 2 hours after breakfast before they are discharged'.[118]

Although there are no surviving comments from the archive which tell us when the new vagrant buildings were first brought into use we do have a report from March 1844 from Thomas Marriott, the Southwell Union clerk, who wrote to the Poor Law Commission stating that the new arrangements were having an effect. Marriott stated that 21 inmates had recently had left the workhouse. The able-bodied men had been confined to work the mill [the hand mill] and consequently there was a much better spirit in the workhouse than that of a week or two earlier. This would put the opening of the new vagrancy facilities at around the end of February 1844.[119]

---

115   Ibid, f 130v, 25 July 1843 and f 134r, 22 August 1843.
116   TNA: MH 12/9527/74, f 114. Letter from Thomas Marriott, Clerk to the Guardians of the Southwell Union, to the Poor Law Commission. 23 August 1843. The plan does not survive. See also MH 12/9527/75, f 115. Draft letter from the Poor Law Commission, to Thomas Marriott, Clerk to the Guardians of the Southwell Union, acknowledging receipt of the proposed plans and specifications for a vagrant ward and mill room and granting approval. 5 September 1843.
117   NA: PUS 1/1/3, f 139v. Southwell Poor Law Union, Guardians' Minute Book, 1841-1845. 5 September 1843, and f 141r. 3 October 1843.
118   Ibid, f 147r. 31 October 1843.
119   TNA: MH 12/9527/152, f 215. Letter from Thomas Marriott,

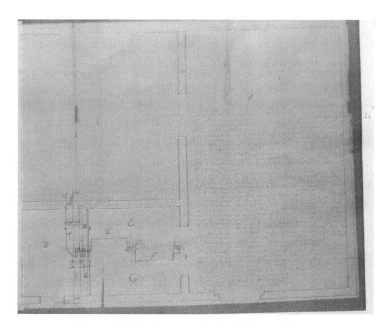

Figure 3/2: TNA: MH 12/9360/303, ff 430-433. Vagrant mill plan in
letter from S Weightman, Southwell Poor Law Union Workhouse
Master, to Robert Weale, Assistant Poor Law Commissioner.
4 November 1844.

The adoption of local initiatives within the Victorian workhouse
system allowed for ideas to be noticed and copied. At Mansfield the
guardians had visited the Southwell workhouse and believed the
adoption of a similar handmill would be useful in regard to their
own casual poor; or at least as they claimed to have none, to ensure
through a deterrent task of work, that this remained the case. A
letter from the Mansfield Union to the Poor Law Commission on
26 October 1844 stated that the local guardians had

> ...visited Southwell Union workhouse on 22 October 1844
> having strongly recommended the wheel [crank] in use at

Clerk to the Guardians of the Southwell Union, to the Poor Law
Commission, 7 March 1844.

that place for the employment of vagrants... [They intended to have a] Similar one to be obtained... With the least possible delay'.[120]

It was at this time that the Poor Law Commission took a renewed interest in the Southwell work scheme. It was Thomas Weightman, the Southwell workhouse master, who had designed the crank mill which had been built in the new vagrant quarters erected in early 1844. However, following the correspondence from Mansfield, Robert Weale, the assistant poor law commissioner responsible for the area, wanted to know more about the machine, and Weightman, in a letter dated 31 October 1844, sent him a set of scale drawings of the mill, the plan of the vagrant quarters, and a very detailed explanation of how the mill worked.[121]

The vagrant mill correspondence showed that Southwell had invested in an unusual solution to the problems of vagrancy, for a rural backwater union. The actual paper on which the plans were drawn, are very large, effectively covering two sides of one long sheet. On the first side the right hand side of the sheet shows the plans of the newly erected vagrants' accommodation. The components of the mill were housed in the room D (Wheel House) at the bottom left corner. Hand cranks in the room C (Shed) next to it were linked to the mechanism through a hole in the wall between rooms C and D. The cranks allowed up to eight people to turn the mill in any one instance. The room B in the top left corner was the ward where the vagrants slept. The whole of the right hand side A was an enclosed yard open to the sky for exercise. This meant that vagrants could sleep, work and exercise with no contact with the other workhouse inmates.

120   TNA: MH 12/9360/302, ff 428-429. Letter from W E Goodacre, Clerk to the Guardians of the Mansfield Poor Law Union, to the Poor Law Commission. 26 October 1844.
121   TNA: MH 12/9360/303, ff 430-433. Letter from S Weightman, Southwell Poor Law Union Workhouse Master, to Robert Weale, Assistant Poor Law Commissioner. 4 November 1844.

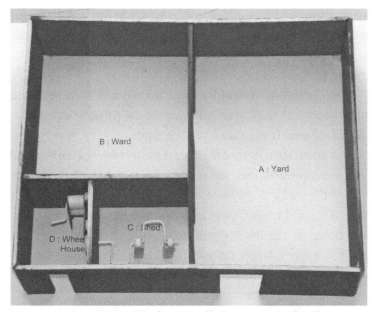

Figure 3/3: Model of Southwell Union vagrants' mill.

Figure 3/4: TNA: MH 12/9360/303, ff 430-433. Vagrant mill plan in letter from S Weightman, Southwell Poor Law Union Workhouse Master, to Robert Weale, Assistant Poor Law Commissioner. 4 November 1844.

From this scale drawing and the written description it has been possible to construct a scale model of the accommodation, see figure 3/3.[122] The detailed specification provides us with the

---

122   This model was produced by Derek Wileman for a Pauper Prisons... Pauper Palaces (Midlands) conference held at the Southwell Workhouse, National Trust, on 1 June 2013.

mechanism which Weightman devised. On left hand side of the same sheet the upper part is a plan of the wheels and the lower drum. The bottom part shows a side view of the brake mechanism, see figure 3/4.

On the second side of the large sheet, not shown here, the right hand end shows the side view of the three wheels and a weighted beam (not to scale) on the right.

An alternative view of the model shows how the parts of the mill, a complicated mechanism, are connected. As the vagrants turned the crank in the shed the brake wheel rotated. This had a band around it which was attached to a long lever. A weight was hung on the lever which could be moved out from the pivot to apply a larger force on the brake. If only one person was operating the crank the weight would be closer to the pivot which would produce a smaller brake force. With eight people operating the system the weight would be furthest from the pivot to give a large force on the drum. The brake wheel itself had a peg protruding from it. As it rotated this peg caught a tooth on the large toothed wheel and moved it a fraction of a turn. Two of the teeth (on opposite sides of the wheel) were larger than the rest. Every half turn of the large toothed wheel engaged with a tooth on the small toothed wheel and turned it a little. In his letter Weightman explained that the men would have to turn the crank 91 times to make the small toothed wheel turn only once. The large teeth touched a small bell every half turn, indicating to the vagrants how many turns they had completed. The small toothed wheel was fixed to an axle which was also fixed to a roller. This roller wrapped some thin rope around it which was taken from another roller above it. Once all the rope was moved from the one roller to the other, the master came along and wound the rope back onto the first roller using the other handle. A detailed perusal of the plans confirm that after building the new vagrants block, designing and constructing the mill itself, and adding the labour power of an unknown number of vagrants, the mill did nothing useful. It was, conceded Weightman, an unpopular task of work. It was designed to have the handles turned 30 times a minute which will roll one '...lap of line from the top roller on to the bottom one'. He pointed out with some satisfaction that some men have tried to turn the handle 40 times a minute to break it but they had not succeeded.[123]

At some point later in 1844 or early 1845 the Mansfield guardians began operating their mill. However, they quickly ran into problems when in February 1845 two vagrants had refused to work the mechanism. As we have seen the workhouse authorities could take those paupers refusing task work to a magistrate for punishment. Indeed this is just what the Mansfield workhouse master did. The two vagrants were punished, but William Wilson, the guardian for South Normanton in the Mansfield Union, who it appears was present at the petty sessions room in the town, was informed by the magistrate that although he had committed a man to the Southwell House of Correction for refusing to work the mill, he would not do so again. The [unnamed] magistrate '... considered the vagrant was only obliged to do some useful work as an equivalent for the food and lodging given them'. This was problematic, stated Williams, as the '...Guardians have erected this Mill at Considerable expense, which if the opinion of the Magistrate is correct will be nearly useless'. The letter was annotated by William Golden Lumley, Assistant Secretary to the Poor Law Commission, who agreed with the view taken by the magistrate and thinks that the '...turning of a wheel without any object & without producing any result is not a task of work' and likened it to '...digging pits & filling them in again'.[124] What

123   TNA: MH 12/9360/303, ff 430-433. Letter from S Weightman, Southwell Poor Law Union Workhouse Master, to Robert Weale, Assistant Poor Law Commissioner. 4 November 1844
124   TNA: MH 12/9361/20, ff 25-26. Letter from William Wilson,

happens now was an unusual u-turn in terms of policy. A letter was drafted to Wilson acknowledging his letter stating that the Commissioners did not agree with the view taken by the magistrate. The Commissioners saw nothing in the terms of the legislation to require that the '...task of work' which may be '... exacted of the paupers should be of a profitable kind'. The words '...in return' for the food etc. appear to them to mean that the labour may be imposed as the '...condition on which the relief will be afforded', and not necessarily seen as a means of securing the reimbursement of such relief. It is the '...task of work' itself, and not the producer of it, that the Commissioners understand be the 'return' for the relief.[125] However, this draft was then crossed out and has '...not to be sent' written across the text. A second draft was produced almost a month later which stated that as the magistrate had taken such a view it might be better to annex to the mill some form of apparatus which would raise water, wash potatoes or perform some other kind of practical work.[126]

It appears the mills at both Southwell and Mansfield continued until the summer of 1845. On 10 July the Poor Law Commission wrote to the Mansfield Union copying them the letter they sent to Wilson and asking the guardians to take steps to act on the suggestions of annexing a useful purpose to the mill. The Commissioners also asked Robert Weale if the wheel used at the Southwell Union workhouse for employing vagrants was similar to that at Southwell, especially with regard to its not being applied to any useful work.[127] The Poor Law Commission

Normanton, Alfreton, Mansfield Poor Law Union, to the Poor Law Commission. 1 February 1845.

125   TNA: MH 12/9361/21, f 27. Draft letter from the Poor Law Commission, to William Wilson, South Normanton, Alfreton, Mansfield Poor Law Union. 24 February 1845.

126   TNA: MH 12/9361/22, f 28. Draft letter from Poor Law Commission to William Wilson, Normanton, Alfreton, Mansfield Poor Law Union. 19 March 1845.

127   TNA: MH 12/9361/116, ff 176-180. Draft letter from the Poor Law Commission to Robert Weale, Assistant Poor Law Commissioner. 10 July 1845

then also wrote to the Southwell guardians and in the minutes for the Southwell guardians meeting in late July 1845 it was recorded that a

> ...letter was read from the Poor Law Comns requesting that the Mill used by the Vagrants and casual poor be so constructed as to do some kind of labour either grinding corn, washing potatoes, casting water etc. That the Clerk consult Mr James Nicholson [local architect] and report the most convenient method to answer the purpose.[128]

No correspondence survives between the Southwell Union and Nicholson but in late September 1845 the Southwell guardians appear to have abandoned the mill altogether, as the minutes record that earlier resolutions concerning the mill be rescinded and that able bodied vagrants

> '...do the following task of work, that is to say to break a quantity of boulders not exceeding half a hundred[weight] to pass through a 3/8 [inch] mesh riddle...' and in early October the guardians confirmed the same with a letter to the Poor Law Commission.[129]

The case of the Southwell hand-crank tells us several things about the New Poor Law and how local boards of guardians might undertake their work. Firstly, it demonstrates how a relatively quiet rural union which had little experience of vagrants was willing to invest much energy and money in creating a prison-like punishing task of work for the casual poor. Secondly, it shows how ideas would spread from union to union

---

128   NA: PUS 1/1/3. Southwell Poor Law Union, Guardians' Minute Book, 1841-1845. 22 July 1845.

129   NA: PUS 1/1/4. Southwell Poor Law Union, Guardians' Minute Book, 1845 -1850. 30 September 1845 and MH 12/9527/311, ff 404-405. Letter from Thomas Marriott, Clerk to the Guardians of the Southwell Union, to the Poor Law Commission. 1 October 1845.

as evidenced by the way that Mansfield picked up the idea, sent a deputation of guardians to the Southwell Union workhouse to assess the mill and then had their own installed in a matter of months. Thirdly, the case illustrates the limitations of poor law authority and the positive agency of the pauper (or paupers) that refused task work which they considered inappropriate or unjust. Fourthly, and finally, the case reveals the dead ends of poor law history, the plans and policies of local government which lasted for very short periods of time and which then dissipated and disappeared. The useless work of paupers set to work on the Southwell hand crank experiment of the 1840s represented one such dead end.

4.

'Shovelling Out Paupers': Emigration under the New Poor Law in Kidderminster

Ann Taylor

Historically, the introduction of the 1834 Poor Law Amendment Act has been firmly attached to the Swing Riots of 1830-31 and this in turn was tied to the perceived surplus of labour in rural parishes. This surplus of labour, part of the social dislocation caused by the enclosure of common lands, the curtailment of small scale cottage industry and the ending of farmers providing lodgings for their unmarried workforce, drove down wages, created unemployment and underemployment in abundance and thus sowed the seeds of the riots themselves.[130] Such being the case it is of little wonder that the act addressed the issue of surplus labour and introduced mechanisms to remove the same. Section 62 of the act stated that

> ...the Rate-payers in any Parish [were able] to direct that such Sum or Sums of Money [may be used] for defraying the Expences of the Emigration of poor Persons having Settlements in such Parish, and willing to emigrate...[131]

This permissive section to the Poor Law Amendment Act may be a little surprising. After all the thrust of the New Poor

---

130 Brundage, English Poor Laws, pp 57-60; Burnett, J. Idle Hands: The Experience of Unemployment, 1790-1990, Routledge, London, 1994, pp 34-41.
131 4 & 5 Will. 4 c 76, s 62. *An Act for the Amendment and better Administration of the Laws relating to the Poor in England and Wales*, 1834.

Law was compulsion not choice. However, the recent history of emigration at the time had not been fertile ground for compulsion. Since the late eighteenth century an intellectual argument, initially developed by Thomas Malthus, which saw a growing population as a potential burden rather than a national resource had taken hold.[132] Parish schemes for emigration developed in the early decades of the nineteenth century to reduce settlements and poor rates.[133] Regardless of the energy of men such as Robert John Wilmot-Horton, politician and later colonial governor, who argued for more state directed and state funded schemes of emigration, such ideas came to little or nothing. The notion of state directed assisted emigration was attacked over fears of the expenditure required to fund and manage such a scheme, its links to notions of deportation and criminal transportation and the fears it might raise within the colonies of Britain ridding itself of those of '...the most worthless class'.[134] Furthermore, it could be interpreted as an admission that the state and the political class had transformed society into something unable to accommodate its own citizens.

The early nineteenth century debates on emigration failed to arrive at a state funded scheme but a state supervised scheme in which '...the vestry of each parish be empowered to order the payment out of the rates raised for the relief of the poor, of the expenses of the emigration of any persons having settlements within such parish, who may be willing to emigrate...' would later become part of the New Poor Law.[135]

132   Malthus, T. An Essay on the Principle of Population, 1798.
133   Snell, K.D.M. Parish and Belonging: Community, Identity and Welfare in England and Wales, 1700–1950, Cambridge U.P., 2009, p 149.
134   Howells, G. Emigrants and Emigrators: A Study of Emigration and the New Poor Law with special reference to Bedfordshire, Northamptonshire and Norfolk, 1834-1860, PhD., University of Leicester, 1996, p 36-40.
135   Report from His Majesty's Commissioners for Inquiring into the Poor Laws, p 357. PP., 1834.

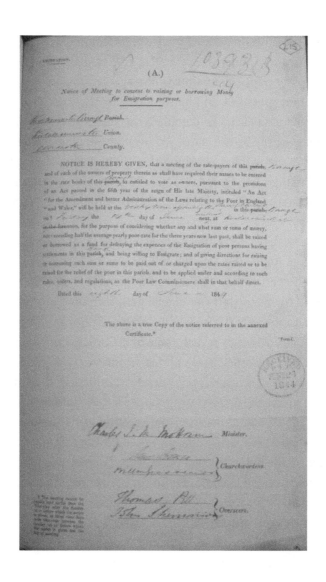

Figure 4/1: Example of one of the forms to be completed by the parish and passed to the central authority via the board of guardians. From TNA: MH 12/14018/130, Folios 214-216. Letter from Henry Saunders, Clerk to the Guardians of the Kidderminster Poor Law Union, to the Poor Law Commission, enclosing copies from the vestry book concerning the emigration [of Lucy Webb and family]. 22 June 1844.

So how was section 62 used by the poor and the local poor law authorities in Kidderminster? Was it a humane safety valve in a rapidly populous nation which allowed society to reduce population pressures and allow wages to rise and civil order to be maintained or, to complete the quote which titles this chapter, was the British state '…shovelling out paupers to where they may die without shocking their betters with the sight or sound of their last agony'.[136] To really get to terms with this we should first understand the process of emigration under the New Poor Law.

As we have seen the responsibility for putting forward emigrants under the New Poor Law was with the parish and it was the parish that would need to provide the union with a series of forms to start the official administrative process. The various forms were devised by the central authority to force the parish officers to sign at each stage of the process and to ensure details were recorded and entered in the vestry minute book (see example at figure 4/1).[137] Therefore, notices of meetings to consent to raising or borrowing money for emigration purposes were called, resolutions from the meeting were recorded and the minister and parish officers would certify that the various forms of the act were complied with.[138] Now that the local requirements had been dealt with the parish was to provide the 'List and Description of the Persons Desirous of Emigrating…'. Here the details of the proposed emigrants would be provided. The details would include the names, gender, ages and marital

136 This was the claim of Charles Buller MP in *Hansard*, LXVIII, 1843, col. 522.
137 These would be Emigration Form A. Notice of meeting to consent to raising or borrowing money for emigration purposes; Emigration Form B. Resolution entered in vestry book, and Emigration form C. Certificate of minister, churchwardens, and overseers, of the forms of the act having been complied with.
138 The form shown here for example is Emigration A: Notice of Meeting to consent to raising or borrowing Money for Emigration purposes from TNA: MH 12/14018/130, ff 214-216. Letter from Henry Saunders, Clerk to the Guardians of the Kidderminster Poor Law Union, to the Poor Law Commission, enclosing emigration forms. 22 June 1844.

status of each person, where they were proposing to emigrate to and significantly the particulars of the amount of parish relief they had received over the previous year. The form was then sent to the central authority via the union secretary to await sanction. The sanction was determined by the data provided by the forms and would be refused if incomplete or not matching the criteria set down by the law. The central authority would only sanction funding to those who wanted to emigrate to what was termed healthy British Colonies such as Canada, Australia, New Zealand and Van Diemans Land (Tasmania). In addition they would not sanction expenditure for the emigration of wives and children of transported convicts, wives and children of soldiers or men who were deemed to have deserted their wives and families and gone to a foreign country.

We can see the detailed supervisory nature of the central authority in the examples of Lucy Webb and Matilda Hillman and it is perhaps worthwhile taking the time to explore the oversight given by them. Matilda Hillman was born on 14 March 1830 and christened on the 19 March at the New Meeting House in Kidderminster.[139] She was the daughter of Samuel and Martha Hillman who married at St Mary's Church in the town on 23 January 1829.[140] In May 1850 Henry Saunders, the union clerk wrote to the central authority stating that the board of guardians had passed a resolution agreeing to the expenditure of £6 to assist the emigration of Matilda to Philadelphia in America and asking whether the money should be charged to the common fund.[141] The central authority replied that the destination was contrary to the regulations to fund emigration to anywhere other than the British Colonies. They also required

139   TNA: RG 4/2738, Kidderminster, New Meeting House (Presbyterian), Births and Baptisms, 1783-1836. 1830.
140   WAAS: 850/8426/5a(i), vol.8. St Mary's Kidderminster Parish Records, 1829.
141   TNA: MH 12/14020/43, ff 56-58. Letter from Henry Saunders, Clerk to the Guardians of the Kidderminster Poor Law Union, to the Poor Law Board, 14 May 1850.

further information as to whether Matilda was eligible to be funded from the common fund.[142] A couple of months later Saunders again wrote to the central authority to ask if they would sanction the expenditure of £6 to assist Matilda, who was now going blind, to join her father in Quebec in Canada.[143] Again the central authority declined to sanction the application, this time they replied that it was impractical for Matilda to go so late in the season. The central authority also wanted to know Matilda's age and whether the board of guardians, due to Matilda's failing eyesight, had considered placing her under the care of a superintendent, or a person emigrating to the same colony. They also asked whether her father was able to care for her.[144] Saunders replied that Matilda was 20 years of age and that the guardians believed her father was able to look after her.[145] The central authority were still not satisfied and in a further letter to Henry Saunders they asked if the board of guardians had received any communication from Matilda's father, and if so would Saunders send it to them. They also still insisted it was too late in the year for Matilda to emigrate.[146] Indeed, we can see from the 1851 census that Matilda had still not emigrated. At this time she was shown living in Broad Street, Kidderminster, with her uncle, a carpet weaver, her aunt and six cousins.[147]

---

142   TNA: MH 12/14020/44, f 59. Draft letter from the Poor Law Board to Henry Saunders, Clerk to the Guardians of the Kidderminster Poor Law Union, 23 May 1850. The latter request for information was presumably on the understanding that Kidderminster may consider changing the place of destination.

143   TNA: MH 12/14020/62, f 90. Letter from Henry Saunders, Clerk to the Guardians of the Kidderminster Poor Law Union, to the Poor Law Board. 2 August 1850.

144   TNA: MH 12/14020/63, f 91. Draft letter from the Poor Law Board to Henry Saunders, Clerk to the Guardians of the Kidderminster Poor Law Union, 5 August 1850.

145   TNA: MH 12/14020/64, f 92. Letter from Henry Saunders, Clerk to the Guardians of the Kidderminster Poor Law Union, to the Poor Law Board, 7 August 1850.

146   TNA: MH 12/14020/65, f 93. Draft letter from the Poor Law Board to Henry Saunders, Clerk to the Guardians of the Kidderminster Poor Law Union, 17 August 1850.

147   TNA: HO 107/2038, f 91, p 31. Census. 1851.

The case of Lucy Webb was a little more complex. She was the widow of Samuel Webb who had served in the 24th Regiment of Foot for 20 years, had been discharged from service at 40 years old and was in receipt of a pension of 1s 6d per day. In a letter to the central authority in April 1842, Saunders had stated that Lucy wanted to emigrate to Springfield, Illinois, in the United States of America, with her five children. On the forms which provided the names and ages of Lucy and her five children, a note stated that Samuel had 'died some time since in a Lunatic Asylum' and that Lucy had relatives in America who wished her to emigrate with her children so that they could take care of them. It was also stated that Lucy was a very respectable woman and as far as circumstances allowed took proper care of her children.[148] As with the case of Matilda Hillman the central authority replied that they could not help her go to America and suggested the guardians contacted Sir Henry Hardinge at the War Office to see if they could help. The central authority was not hopeful that any assistance would be forthcoming from the government.[149] Saunders again wrote to the central authority and stated that the guardians wished to pay the £25 necessary for Lucy and her family who had now applied for the means to emigrate to Kingston, Canada. If the family remained in Kidderminster the guardians feared any future costs of relief would be considerable.[150] At the end of the month Saunders forwarded the completed parish forms for Lucy and her family to the central authority which responded that they had no objection to the £25 being paid out of the rates as long as the

148   TNA: MH 12/14018/105, ff 158-159. Letter from Henry Saunders, Clerk to the Guardians of the Kidderminster Poor Law Union, to the Poor Law Board. 23 April 1844.
149   TNA: MH 12/14018/106, f 160. Draft letter from the Poor Law Board to Henry Saunders, Clerk to the Guardians of the Kidderminster Poor Law Union, 29 April 1844.
150   TNA: MH 12/14018/124, f 202. Letter from Henry Saunders, Clerk to the Guardians of the Kidderminster Poor Law Union, to the Poor Law Board. 3 June 1844.

rate payers agreed.[151] Although the emigration for Lucy Webb and her family was agreed by both the parish and the central authority we find that that almost three years later the money authorised was not raised '...in consequence of the persons in whose favour it was intended to be applied having afterwards declined to Emigrate...'.[152]

For the 1830s, 1840s and up to the early 1850s emigration at Kidderminster was a side show in poor law terms with only one further unsuccessful attempt to raise money for Eliza, William and Jane Tyler in May 1850 being added to the cases of Hillman and Webb. The Tylers, like Hillman and Webb, also proposed emigration to America. In this instance New York was the preferred destination.[153]

By this time Kidderminster and carpet weaving were inextricably linked. From the employers' perspective at least, this was a matter of some pride with one of the Kidderminster carpet manufacturers visiting the 1851 Great Exhibition and proclaiming that

> Kidderminster had nothing to fear from British or foreign competition in the Crystal Palace. He had gone through the whole display of carpet goods and is thoroughly satisfied that Kidderminster must beat the palm for excellence in drawing, colouring, materials and weaving, above all other rivals.[154]

Yet, the period was also difficult with new technology affecting labour and wages. In the 1850s some 2,000 handlooms were

---

151   TNA: MH 12/14018/130, ff 214-216. Letter from Henry Saunders, Clerk to the Guardians of the Kidderminster Poor Law Union, to the Poor Law Board. 22 June 1844.
152   TNA: MH 12/14019/17, f 20. Letter from Henry Saunders, Clerk to the Guardians of the Kidderminster Poor Law Union, to the Poor Law Board. 12 February 1847.
153   TNA: MH 12/14020/49, ff 64-66. Letter from Henry Saunders, Clerk to the Guardians of the Kidderminster Poor Law Union, to the Poor Law Board. 23 May 1850.
154   *Worcester Chronicle and Provincial Railway Gazette*, 7 May 1851.

replaced by 700 Brussels power looms.[155]. The weavers sought some protection from John Downall who became the vicar of St Georges, Kidderminster in 1847.[156] They must have been dismayed when he allied himself with the manufacturers claiming that 'Had the weavers been more frugal they would… have had no need to seek more money'.[157]

However, in noting that thus far we see little appetite or enthusiasm for emigration under the poor law, we must be careful in how we draw our conclusions. Emigration under the poor law was bureaucratic and depended not only upon people agreeing to emigrate but upon the parish, union and central authorities authorising the expenditure from the poor rates. In 1852, in a single year, everything changed. In that year carpet weavers from Kidderminster applied *en masse* to emigrate to Australia.[158] On the morning of 20 April 1852 the Kidderminster bellman was sent to summon the carpet weavers to a meeting at the Plough Inn to hear of a proposal, by Mr B Woodward, to cut the rate he paid to his weavers by ½d a yard. At a delegate meeting the previous evening a deputation from the firm outlined the proposal to the workers; the proposition was met with a resounding no. So many weavers had turned up for the meeting that it was proposed that it was reconvened at the Vine Inn, Horsefair, where there was a bigger yard. At this meeting various resolutions were made by Messrs Blowen, Williams, Link, Baylis and Barber

…the first reprehending the conduct of Mr B Woodward in offering to reduce the wages of his men; the second declaring the deductions proposed to be on the hardest money earned by the men and therefore the most unjustifiable that could have been proposed; the third accusing the manufacturers of using unfair means to entrap their men.

155   Thompson, Woven in Kidderminster, p 44.
156   Marsh, A. The Carpet Weavers of Kidderminster, 1995, p 43.
157   Ibid, p 43.
158   *Fifth Annual Report of the Poor Law Board*, Appendix 2, pp 138-139. PP., 1852.

The outcome was that a resolution was carried in which the weavers promised to support the men from Woodwards. After the meeting dispersed in an orderly manner a deputation waited upon Woodward himself to acquaint him with the situation. Woodward promised to 'relinquish any attempt either at present or in the future to bring about any reductions'.[159]

It appears that some of the weavers still feared for their working conditions and their jobs. In May 1852 Thomas Miles wrote to the Poor Law Board on behalf of Henry Saunders, the union clerk, stating that a large number of carpet weavers across the union were unemployed and many, up to 50 persons, had expressed a wish to emigrate to Australia if means were provided for them to do so.[160] The board of guardians appeared anxious to do all they could to assist the applicants and asked the Poor Law Board for advice and suggestions. The Poor Law Board answered that the guardians should get in touch with the Colonial and Emigration Commissioners for their assistance as they might be able to fund some of those wishing to emigrate. In addition the Poor Law Board asked questions concerning the settlement, and thus the entitlement, of those wishing to leave.[161] In June 1852 it was reported that a petition, 'very numerously signed', had been sent to the Emigration Commissioners, from the carpet weavers of Kidderminster, asking for free passage to Australia. The petition stated that the introduction of steam power in the carpet weaving process would lead to much unemployment. The Kidderminster guardians had appointed a committee, and found that 50 men, who with their wives and children totalled almost 200 people, had already applied

159   *Worcester Chronicle*, 21 April 1852.
160   TNA: MH 12/14020/231, f 314. Letter from [Thomas Miles], for Henry Saunders, Clerk to the Guardians of the Kidderminster Poor Law Union, to the Poor Law Board. 25 May 1852.
161   TNA: MH 12/14020/232, f 315. Draft letter from the Poor Law Board to Henry Saunders, Clerk to the Guardians of the Kidderminster Poor Law Union. 29 May 1852.

to emigrate.[162] Towards the end of the month the Emigration Commissioners had indicated a willingness to send a '…limited number of respectable weavers' where the families did not have too many children. The carpet weavers themselves had established an emigration society to ask for subscriptions. The Kidderminster guardians reported that they had held a meeting on the subject only to adjourn it to give Robert Wilkinson, relieving officer, further time to look into and report back on any cases.[163]

By the beginning of July the relieving officer had reported that 96 men, 71 women and 136 children were looking to emigrate and that the Kidderminster guardians were looking to send the Emigration Commissioners applications for 41 families.[164] Two weeks later it was reported that 35 out of the 41 families were to be given assistance to emigrate. It was noted by the *Bradford Observer* that the six rejected families, made up of woolcombers, who sought aid from the Emigration Commissioners 'May be rejected as *unfit* to be emigrants; just as some of the candidates for emigration among the Paisley weavers and Kidderminster carpet makers have been rejected'.[165] Tellingly, as we will see, General Lygon, MP for West Worcestershire, which included Kidderminster, provided a donation of £20 towards the emigration fund.[166] An examination of the initial list of those applying to emigrate shows that it was mainly those with young families who wished to take the step of leaving the people and places they knew for the unknown.[167] Out of 102 persons listed 38 were children under the age of seven years and nine of those children were under a year. In mid-July 1852 Henry Saunders

---

162   *Berrow's Worcester Journal*, issue 7802, 10 June 1852.
163   Ibid, issue 7804, 24 June 1852.
164   Ibid, Issue 7805, 1 July 1852.
165   *The Bradford Observer*, issue 966, 9 September 1852.
166   Ibid, issue 7807, 15 July 1852.
167   TNA: MH 12/14020/245, ff 333-340. Letter from Henry Saunders, Clerk to the Guardians of the Kidderminster Poor Law Union, to the Poor Law Board. 15 July 1852.

sent a copy of a report of a meeting held by the local board of guardians to the Poor Law Board. The Kidderminster guardians asked that their request be sanctioned for eight families, all irremovable, to be given permission to emigrate with no more than £2 per person being charged to the common fund.[168]

As well as the financial, and so open, support of local emigration by Lygon as their county member of parliament, a new local advocate of emigration was Robert Lowe. Lowe had held a seat on the New South Wales Legislative Council in the 1840s and returned to England in 1850. In 1852 he was elected as the member of parliament for Kidderminster. In September 1852 he spoke collectively of the increased progress of emigration, the rapid increase of wages and the need of popular education.[169] For Lowe the wages and standards of living of the labourer were inextricably linked and that

> A large emigration to Australia had taken place: but he did not think it would stop there; 'we were in the beginning of the end'. It was a most serious thing for all persons employing labour, what the end of that emigration would be. The temptations held out were so manifest, and the resources of the country [Australia] so manifold, that it was difficult to anticipate the extent of that emigration. Already it had begun to raise wages; but it was not to be supposed that a little alteration would tempt those who contemplated emigration to give it up. The habit of emigration once afloat, it would probably continue until wages should be very considerably raised.

More enthusiastically, Lowe claimed that emigration would see the end of pauperism for the able-bodied and that such people would never know '…what it was to want the necessities or even

---

168   TNA: MH 12/14020/246: 341-343. Letter from Henry Saunders, Clerk to the Guardians of the Kidderminster Poor Law Union, to the Poor Law Board. 17 July 1852.
169   *Daily News*, issue 1972, 16 September 1852.

the comforts of life…'.[170] Indeed, he thought, the industrious labourer '…might there realise the nearest thing which the world afforded to an earthly paradise'.[171]

For all the vigorous emigration activity in Kidderminster during the summer of 1852 and regardless of the recent, solid local political support from Lygon and Lowe, there was some delay in the people leaving. In early November 1852 Saunders asked the Poor Law Board if it was possible to '…expend an extra amount, not exceeding 15s per head, to provide outfits and to pay for their passage'.[172] Originally 102 people were emigrating but at the time of the letter only 85 still wished to go. A resolution, signed by a majority of the guardians, regarding the emigration of poor persons to Moreton Bay, Australia, was sent to the Poor Law Board. As a result of this letter and the resolution the Poor Law Board issued an emigration order giving sanction for an additional 15s in addition to the £2 already sanctioned to be spent.[173]

Postscript

We know that all who expressed a very definite opinion that they wanted to emigrate and were listed on the description form (see Appendix 1) did not leave. James Marshall left the carpet industry and he became a grocer living with his wife and children in Blackwell Street, Kidderminster.[174] John and Charlotte Harrison and their two children can be found on the

---

170   *The Sheffield and Rotherham Independent*, Issue 1730, 25 September 1852.
171   *Reynold's Newspaper*, issue 114, 17 October 1852.
172   TNA: MH 12/14020/263, f 366. Letter from Henry Saunders, Clerk to the Guardians of the Kidderminster Poor Law Union, to the Poor Law Board. 2 November 1852.
173   TNA: MH 12/14020/265, ff 368-371. Letter from Henry Saunders, Clerk to the Guardians of the Kidderminster Poor Law Union, to the Poor Law Board. 3 November 1852.
174   TNA: RG 9/2078, f 7, p 9. Census. 1861.

1861 census.[175] Others found their agreed emigration under threat. In the guardians' minutes in October 1852 we find that James Cox was called before the local board and told that unless he paid the money he owed to Joseph Murdock and John Squires his embarkation order might be withdrawn.[176] Earlier in the year William and Adelaide Moore and their two children were also noted in the guardians' minutes as eventually declining to leave.[177]

175   Ibid, f 13, p 19.
176   WAAS: b251/ BA 403/9, Kidderminster Guardians Minute Book, 12 October 1852.
177   Ibid, 13 July 1852.

Appendix 1

List of carpet weavers and their families desirous to emigrate from the Kidderminster Union to Moreton Bay. MH 12/14020/245, ff333-340. A record of the meeting of the guardians with several lists and descriptions of persons seeking to emigrate from the Kidderminster Borough in the Kidderminster Poor Law Union to Moreton Bay [Australia]. July 1852.

Name	Age	M/S	Comment	Name	Age	M/S	Comment
Samuel Bartle	22	M	Crossed through	Alice Cox	8 months		
Joseph Butcher	31	M	Crossed through	Ann Jane Crump	25		
Joseph Butcher	2			Mary Jane Crump	11 months		
Charles Cook	34	M		Emily Francis	19		
John Cox	27	M		Catherine R Francis	8 months		
John Crump	32	M		Emma Hampton	24		
William Francis	22	M		Charlotte Harrison	27		
John Hampton	24	M		Maria Hawthorn	20		
Thomas Hampton	5			Mary Elizabeth Hawthorn	1		
George Hemming Hampton	3			Sarah Hill	21		
John Harrison	28	M		Emma Hill	1		

Name	Age		Note	Name	Age		Note
John Hawthorn	27	M	Crossed through	Elizabeth Hooper	39	M	
Edmund Hill	25	M		Eliza Jordan	27		
Edmund Hill	10 weeks			Lavinia Jordan	6		
Henry Hooper	27	M		Martha Lewis	26	M	
Henry Jordan	29	M		Maria Lewis	4		
William Henry Jordan	4			Eliza Lewis	1		
Thomas Lewis	24	M		Hannah Lloyd	32	M	
Richard Lloyd	32	M		Martha Lloyd	11		
Thomas Lloyd	9			Elizabeth Lloyd	4 months		
Henry Lloyd	5			Hannah Lock	30	M	Crossed through
John Llock	33	M	Crossed through	Mary Ann Long	25	M	Crossed through
Charles Alfred Long	28	M	Crossed through	Sarah Manton	26	M	
William Manton	28	M		Selina Manton	6		
John Manton	4			Elizabeth Manton	2		
James Marshall	24	M	Crossed through	Leah Ann Marshall	25	M	Crossed through

William Martin	44	M	Crossed through	Ann Marshall	10 months	M	
James Martin	10		Crossed through	Cordelia Martin	44		Crossed through
William Mason	44	M	Phoebe Martin		8		Crossed through
William J Mason	13			Louisa Martin	2		Crossed through
Enoch Mole	31	M		Mary Ann Mason	44	M	
Samuel Mole	4			Eliza Martin	10		
William Moore	27	M	Crossed through	Maria Martin	7		
William Moore	3		Crossed through	Harriet Mole	26	M	
William Murliss	36	M		Hannah Mole	6		
Samuel Murliss	7 months			Selina Mole	1		
Thomas Price	22	M	Crossed through	Adelaide Moore	21	M	Crossed through
James Rutter	34	M	Crossed through	Ann Moore	4 months		Crossed through
John Smith	28	M		Ann Murless	35	M	

Name	Age	Status	Name	Age	Status	Notes
Benjamin Southall	21	M	Frances Male	17	S	
James Steward	34	M	Jemima Price	24	M	
Charles Steward	1		Mary Ann Price	5		
Emma Bartle	21	M	Harriet Price	3		
Mary Ann Butcher	30	M	Alice Price	1		
Elizabeth Butcher	4		Sarah Rutter	34	M	Crossed through
Ellen Cooke	28	M	Sarah Smith	22	M	
Mary Ann Cooke	2		Mary Ann Southall	20	M	
Agnes Guest Cooke	6 weeks		Susan Southall	8 months		
Jemima Cox	26	M	Harriett Steward	27	M	
Jane Elizabeth Cox	5		Catherine Steward			
Emma Cox	2		Ellen Steward			

5.

Who Cared? Death, Dirt and Disease in the Bromsgrove Poor Law Union

Sarah Bradley, Pam Jones and Jane Somervell

Introduction

Mention the workhouse and images of Oliver Twist, begging for more, spring to mind. In Dickens' world, the 1834 New Poor Law system starved and neglected the poor.[178] Undoubtedly, bad practice occurred in the real world, too. In Bridgwater, Somerset, in 1840, for instance, a scandal arose when the guardians failed to respond to high death rates caused by poor diet and disease.[179] But just how widespread was this, and did it mean that the system itself was cruel? Could it be that some people actually cared? By investigating what happened when the Bromsgrove Poor Law Union faced death, dirt and disease, we seek to discover whether, and by whom, anything approaching human kindness was shown to the poor in this one area of the West Midlands.

The cruel nature of the workhouse system has been the subject of debate ever since its inception in 1834. In June 1834

---

178   However, *Oliver Twist* was published as early as 1838 and so was undoubtedly also influenced by the Old Poor Law.
179   Shave, S. "'Immediate Death or a Life of Torture Are the Consequences of the System': The Bridgwater Union Scandal and Policy Change' in Reinarz, J. and Schwarz, L. eds. Medicine and the Workhouse, University of Rochester Press, 2013, ch 8, pp 164-191.

The Manchester and Salford Advertiser, taking its lead from the official title of the 1834 Act,[180] dubbed it 'An Act for further debasing and degrading English labourers, and for the better encouragement of seduction, and the propagation of bastardy and infanticide'. The following month the *Leeds Advertiser*, which had initially supported the bill, saw the detailed implications of the 1834 Act as '…bad in principle… [and] cruel in spirit'. At Barnsley in 1836 the local radical association stated they had examined the leading features of the New Poor Law and its '…cruel operations on the suffering poor' and called for a vote of censure on the 1834 Act as well as the Parliament that created it.[181] Even as the New Poor Law was further entrenched by the Poor Law Board in the late 1840s criticisms continued and in 1851, John Cobden wrote of '…the horrible system under which paupers are held in these establishments'.[182]

The debate did not end there. Reviewing the evidence over a century later, David Roberts suggested that the Poor Law Commission was not, in fact, ruthless and that tales of cruelty were either exaggerated, notably in a campaign waged by *The Times* from 1837-1842,[183] or the result of local abuses.[184] While Anne Crowther suggests that Roberts may have been too quick to accept the assurances of the Poor Law Commission, she points out that, in trying to understand what really happened, we have to contend with a deliberate attempt by the Poor Law Commission '…to make the workhouses seem repulsive'.[185] They were, after all, meant to be a deterrent. Furthermore, as Ursula Henriques reminds us, cruelty does not have to be 'sadistic'; it can also arise from 'insensitivity'.[186] It is true that The Poor Law Commission

---

180   The title being *An Act for the Amendment and Better Administration of the Laws Relating to the Poor in England and Wales.*
181   Knott, Popular Opposition to the 1834 Poor Law, pp 66, 88, 93.
182   Cobden, John. The White Slaves of England, Auburn, 1853, p 206.
183   Roberts, David. 'How Cruel was the Victorian Poor Law?', The Historical Journal, 6, 1963, p 101.
184   Ibid, p 107.
185   Crowther, Workhouse System, pp 33-34.
186   Henriques, Ursula. 'How Cruel was the Victorian Poor Law?'. The

expected, for instance, that workhouses should be hygienic, clean and well ventilated. Yet workhouses were also designed to deter applications and thus introduced regulations, such as the separation of family members, a particularly hated aspect of the system, to do just that.[187] The 'dreadful' workhouse is not as simple as it seems. We should also remember that a version of paternalism continued to colour the attitudes of some Victorians to the poor. Calls for reform of the Old Poor Law came not just from Benthamite utilitarians and economists who wanted to control the cost of out-relief and make it more efficient; there was also a concern for human values.[188] Anthony Brundage argues that the framers of the new law, and many guardians, saw themselves both as '…good capitalists *and* good paternalists'.[189]

This can be seen particularly in the New Poor Law's approach to the sick. Designed to deal with the problem of the able-bodied pauper, the new rules were to be applied less stringently to the infirm or impotent. Indeed, reducing sickness could cut the cost of relief and Derek Fraser describes attempts to do this as 'a pragmatic response to a practical need'.[190] Not all guardians were ready to make the connection, however, as Anne Digby found in Norfolk.[191] Furthermore, medical officers had a special status. Despite being under the direction of the guardians and the workhouse master,[192] they acquired a degree of autonomy in treating the poor as a result of their increasing professionalisation and prestige.[193] Some, most notably Joseph

Historical Journal, 11, 1968, p. 365.
187   Crowther, Workhouse System, p 42.
188   Checkland, S. G. and E. O. A. eds., The Poor Law Report of 1834, Penguin Books Ltd, Aylesbury, 1974, p 22.
189   Brundage, Anthony and Eastwood, David, 'Debate: The Making of the New Poor Law Redivivus', Past and Present, 127, 1990, p 185.
190   Fraser, Derek, The Evolution of the British Welfare State: A History of Social Policy since the Industrial Revolution 2nd edn., Basingstoke: Macmillan, 1984, p 94.
191   Digby, Anne, Pauper Palaces, Routledge & Kegan Paul Ltd, London, 1978, pp 173-75.
192   Crowther, Workhouse System, p 160.
193   Crowther, M. A., Paupers or Patients? Obstacles to Professionalization

Rogers, were active reformers. Rogers found himself seriously at odds with the local guardians in his efforts to improve the appalling conditions, and reduce disease, in the Strand workhouse, and was eventually forced to resign.[194] While few medical officers went as far as Rogers, M W Flinn talks of '…a perpetual guerrilla warfare' on the part of individual medical officers struggling, with limited success, to persuade reluctant guardians to make improvements locally.[195] If we are to find evidence of individual acts of kindness then, it is most likely to be in the area of healthcare. We have therefore chosen to look at what happened when the Bromsgrove Union was faced with three medical challenges in the mid-nineteenth century, namely accusations of medical negligence; significant, new responsibilities in respect of smallpox vaccination; and an outbreak of typhus in the workhouse.

The three key sets of players are the Poor Law Commission and, in particular, the assistant poor law commissioners who acted as their intermediaries with the unions; the guardians, who were responsible for operating the New Poor Law system; and the medical officers who, while part of the system, retained some independence from it. From their responses to the three challenges, we seek to identify whether, and to what extent, any of them 'cared'. Limited as it is to three case studies, this does not claim to be a comprehensive survey. Nor should it be seen as a defence of the New Poor Law system. However, by posing a question which apparently turns the common perception of the workhouse system on its head, we seek to offer a slightly different perspective to the debate on just how cruel it was.

in the Poor Law Medical Service before 1914, The Journal of the History of Medicine and Allied Sciences, 39, 1984, p 47.
194   Richardson, Ruth, and Hurvitz, Brian, 'Joseph Rogers and the Reform of Workhouse Medicine', British Medical Journal, 299, 1989, pp 1507-1508.
195   Flinn, M. W. 'Medical Services under the New Poor Law' in Fraser, Derek, ed., The New Poor Law in the Nineteenth Century, The Macmillan Press, 1976, p 61.

The Bromsgrove Poor Law Union

First, however, we must introduce the Bromsgrove Poor Law Union and say a little about how medical care was organised. The union was formed in the autumn of 1836 from 13 north-east Worcestershire parishes,[196] and was situated immediately to the south of the Black Country. Whilst mainly agricultural, there were two important industrial centres: Bromsgrove, where about a third of the population was engaged in the hand-made nail trade, and Redditch, world famous for making needles and fishhooks.[197] By the 1840s, the cottage hand-made nail industry was in decline, replaced by machine cut nails,[198] resulting in considerable poverty in Bromsgrove, and consequent demands on the union for relief.

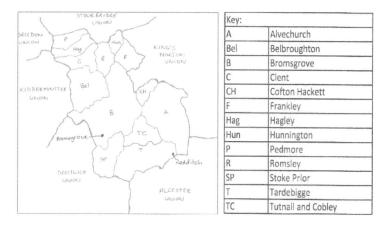

Key:	
A	Alvechurch
Bel	Belbroughton
B	Bromsgrove
C	Clent
CH	Cofton Hackett
F	Frankley
Hag	Hagley
Hun	Hunnington
P	Pedmore
R	Romsley
SP	Stoke Prior
T	Tardebigge
TC	Tutnall and Cobley

Figure 5/1: Map of the Bromsgrove Poor Law Union.[199]

---

196   Tutnall and Cobley, part of Tardebigge, had its own guardian and overseers from the start, while the rest of the parish was divided into the separate townships of Bentley Pauncefoot, Redditch and Webheath in 1840.
197   http://www.forgemill.org.uk/forgemill.htm [accessed 11 June 2014].
198   *Sanitary Inquiry: England. Local Reports on the Sanitary Condition of the Labouring Population of England, in Consequence of an Inquiry Directed to be made by the Poor Law Commissioners*, p 103, 1842 (007).
199   Bradley, Sarah, Welcoming the New Poor Law, Unpublished MA dissertation, University of Birmingham, 2014, p vi. Created from Ordnance Survey, Unions Series, Worcester Sheet (1830), [http://www.visionofbritain.

The Bromsgrove guardians were mainly local tradesmen and farmers, with a couple of clergymen. They were enthusiastic about the new system from the start, declaring in May 1837 that '…it will prove highly conducive to the public welfare'.[200] They appear to have made a genuine effort to administer the system according to the rules, and saw the Poor Law Commission as a support rather than an intrusion, in contrast to many unions which resented encroachments on their independence.[201] Among other things, they were quick to decide that they needed a new purpose-built workhouse,[202] unlike many northern unions which resisted such expenditure. Bromsgrove's design was described as 'efficient',[203] and in March 1839, the workhouse was certified to be '…in a dry, fit and proper state for the reception of the Paupers'.[204]

Although the 1834 Poor Law Amendment Act did not explicitly direct the appointment of medical officers, in practice most unions appointed them.[205] The Bromsgrove guardians had no hesitation in doing so, and by mid-December 1836, three medical officers had been appointed. Their duties were to

> …attend all cases of sickness and surgery, and provide leeches vaccination medicines and applications for all poor persons falling ill within their respective Districts … for attendance

org.uk/maps, accessed 1 May 2014]; 'Index Map to the Hundred of Halfshire' in A History of the County of Worcester, Vol 3 (1913) [http://www.british-history.ac.uk/ accessed 1 May 2014].

200   TNA: MH 12/13903/87, f 149, Extract from the minutes of a guardians' meeting. 13 May 1837.

201   Bradley, Welcoming the New Poor Law, p 66.

202   TNA: MH 12/13903/32, ff 62-66. Letter from Joseph Granger, Clerk to the Guardians of the Bromsgrove Poor Law Union, to the Poor Law Board. 23 November 1836.

203   TNA: MH 12/13903/71, f 131. Letter from C. W. Savage, Poor Law Board. 30 March 1837.

204   TNA: MH 12/13904/17, ff 20-21. Letter from Thomas Day, Clerk to the Guardians of the Bromsgrove Poor Law Union, to the Poor Law Commission. 12 March 1839.

205   4 & 5 Will. 4 c. 76. s. 46 An Act for the Amendment and better Administration of the Laws relating to the Poor in England and Wales, 1834.

on whom they shall receive a written order from the Relieving Officer.[206]

Some historians have found unions which encountered difficulties finding suitable candidates, particularly when the guardians refused to pay adequate salaries.[207] However, this does not generally seem to have been the case in Bromsgrove where there was competition for some of the posts.[208] One irate, defeated candidate even claimed that Dr Hobbes[209] (who had a diploma from the Royal College of Surgeons but was not a Licentiate of the College of Apothecaries) '…is no more qualified to practice … than my horse',[210] an objection rejected by the Poor Law Commission.[211]

Medical Negligence

Most unions had to deal with accusations of negligence against their medical officers, suggesting many were careless in the attitudes towards their patients, rather than caring. However, such accusations frequently related to *attendance* on the sick and Kim Price suggests that this, rather than a failure to provide good medical treatment, '…was *the* negligence issue of the nineteenth century'.[212] He ascribes this in part to

---

206   TNA: MH 12/13903/32, ff 62-66. Letter from Joseph Granger, Clerk to the Guardians of the Bromsgrove Poor Law Union, to the Poor Law Commission. 23 November 1836.
207   Dunkley, P. 'The "Hungry Forties" and the New Poor Law: A Case Study', The Historical Journal, 17, 1974, pp 341-342.
208   Bradley, Welcoming the New Poor Law, p 22.
209   Medical officers were normally referred to as 'Mr', but we have used the term 'Dr' to make clear their status.
210   TNA: MH 12/13903/47, ff 96-97. Letter from Edward Jackson, Medical Officer, to the Poor Law Commission. 12 December 1836.
211   TNA: MH 12/13903/44, f 90. Draft letter from the Poor Law Commission to Edward Jackson, Chaddesley Corbett, Kidderminster. 16 December 1836.
212   Price, Kim, A Regional, Quantitative, Qualitative Study of the

the impossible position of medical officers who had a duty to care for both their private and their pauper patients 24 hours a day.[213] An additional factor was that medical care and the duties of a medical officer were not well defined in the first half of the nineteenth century. What constituted negligence was therefore open to interpretation by Poor Law Commission staff and guardians.[214] While cases were often investigated by the guardians or assistant poor law commissioners, suggesting a level of concern on their part, guardians were often reluctant to dismiss, as Digby found to be the case in Norfolk,[215] so perhaps complacency, or practical considerations such as the ability to find a replacement, prevailed.

A number of cases of alleged negligence occurred in the Bromsgrove Union between 1840 and 1850. Several related to Dr Fletcher, medical officer for the Bromsgrove District and the workhouse. He was an interesting character. Like many medical officers, he was only in his late twenties when he was appointed, and was an apothecary, but not a qualified surgeon.[216] It was only in 1842, under the General Medical Order of 1842, that it became compulsory to have both qualifications.[217] Despite the accusations of negligence, he seems to have attracted considerable respect.

The first negligence case we come across is that of Henry Cartwright who died in the workhouse on 5 February 1842, aged five. The story was told in a letter from Ralph Docker, Coroner for Worcestershire, which enclosed detailed testimony from

employment, disciplining and discharging of workhouse medical officers of the New Poor Law throughout nineteenth century England and Wales, Unpublished PhD thesis, Oxford Brookes University, April 2008, p 67.
213   Price, A Regional, Quantitative, Qualitative Study, p 85.
214   Price, A Regional, Quantitative, Qualitative Study, pp 128-132.
215   Digby, Pauper Palaces, p 167.
216   TNA: MH 12/13905/42, ff 72-78. Letter from Thomas Day, Clerk to the Guardians of the Bromsgrove Poor Law Union, to the Poor Law Commission. 12 April 1841.
217   Hodgkinson, Ruth, 'Poor Law Medical Officers of England 1834-1871', Journal of the History of Medicine, 11, 1956, pp 300-301.

witnesses.[218] Some three weeks before Henry's death, Fletcher had been called in to treat a number of patients for 'the itch', or scabies, a nasty, but common, complaint in workhouses. After treatment with an ointment which caused pain, swelling and loose teeth, and with brimstone and treacle, both of which failed, Fletcher prescribed a sulphur bath. This was prepared by Sarah Chambers, the nurse, who proceeded to immerse a number of children in it. Henry complained of pain and was put to bed, but despite frequent visits by Fletcher, including three during the night of the bath, the child died three days later. His body looked as if it had been scalded. Three other children were also affected, but none as seriously as Henry.

The ensuing inquest heard from an impressive collection of medical men, including John Percy, a physician in Birmingham and lecturer on organic chemistry at the School of Medicine, and David Bolton, a demonstrator of anatomy at the Birmingham School of Medicine. Their evidence illustrates just how uncertain medical knowledge was at the time. It revealed that a solution of potassium sulphate was known as a cure for the itch, but that its use was not universal, and the quantities to be used were uncertain. It was suggested that too strong a solution might have been used, or that some patients may be more susceptible in unpredictable ways. On the other hand, a bath of the solution used could even be a gentle stimulant to healthy skin, though it might be 'injudicious' if the skin were broken.

The jury decided (unsurprisingly) that Henry died as a result of being immersed in a solution of '…sulphinet of potassium' but, despite the inconclusive medical evidence, they went on to find Fletcher's conduct '…injudicious and negligent'.[219] The *Worcestershire Chronicle* was more sympathetic to Fletcher, reporting

---

218   TNA: MH 12/13905/153, ff 256-271. Letter from Ralph Docker, Coroner for Worcestershire, to the Poor Law Commission. 17 February 1842.
219   TNA: MH 12/13905/149, f 248. Alfred Power, Assistant Commissioner, to the Poor Law Commission, 12 February 1842.

We understand that, though the bath had so lamentable an effect upon one of the children, its effect upon most of the others has been very successful; and we may add that Mr Fletcher is much respected by the poor generally, for his kind and humane conduct towards them.[220]

The guardians agreed that he could be blamed for having left the application of a powerful remedy to Nurse Sarah Chambers but decided to retain his services because of his '... hitherto unblemished professional record...', and kindness to pauper patients.[221] The Poor Law Commission recognised the inconclusive nature of the depositions and, on the advice of Alfred Power, assistant poor law commissioner, decided that the fatal result could not have been anticipated. They endorsed the guardians' resolution.[222]

In the summer and autumn of 1843, the guardians had to deal with four further cases. Two (neither involving Fletcher) got barely a mention in the guardians' minutes, which record simply that the medical officers' explanations were accepted.[223] Both of the other two involved an alleged failure by Fletcher to visit a patient, and in both cases the guardians admonished him *and then* decided to carry out an inquiry.[224] In the first case, a pauper, Mr Ward, complained that Fletcher had failed to visit his sick wife for ten days between 18 and 27 September. Eventually Ward called on Dr Horton, another local doctor, who drained six half pints of water from his wife and prescribed

220   *Worcestershire Chronicle*, 9 February 1842.
221   TNA: MH 12/13905/151, ff 250-251. Letter from Thomas Day, Clerk to the Guardians of the Bromsgrove Poor Law Union, to the Poor Law Commission. 14 February 1842.
222   TNA: MH 12/13905/153, ff 252-255. Draft letter from the Poor Law Commission to Thomas Day, Clerk to the Guardians of the Bromsgrove Poor Law Union. 2 March 1842.
223   Worcester Archive and Archaeology Service (henceforward WAAS): 251BA400/ii Minutes, Bromsgrove Guardians' minute book, 1840-1844. 31 July 1843 and 14 August 1843.
224   WAAS: 252BA400/ii Minutes. Bromsgrove guardians' minute book, 1840-1844. 11 September and 16 October 1843.

castor oil, port wine, beef tea and egg pudding, and gave them a note for the relieving officer. When Fletcher visited two days later, he found Mrs Ward ill with inflammation of the brain; she died shortly afterwards.[225] Fletcher's response was that he had regularly treated the Ward family to their satisfaction in recent months, that he had refused to prescribe port wine as it would harm her, and that he had not been told the case was urgent.[226] The second case relates to Mrs Pratt, who Fletcher also apparently declined to visit. Her husband complained to Mr Tolley, one of the neighbouring Droitwich Union guardians, who suggested that Horton should be summoned instead. The case came to light as a result of a dispute between Bromsgrove and Droitwich over who should pay for Horton's services. Fletcher argued that, despite having a note from the relieving officer, the Pratts were able bodied (Mr Pratt could apparently thatch truss-hay), and that they would not have thought of claiming medical assistance from the parish if Tolley had not suggested it.[227]

The guardians sent the results of their inquiries to the Poor Law Commission and asked for their opinion. In the Pratt case, the concerns of both the Bromsgrove and the Droitwich guardians focused on the financial question. However, Alfred Austin, the assistant poor law commissioner who investigated the case, picked up on the question of neglect, which he suggested might justify the 'interference' of the Poor Law Commission. In the event, he concluded that there was no serious case to answer in either incident. He found Ward's evidence unreliable, and that the neglect in the Pratt case was 'nothing more' than

225   TNA: MH 12/13906/116, ff 203-207. Letter from Thomas Day, Clerk to the Guardians of the Bromsgrove Poor Law Union, to the Poor Law Commission. 18 October 1843.
226   TNA: MH 12/13906/121, ff 215-218. Letter from Thomas Day, Clerk to the Guardians of the Bromsgrove Poor Law Union, to the Poor Law Commission. 24 October 1843.
227   TNA: MH 12/13906/130, ff 233-244. Letter from Thomas Richards, Clerk to the Droitwich Poor Law Union, to the Poor Law Commission. 25 October 1843.

an 'erroneous opinion' by Fletcher that he could use his own judgement as to whether the couple were destitute.[228] The Poor Law Commission concurred, although they did warn Fletcher that '...mischievous consequences' could arise if he failed to comply with a relieving officer's order.[229]

News of these cases obviously spread, and two letters and a memorial or petition were sent in Fletcher's support. The memorial signed by 50 '...respectable ratepayers', said that he '...has been unremitting in his care and attention to the Poor Patients' and testifies to the widespread regard in which he was held.[230]

Seven years later, in December 1850, Dr Hobbes, medical officer for the Belbroughton and Hagley District, was accused of negligence for failing to attend Isaac Burton who died in an emaciated state, despite being helped by neighbours in his final days. Although the verdict was that he had died by a '... visitation from God', the jury also felt there had been great neglect on Hobbes's part.[231] He had been called to Burton twice, and had received a note from the relieving officer which should have obliged him to attend. The second time he was called, he was dining with his friend, Mr Rufford, the banker, and clearly resented the interruption, merely sending an assistant to visit Burton the next morning.[232] Hobbes attempted to excuse his behaviour by saying that to avoid frequent calls upon him by

228   TNA: MH 12/13906/135, ff 251-254. Letter from Alfred Austin, Assistant Commissioner, to the Poor Law Commission. 23 November 1843.
229   TNA: MH 12/13906/137, ff 257-258. Letter from the Poor Law Commission to Thomas Fletcher, Medical Officer, Bromsgrove Poor Law Union. 28 November 1843.
230   TNA: MH 12/13906/119, ff 211-213. Letter from W. A. Greening (with enclosure) to the Poor Law Commission. 19 October 1843.
231   TNA: MH 12/13909/259, ff 356-361. Letter from Thomas Day, Clerk to the Guardians of the Bromsgrove Poor Law Union, to the Poor Law Board. 24 December 1850.
232   TNA: MH 12/13909/260, ff 362-377. Document of complaint against Jonathan Lord Hobbes, Medical Officer, Bromsgrove Poor Law Union. 8 January 1851.

people who knew nothing of illness, he had an arrangement by which he would only respond to certain requests. Once again the central authority, this time the Poor Law Board, on receiving a report about the case, sent a poor law inspector, John Graves, to investigate. He found Hobbes to be '...a skilful though not very attentive officer', and commented that there was a want of the '...punctual attendance' which the Poor Law Board required. He recommended calling for Hobbes's resignation,[233] and the Poor Law Board agreed, unless his future conduct could be assured.[234] In March 1851, however, he was reappointed as he was the only local candidate; the guardians expressed confidence that he would be more attentive to his duties following his admonishment.[235]

These negligence cases support the view that the New Poor Law was not deliberately cruel to the sick. In the first place, the number of reported and investigated cases was relatively low, given the high incidence of sickness among the poor. It is possible that negligence was under-recorded, either because most people had low expectations of the care they should receive and were reluctant to complain, or because the guardians preferred to cover up poor practice. However, there is no evidence that the latter was systematically the case. This points to a potential for further research.

The relative speed and thoroughness, with which cases were investigated by assistant poor law commissioners and inspectors on behalf of the central authority, show a desire on the part of the central authority to identify and investigate shortcomings, and recommend remedial measures. Allegations could not simply

---

233   TNA: MH 12/13909/261, ff 381-382. Letter from J. T. Graves, Poor Law Inspector, to the Poor Law Board. 10 January 1851.
234   TNA: MH 12/13909/262, f 383. Draft letter from the Poor Law Board to Thomas Day, Clerk to the Guardians of the Bromsgrove Poor Law Union. 13 January 1851.
235   TNA: MH 12/13909/288, ff 415-416. Letter from Thomas Day, Clerk to the Guardians of the Bromsgrove Poor Law Union, to the Poor Law Board. 19 March 1851.

be ignored. However, they also tend to confirm Price's view that neither what was expected of a medical officer, nor what constituted negligence, were well-defined, giving guardians considerable leeway in how they acted. In failing to dismiss Hobbes for what was clearly a neglect of his duty, the guardians demonstrated that they were prepared to accept second best on behalf of the poor rather than deal with the practical problem of replacing him. We are also faced with the curious series of four negligence cases in 1843. Why were two barely mentioned, while in the others Fletcher was admonished and then investigated, only to be broadly exonerated? We know from correspondence in the 1860s that he had a particular interest in the workhouse diet which went back to the 1830s. In 1868 he states that he was first alerted to the insufficiency of the then Bromsgrove dietary in 1837 by '…an Idiot eating gravel "because he was hungry"'. Before suggesting any alteration Fletcher lived a week on the workhouse diet for the able-bodied inmates. He stated that 'My cravings of hunger were more than I could possibly have imagined or can describe'. He had since known the inmates as well as idiots eat '…putrid horse flesh and Oilcake intended for the dogs', others have eaten their poultices'.[236] Were the guardians of 1843 concerned that he was being too attentive to the poor and that, if he had his way, costs, and therefore rates, would go up?

The death of Henry Cartwright might suggest a careless attitude on Fletcher's part. However, there is some evidence that he was making a genuine effort to cure inmates of a nasty complaint, using a recognised, if not fully understood, treatment. When the child became ill, his frequent visits show a real concern. Furthermore, he was not put off by what happened, and in October 1842, he reported that the workhouse was free

---

236   TNA: MH 12/13913/175, f 241. Letter from John Humphreys, Clerk to the Guardians of the Bromsgrove Poor Law Union, to the Poor Law Board. 22 September 1868.

of the itch, a huge achievement.[237] This is consistent with the memorial and letters which speak of his kindness to the poor. By contrast, the accusation against Hobbes seems to reveal a very casual attitude towards his pauper patients.

Vaccination

As Joan Thirsk and Edward Collins have commented, medical services under the New Poor Law were mainly curative rather than preventative. The one exception was vaccination against smallpox.[238] Initially this was part of a medical officer's general duties in respect of the poor. But in 1840, in an effort to increase coverage, new legislation required guardians to make vaccination available to all, whether or not they were dependent on relief.[239] This, as Digby explains, also made it exceptional in being a free service which did not confer pauper status on the patient.[240] The Poor Law Commission expressed their support for the new provisions in their *Seventh Annual Report* stating, 'The benevolent object of the statute is ... to prevent as far as possible the mortality and sufferings occasioned by smallpox'.[241] They described how they had

'...endeavoured by every means within their power to obtain and convey to the Boards of Guardians the best information from the highest authorities on the subject of vaccination.[242]

---

237   WAAS: 251BA400/ii. Bromsgrove Guardians' Minute Book, 1840-1844. 10 October 1842.
238   Thirsk, Joan, and Collins, Edward, eds. The Agrarian History of England and Wales, Cambridge University Press, Vol 7, Pt 2, p 1445.
239   3 & 4 Vict., c 29. *An Act of Parliament to Extend the Practice of Vaccination*, 1840.
240   Digby, Pauper Palaces, p 176.
241   Seventh Annual Report of the Poor Law Commissioners, with appendices, London 1841, p 95. Circular letter from the PLC to Boards of Guardians 20 August 1840.
242   *Seventh Annual Report of the Poor Law Commissioners*, with

They trusted that, in addition to their duties, guardians would, '...as private individuals ... voluntarily ... exert their influence to remove prejudice, and ... promote vaccination'.[243] The central authority monitored take-up and required explanations when levels were low. In spite of their efforts, however, few people availed themselves of the service, and in 1853 vaccination was made compulsory for all children shortly after birth.[244] This seems to have had an effect as in 1854 the ratio of vaccinations to births was 112%, the only year between 1852 and 1870 when there were more vaccinations than births.[245]

The Bromsgrove guardians responded positively to the 1840 Act, establishing new arrangements for vaccination, and setting up new contracts with their medical officers.[246] They displayed posters informing people of the necessity of having their children vaccinated, telling them where and when it would be done, and warning of the dangers, including death and disfigurement, of not doing so. In 1845, a poster claimed that as many as 30,000 people had succumbed in the last two-and-a-half years. It also set out the dangers of inoculation,[247] including the high risk of spreading the disease, and declared that anyone found practising it, would be subject to one month's imprisonment. Just how much of the detail a labourer, who had received little or no education, would have been able to take on

appendices, p 36. PP., 1841.
243 *Seventh Annual Report of the Poor Law Commissioners*, with appendices, p 95. PP., p 95. Circular letter from Poor Law Commission to Boards of Guardians, 20 August 1840.
244 16 & 17 Vict., c 100. *An Act further to extend and make compulsory the Practice of Vaccination*, 1853.
245 *Twenty-third Annual Report of the Poor Law Board*, p 515, Appendix 59. Table showing number of people vaccinated in England & Wales 1852-1870. PP., 1871.
246 TNA: MH 12/13904/302, ff 439-441. Letter from Thomas Day, Clerk to the Guardians of the Bromsgrove Poor Law Union, to the Poor Law Commission. 18 December 1840.
247 In vaccination patients were immunised against smallpox using the cowpox virus; in inoculation a weakened live smallpox virus was used.

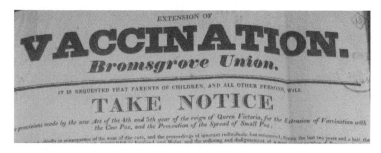

board is debatable, but the message to vaccinate must have been clear.

Figure 5/2: MH 12/13907/8, f 13. Printed Vaccination Poster, 1845.[248]

Despite these very direct messages, it is evident that ensuring good take-up was not straightforward and that there was significant public resistance. A return for the year ended 29 September 1844 shows that only 293 people were successfully vaccinated out of a total of 791 live births, and that one of the medical officers, Dr Gaunt, had failed to vaccinate anyone in his district.[249] The Poor Law Commission's request for an explanation, coming as it did on a pre-printed proforma, illustrates that Bromsgrove was not the only union where vaccinations were lower than they should have been.[250] The local evidence suggests that the programme faced two main problems. First, as is often the case, was money. When asked in 1845 about his low vaccination rate, Gaunt explained that he had vaccinated the three or so children who came to his residence but that he could not be expected to go to

<hr />

248 TNA: MH 12/13907/8, f 13. Notice from Thomas Day, Clerk to the Guardians of the Bromsgrove Poor Law Union, to the Poor Law Commission. 30 January 1845.
249 TNA: MH 12/13907/7, ff 10-12. Letter from Thomas Day, Clerk to the Guardians of the Bromsgrove Poor Law Union, to the Poor Law Commission (enclosing vaccination return for 29 September 1844). 20 January 1845; Bradley, Welcoming the New Poor Law, p. 50.
250 TNA: MH 12/13907/9, f 14. Draft letter from the Poor Law Commission to Thomas Day, Clerk to the Guardians of the Bromsgrove Poor Law Union, 3 February 1845.

the homes of the poor for 'the trifling sum of one shilling and six pence'.[251] His opinion was clearly shared by others and in a later debate on the Vaccination Bill in the House of Commons on 31 March 1856, the President of the Board of Health, Mr Cowper, proposed to increase the rate of remuneration to 2s 6d per case.[252]

More serious perhaps, were public attitudes. Resistance to vaccination was clearly widespread, despite the devastating effects of the disease being so well known, and we can see the efforts of the authorities to try to increase take up. For example, in 1852 there was a decrease in successful vaccinations in Worcestershire of 7.9%, and the Poor Law Board deemed it necessary to call attention to the tables of mortality published by the Registrar General stating many deaths were through neglect on the part of parents to have their children vaccinated.[253] Writing to the Poor Law Commission in 1845, Fletcher said that many people refused vaccination in the belief that inoculation was more efficacious and less likely to spread scrofula and other diseases. Furthermore, he generally found that when smallpox was in a house people believed it was

> ...too late for the inmates or the immediate neighbours to be vaccinated and the consequence is that one suffers then others fall ill, keeping up a succession of this long and fatal disease.

He concluded that the law ought to allow 'medical men' to inoculate where they could not overcome prejudice to vaccination.[254] A few years later, he and William Smith, then

251   TNA: MH 12/13907/15, ff 20-21. Letter from Thomas Day, Clerk to the Guardians of the Bromsgrove Poor Law Union, to the Poor Law Commission. 12 February 1845.
252   *Association Medical Journal*, 5 Apr. 1856.
253   *Fifth Annual Report of the Poor Law Board*, p 7, summary of vaccination returns for year ended 29 September 1852. PP., 1853.
254   TNA: MH 12/13907/7, ff 10-12. Letter from Thomas Day, Clerk to the Guardians of the Bromsgrove Poor Law Union, to the Poor Law

medical officer for Redditch, reported that smallpox was rife in the area, and bemoaned the ignorance and prejudice that prevailed among the poor on the subject. They said that people had become complacent about the disease, not bothering to get vaccinated and not realising that during an epidemic, it was always the unvaccinated who succumbed. They argued strongly for compulsory vaccination.[255]

By October 1853, compulsory vaccination was established and the Bromsgrove guardians again responded promptly by reviewing their vaccination arrangements. They extended the contracts to include two other medical practitioners in the area, and gave parents the choice of who should vaccinate their children. They ensured that the vaccination stations were convenient for the public and included the medical officers' own residences, school rooms in a number of the parishes, and several public houses.[256] By 1861, the situation in Bromsgrove had improved considerably, and a report by Mr Graves, Poor Law Inspector, stated that the vaccinators had been generally very vigilant with 861 vaccinations carried out from 886 births.[257]

There was undoubtedly a national concern for widespread vaccination to prevent 'the evils' of death and debility caused by smallpox.[258] While this may have been prompted to some degree by a regard for the public purse, it is clear that there was a strong humanitarian impulse behind it. The central authority and the

---

Commission. 20 January 1845.

255   TNA: MH 12/13910/24, ff 29-31, Letter from Thomas Day, Clerk to the Guardians of the Bromsgrove Poor Law Union, to the Poor Law Board (with enclosures). 7 February 1852.

256   TNA: MH 12/13910/325, ff 453-454, Letter from Thomas Day, Clerk to the Guardians of the Bromsgrove Poor Law Union, to the Poor Law Board. 21 October 1853.

257   TNA: MH 12/13911/551, ff 755-758. Workhouse Inspection Report Form from John Thomas Graves, Poor Law Inspector, to the Poor Law Board. 29 October 1861.

258   Seventh Annual Report of the Poor Law Commissioners, with appendices, p 95, circular letter from the Poor Law Commission to Boards' of Guardians, 20 August 1840. PP., 1841.

Bromsgrove guardians all sought to secure high levels of take-up. While some medical practitioners were more concerned about pay than public welfare, notably Gaunt in Bromsgrove, others were keen to ensure the eradication of a terrible disease. Fletcher's suggestion about inoculation, if misguided, shows his anxiety to ensure that at least people had some form of protection. His subsequent support for compulsory vaccination anticipated national legislation.

Typhus in the Workhouse

As we have seen, the Poor Law Commission had not intended workhouses to be as insanitary as the homes of the poor, and guardians were therefore required to maintain sanitary, well-run workhouses. However, this often conflicted with their wish to save money and Digby describes the pressure on guardians to reduce the burden on ratepayers as 'intense'.[259] The visiting committees set up by guardians were responsible for regularly inspecting the workhouses, but in some unions their visits were infrequent and cursory and were criticised by the assistant poor law commissioners.[260] The Poor Law Commission may have had good intentions but the conditions in each workhouse depended very much upon the attitudes and actions of their guardians. Standards varied enormously and outbreaks of disease were not uncommon.

So how then did the Bromsgrove Union respond when it faced an outbreak of typhus in 1844 and can we discern any real humanitarian impulse in regard to paupers affected by the disease? The new Bromsgrove Union workhouse was considered a satisfactorily sanitary place in 1842, when Fletcher reported that, apart from a few cases of measles, '…

---

259   Digby, Pauper Palaces, p 75.
260   Ibid, p 79.

the house ... is generally healthy'.[261] However, two years later its first case of typhus appeared. In the first week of May 1844, Lucy Owen, the matron, became ill with diarrhoea and fever. The sickness quickly spread to the inmates and for the next few weeks the guardians, the workhouse staff and Fletcher, the medical officer, battled with the epidemic. Throughout the period, Fletcher made frequent visits to the workhouse, writing weekly reports to the guardians about the progress of the sickness and making recommendations about actions to be taken to relieve the situation. In his report of 10 June Fletcher ordered rum punch and an improved diet of bread and meat for the inmates, and recommended giving out-relief wherever possible to restrict entry into the workhouse.[262] A week later, on 17 June, he recommended that those with fever should be kept separate from other inmates and asked the guardians to consider building a new ward for the hospital.[263] On 24 June he requested that the hospital rooms be lime-washed.[264]

The Poor Law Commission gave the guardians permission to improve the diet and to provide out-relief for able bodied paupers. They requested weekly reports and asked Alfred Austin, assistant poor law commissioner, to visit the workhouse. Austin reported back, approving the actions taken to control the disease but stipulating that the out-relief should only be given for as long as necessary, due to the difficult economic conditions in the union.[265]

261   TNA: MH 12/13905/230, ff 402-403. Letter from Thomas Day, Clerk to the Guardians of the Bromsgrove Poor Law Union, to the Poor Law Commission (with enclosure). 23 June 1842.
262   TNA: MH 12/13906/188, ff 332-334. Letter from Thomas Day, Clerk to the Guardians of the Bromsgrove Poor Law Union, to the Poor Law Commission. 18 June 1844.
263   MH 12/13906/188, ff 332-334. Letter from Thomas Day, Clerk to the Guardians of the Bromsgrove Poor Law Union, to the Poor Law Commission. 18 June 1844.
264   MH 12/13906/206, f 358. Letter from T S Fletcher [Thomas Swindell Fletcher], Medical Officer, to the Poor Law Commission. 24 June 1844.
265   MH 12/13906/189, f 335. Letter from Alfred Austin, Assistant Poor Law Commissioner, to the Poor Law Commission. 24 June 1844.

In early July, Fletcher reported that the rooms had been lime-washed, and the tanks, which received the soil and dirt from the water closets and sinks, had been cleaned and had quick lime put into them.[266] He gave details of individual sufferers.

Sarah Hodgkiss (who is ill) had a child four years old taken yesterday morning with very violent diarrhea [diarrhoea] and I fear it will not live many hours.[267]

The child of Hodgkiss I spoke of last week died about noon on Monday last and the infant of Sarah Waldron has since the death of its mother gradually sunk and died on Saturday.[268]

By the middle of July the worst was over and Fletcher reported that the inmates could return to their usual diet and the workhouse could begin to receive new paupers.[269] However the typhus and diarrhoea did not just affect the workhouse inmates - several guardians were taken ill and three of them died. By September this was worrying enough for the guardians to ask the Poor Law Commission to carry out an enquiry into the origins and progress of the disease. It was getting difficult to convene meetings as several guardians had '…absented themselves from their duties'.[270] They needed to be reassured that the workhouse was now safe.

---

266   MH 12/13906/197, ff 346-348. Letter from Thomas Day, Clerk to the Guardians of the Bromsgrove Poor Law Union, to the Poor Law Commission. 8 July 1844.
267   MH 12/13906/1938, f 340. Letter from Thomas Day, Clerk to the Guardians of the Bromsgrove Poor Law Union, to the Poor Law Commission. 1 July 1844.
268   MH 12/13906/197, ff 346-348. Letter from Thomas Day, Clerk to the Guardians of the Bromsgrove Poor Law Union, to the Poor Law Commission. 8 July 1844.
269   MH 12/13906/207, f 359. Letter from T S Fletcher [Thomas Swindell Fletcher], Medical Officer, to the Poor Law Commission. 15 July 1844.
270   MH 12/13906/214, ff 368-369. Letter from Thomas Day, Clerk to the Guardians of the Bromsgrove Poor Law Union, to the Poor Law Commission. 23 September 1844.

Austin's enquiry on 16 October 1844 was thorough and concluded that the disease was caused by the '...extreme foulness...' of the drainage and sewage tanks in the workhouse. These tanks were situated in the exercise yards (see figure 5/3), which would have been used by the inmates on a daily basis. Austin reported that the tanks had not been emptied or cleared for nearly two years

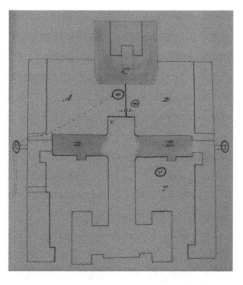

Figure 5/3: Ground Plan of Bromsgrove Poor Law Union Workhouse. A: Old Men's yard; B: Old Women's yard; C: Hospital; D: Ward containing old men's and children's day rooms; E: Ward containing old and young women's day rooms; 40: Well supplying pumps a and b; 41-44: Tanks.

and one tank had a small open grate and drained only when the soil accumulated to a depth of at least six feet. William Owen, the master of the workhouse, had noticed a foul smell coming from the grate and on 4 May, 6 July and 24 July the tanks were opened, cleaned out and emptied. Mr Woodhouse, the tradesman who carried this out, described it as one of the most offensive jobs he had ever undertaken.[271] Lucy Owen, William's wife, had been taken ill shortly after the first tank was opened and no new case had appeared after 24 July so Austin's conclusions about the causes of the illness seem reasonable.

The guardians' visiting committee made recommendations

271   MH 12/13906/234, ff 395-399. Report from Alfred Austin, Assistant Poor Law Commissioner, to the Poor Law Commission. 28 October 1844.

about improving the workhouse drainage, including examining and emptying the tanks at least twice a year, and the Poor Law Commission approved the plans.[272] A few years later, in 1847, the union decided to build a separate, detached building to house inmates suffering from infectious diseases. Apparently it had already proved its worth before it was completed, enabling two destitute Irishmen, one with typhus fever, to be isolated. In requesting (retrospective) sanction for the expenditure, they commented that 'If such building had not been at the disposal of the Guardians, the Health of the Inmates of the Workhouse might have been endangered'.[273]

Looking at how this outbreak of typhus and diarrhoea was dealt with in Bromsgrove, can we see who actually cared about the paupers in the workhouse? From his actions during the outbreak it is clear that Fletcher cared about the inmates. He visited the workhouse frequently, not seeming to worry about his own personal health, and continually pressed the guardians to carry out measures to help the inmates. His reports about the sick, especially when he refers to them by name, convey his humanity in witnessing their illnesses and their deaths.

The Poor Law Commission showed less humanitarian feeling but aimed at safeguarding administrative effectiveness through ensuring the workhouse continued to be run in line with their central regulations. They responded relatively quickly to the situation by sending in an inspector a month into the outbreak, and were concerned enough to require weekly reports from the guardians. They allowed an improved diet as well as the provision of out-relief for the able bodied, though only for as long as the outbreak lasted. The inspection by Austin in October 1844 was thorough and identified the source of the disease.

272   MH 12/13906/249, ff 416-417. Letter from Thomas Day, Clerk to the Guardians of the Bromsgrove Poor Law Union, to the Poor Law Commission. 19 November 1844.
273   TNA: MH 12/13908/, ff 157-158. Letter from Thomas Day, Clerk to the Guardians of the Bromsgrove Poor Law Union, to the Poor Law Commission. 11 October 1847.

The guardians appear to have cared less about the paupers in that they seem to have made improvements to their living conditions only when requested to do so by Fletcher. They were willing to sanction the expenditure for improved food during the outbreak and, later, for a separate building for those with infectious diseases, but seem to have been less concerned with the everyday standards in the workhouse, their visiting committee failing to see that the tanks had not been emptied for two years. Unlike Fletcher, the guardians preferred not to risk their health by attending meetings at the workhouse during the outbreak and it was this administrative problem, rather than concern for the paupers, that seems to have led them to request an enquiry into the causes of the disease.

Conclusion: Who Cared?

Like all unions, Bromsgrove faced its share of dirt, death and disease. However, this, of itself, did not mean that nobody cared about the health of its poor. Dr Fletcher, medical officer for Bromsgrove and the workhouse, apparently did. We saw this in his concern for patients in the workhouse during the typhus outbreak, in the tenderness of his reports on Sarah Hodgkiss's child, and in the improved diet he ordered for those who remained well. His anxiety to ensure that all should be protected against the scourge of smallpox showed his concern for public health, even if his desire to allow inoculation instead of vaccination might have been misguided medically. The public memorial raised when he was accused of negligence, with its reference to his 'unremitting' care for his poor patients, demonstrated the high regard in which he was held locally. By contrast, Dr Hobbes, with his concern for his dinner, and Dr Gaunt, reluctant to vaccinate if not better paid, illustrated that at times self-interest prevailed over professional duty among union medical officers.

The central authority 'cared' to ensure a well-run system. They were quick to investigate these accusations of negligence, sickness in the workhouse or low levels of vaccination, sending in an inspector where necessary to report back to them, and requiring detailed reports from the guardians. Depending on the findings, they might make recommendations for remedial measures, such as the dismissal of Dr Gaunt (though they failed to follow this through). This apparent concern for efficiency cannot, of course, be assumed to show that the centre 'cared' for the individual paupers they were responsible for. They also had other motivations such as the public purse and public opinion. They allowed an improvement in the diet, for instance, only in exceptional circumstances, where they thought it would lead more quickly to life in the workhouse returning to normal. Nonetheless, the actions of the assistant commissioners and inspectors, in particular, suggest a degree of genuine concern for the health of the poor.

It is difficult to judge just how much the guardians, who should perhaps have been the central figures in this, were motivated by the welfare of local paupers. In general they appear to have reacted to events rather than working to ensure good standards in their area. It seems shocking, for instance, that the visiting committee, who were supposed to inspect the workhouse on a regular basis, should not have noticed that the drains had not been emptied for two years. And, unlike Fletcher who made frequent visits to the workhouse to deal with the outbreaks of sickness, some of the guardians preferred to step back from their duties and absented themselves from meetings, rather than risked becoming ill themselves. On the other hand, they took action to avoid a further outbreak of fever in the workhouse, by building a separate isolation ward, possibly preventing a new outbreak of typhus in 1847. It is also evident that they took steps to try to improve take-up of vaccination in the union, which would undoubtedly have brought benefits to the community as a whole.

In conclusion then, we see a system, at least in part, which had tried to ensure a basic level of public health and professional practice. If concern for individuals appeared to be somewhat absent, overall the poor would have had some protection from negligent practitioners, and the spread of disease. Perhaps the real honours in this story should go to Thomas Swindell Fletcher who, despite accusations of negligence, appeared to have shown a genuine and effective concern for the sick.

6.

Ambrose Taylor of Newcastle under Lyme: A Victorian Tale of Immorality

Julie Bagnall

In the spring of 1857 allegations of immorality were made against Ambrose Taylor, who held the joint positions of porter and baker at the Newcastle under Lyme Union workhouse. The charges were made on behalf of Sarah Hand, reportedly a '… respectably connected…' woman of the town, who had recently died '…in distressing circumstances'.[274] The case outraged the townspeople who demanded Taylor's dismissal; public meetings and disquiet clouded the town. The local guardians requested an inquiry and Andrew Doyle, one of the Poor Law Inspectors, duly attended their next two meetings. However, as I have already indicated, this was not a case of pauper neglect or improper behaviour towards a female workhouse inmate. Taylor and Hand had been in a relationship which ended with tragic consequences and Taylor was now the subject of public outrage and Poor Law Board scrutiny. But, what lay behind the allegations? What can we learn about Sarah Hand's respectable connections and the circumstances of her death? Were the townspeople able to have Taylor dismissed? And is it possible at this late stage to trace the actions of local people, the local poor law union officials and central government officers in such a case?

---

274   TNA: MH 12/11366/22, ff 35-36 Letter from Thomas Twemlow, Chairman of the Board of Guardians, Newcastle under Lyme Poor Law Union, to the Poor Law Board. 30 March 1857.

The charge against Ambrose Taylor

The guardians of the Newcastle under Lyme Union held their usual fortnightly meeting on 30 March 1857. Two outraged townsmen also attended. John Hand and Thomas Heath were there on behalf of Sarah Hand, John's sister, who had recently died '…in distressing circumstances'. Their purpose was clear; they brought a verbal charge of immorality against Ambrose Taylor, baker and porter at the union workhouse, whom they held responsible for Sarah's death. Hand and Heath, described as '…two gentlemen of Newcastle' made a brief yet condemning statement to the board. Succinct and to the point they claimed that Sarah had been '…in the family way by him [and] just confined of three children at one birth…the children and mother are dead…which [h]as caused a good deal of observation in the Town…'.[275] They demanded action be taken against Taylor in the form of his dismissal. Taylor was called into the meeting where he admitted he had courted Sarah for a considerable time and said that he had proposed marriage on several occasions but that she had always refused.

After the meeting Thomas Twemlow, the union chairman, wrote to the Poor Law Board informing them of the resolution passed; that a copy of the charge be sent to them with a request that they '…send down an Inspector to enquire into the truth of such alleged charge…'.[276] A copy of the allegations was written out, signed by Heath and Hand and duly sent to the Poor Law Board. In his letter Twemlow set out the circumstances leading to the allegations. Citing the statement made by John Hand and Thomas Heath, Twemlow informed the board that '…for some

275   TNA: MH 12/11366/25, ff 39-40 Letter from Samuel Harding, Clerk to the Guardians of the Newcastle under Lyme Poor Law Union, to the Poor Law Board, which includes the statement by Thomas Heath and John Hand. 2 April 1857.
276   TNA: MH 12/11366/22, ff 35-36 Letter from Thomas Twemlow, Chairman of the Board of Guardians, Newcastle under Lyme Poor Law Union, to the Poor Law Board. 30 March 1857.

time an intimacy existed' between Sarah Hand and Taylor and that his proposals of marriage had been rejected. He also stated that during her pregnancy Sarah had travelled to Sheffield '... when a correspondence was kept up...' then to Congleton where Taylor had visited her the day before she gave birth to triplets. On returning to Newcastle, she died '...about a week ago'.

Doyle attended the next meeting of the Newcastle guardians on 13 April. Again, John Hand and Thomas Heath, the latter described by Doyle as a dissenting clergyman,[277] attended and were accompanied into the board room by a number of ratepayers who were now calling for a public meeting. Yet it seems that public outrage outweighed official concern as only eight of the 18 guardians attended.[278] Taylor was called in and again the facts set out. In Doyle's words Taylor

> ...had recently kept company (which in the Dialect of the District means had carried on an illicit intercourse) with her. The result was that she became pregnant and was delivered of three children and shortly afterwards died.[279]

Taylor did not deny any of this. Despite an eagerness for the matter to be cleared up quickly and Doyle's inquiry completed at this meeting, the guardians could not agree on what course of action to take against Taylor. A resolution was passed stating he should be dismissed but it was not carried by a majority and the resolution was withdrawn. Another was made censuring Taylor's conduct and it seems the guardians were willing to leave it at that

> ...the board feeling deeply the bitter consequences of his

---

277   TNA: MH 12/11366/24, f 38. Report from Andrew Doyle, Poor Law Inspector, to the Poor Law Board. 15 April 1857. I can find no record of a minister in Newcastle under Lyme named Thomas Heath at this time.
278   SRO: D339/1/6 p 76. Newcastle under Lyme Guardians' Minute Book, April 1856-April 1861. 13 April 1857.
279   TNA: MH 12/11366/24, f 38. Report from Andrew Doyle, Poor Law Inspector, to the Poor Law Board. 15 April 1857.

conduct, though unwilling to proceed to the extremity of discharge[ing] him considered him deserving of the severest condemnation decided that [he] should be strongly reprimanded and cautioned as to his future conduct.[280]

Although the poor law officers at local level had requested their chiefs in London to inquire into a case which they felt warranted investigation Doyle went along with the guardians' decision: '… It does not appear to me that the case is one in which the Board are called upon to set aside the Resolution of the Guardians by calling on the Porter to resign his office'.[281] He concluded his report by advising the central authority in London they need not take the matter further or overrule the guardians. It seems that their words of condemnation were adequate punishment for what they saw as a private matter.

However, the case was certainly causing '…much rancour in the town…'.[282] Unlike the more usual cases of pauper neglect or conflict over relief, the Poor Law Board had been called in to deal with an issue with a solely social impact; a case involving an employee and a highly thought of townswoman. Doyle's report states that Sarah Hand '…appears to have been rather respectably connected…' her case being '…taken up very warmly…' by her friends and family who '…expressed themselves very strongly…'.[283] Yet Twemlow did not merely allow the statement of Hand and Heath to stand alone. He seemed keen to present mitigating factors in defence of Taylor, making it public knowledge that proposals of marriage had been made and refused and that contact with Sarah was maintained right up to the time she gave birth. If Taylor's accusers, led by

280   SRO: D339/1/6, p 76. Newcastle under Lyme Guardians' Minute Book, April 1856-April 1861. 13 April 1857.
281   Ibid.
282   TNA: MH 12/11366/22, ff 35-36 Letter from Thomas Twemlow, Chairman of the Board of Guardians, Newcastle under Lyme Poor Law Union, to the Poor Law Board. 30 March 1857.
283   Ibid.

Sarah's brother John and Thomas Heath, thought him guilty of abandoning her while pregnant, his behaviour seems hardly that of a wayward lover or a lecherous womaniser. Though he and Sarah may not have had a stable relationship it was clearly more than a mere dalliance. There is no doubt that the loss of Sarah and her three babies was a family tragedy with a social impact for which Taylor was held responsible.

The correspondence into the case against Taylor lasted for just three weeks, from Twemlow's letter to the Poor Law Board on 30 March 1857 to the latter's acknowledgment of the guardians' resolution to censure Taylor's behaviour on 21 April. Yet two chance remarks within these letters and referring to Sarah Hand are worth considering as they raise issues of the poor law experience outside this case. Firstly, Twemlow states that Sarah was '...some time ago a schoolmistress in the workhouse...'. On arrival at the Poor Law Board this letter was annotated. Doyle scribbled on the back confirming he was to travel to Newcastle under Lyme and attend the guardians' next meeting. He also enquired '...are there any papers in the office with reference to the appt or resignation of Sarah Hand as schoolmistress in the WH?'. Another hand scribbled '...Sarah Hand does not appear to have held the office of schoolmistress at the Whouse of Newcastle under Lyme Union'.[284] Secondly, Andrew Doyle's comment regarding Sarah Hand's social standing in the town - that she was '...rather respectably connected' hints at the crux of the case which became embroiled in the attitudes and perceptions of respectability in a midlands market town in the mid-nineteenth century.

A very new union

The case brought against Taylor in 1857 takes us back to the very first days of the Newcastle under Lyme Poor Law Union.

---

284   Ibid.

Despite the Poor Law Board finding no record in their office, Sarah was, indeed, a workhouse schoolmistress; in fact she was the first to hold this office, appointed shortly after the union's formation in 1838.[285] Created from nine parishes the union comprised the town of Newcastle under Lyme and the surrounding parishes of Audley, Whitmore, Madeley, Chorlton, Keele, Maer, Betley and Balterley. These areas provided a mix of rural and urban, agriculture and industry, established county gentry and incoming migrant workers. Eighteen guardians had been elected by the first meeting, which had been held on 4 April 1838.[286] Thomas Stevens, one of assistant poor law commissioners, had arrived from London and chaired the meeting.[287] It was observed that '...many from the working class...' attended the open meeting in Newcastle Town Hall.[288] Clearly, local public interest was aroused. It was decided, on Stevens' recommendation, that weekly meetings should be held initially as there would be so much administrative work and organisation for the new union to deal with in the first year. The main business in the early stages was to appoint officers for the forthcoming year, with the positions of chairman, vice chairman and clerk taking priority. Captain R Mainwaring, of Whitmore Hall and guardian of Whitmore, was elected chairman and the Reverend John Daltry, guardian of Madeley, was elected vice chairman.[289]

The election of clerk was deferred until the next meeting, which was again attended by Thomas Stevens.[290] Yet it seems the guardians faced a dilemma; what class of man would be

---

285   Paid staff registers compiled by the Poor Law Commission appear to have been maintained only from the 1840s onwards and this explains (at least in part) the Poor Law Board's inability to find her in their own records.
286   SRO: D/339/1/1, p 1, Newcastle under Lyme Guardians' Minute Book, April 1838-December 1839. 4 April 1838.
287   Ibid.
288   *Staffordshire Advertiser*, p 3, 7 April 1838.
289   SRO: D/339/1/1, p 1, Newcastle under Lyme Guardians' Minute Book, April 1838-December 1839. 4 April 1838.
290   Ibid, p 5, 16 April 1838.

most suited to the role? The clerk's job was to be full time and salaried, therefore the guardians needed a man who could devote his whole time to the duties of the union. There was much debate and discussion. The question was how to balance adequate competency with existing commitment. On the one hand, a professional man would be more suitable as he would have a higher standard of education but would not be able to provide his full attention to the role, having his own business to attend to. A lesser qualified man would have no personal business demands but would be less capable of fulfilling the duties required of him.

Stevens pointed out that the Poor Law Commission would be supplying standard printed forms and documents for union clerks to work with and therefore a less qualified man would be just as able to do the work. Also, a less qualified man would be more likely to devote all his time to union business, not having any of his own to run. There were arguments both for and against. It was left to the guardians to decide the matter. Their advertisement for the clerk's position invited written applications with testimonials from those with '… perfect competency in bookkeeping and accounts…' who was required to '…spend the whole of his time to the service of the Union'.[291] There were two such applications. One from a Captain McDermott of Betley, and one from a Mr Henry Sneyd of Madeley. A third candidate,[292] Samuel Harding, had '…been in the field from the first…' but had failed to make written application and had no written testimonial due to an oversight.[293] Harding, on being proposed and seconded, hastily wrote out an application as the meeting continued, whilst at the same time Henry Sneyd withdrew his application.

---

291   *Staffordshire Advertiser*, p 1. 14 April 1838.
292   Only McDermott and Harding are named in the minutes of the meeting. SRO D339/1/1 p 5. Newcastle under Lyme Guardians Minute Book, April 1838-December 1839. 16 April 1838.
293   *Staffordshire Advertiser*, p 3. 21 April 1838.

Thomas Stevens pointed out that this was not the accepted manner and Harding should have made his application as advertised. Yet once again, he left the decision to the guardians. After many verbal testimonials praising Harding's integrity and performance as '... registrar of births etc and clerk to Newcastle Vestry (though not formally appointed)...',[294] he was appointed as union clerk. With the three offices of chairman, vice chairman and clerk now filled it became the union's business to appoint other workhouse staff. In June the guardians advertised for '...a person to act as schoolmistress... required to reside in the house...'.[295] There were two applicants, Sarah Hand and Harriet Worth. Sarah, with her application supported by written testimonials, whereas Harriet Worth's was not, was unanimously elected to the post.[296] However, she did not stay long in the job and by August she had sent in her resignation which caused the guardians to advertise again for a schoolmistress.[297] The lack of record in the Poor Law Board office in 1838 regarding Sarah's appointment and resignation means we can only speculate about her reasons for leaving.[298] Perhaps the reason behind Sarah's resignation was financial. She had been appointed at a salary of £10 per year plus board in the workhouse. The guardians sanctioned that a new schoolmistress should be appointed at a salary of £12.[299] Advertisements placed by the Newcastle under Lyme guardians did not go into any detail regarding the qualities necessary in applicants to the position of schoolmistress, or even the duties she would be required to perform. However, we may get an

---

294   Ibid.
295   *Staffordshire Advertiser*, p 1. 16 June 1838.
296   SRO: D339/1/1, p 86. Newcastle under Lyme Guardians' Minute Book, April 1838-December 1839. 18 June 1838.
297   Ibid. p127. 27 August 1838.
298   Neither did the guardians record a reason in the minutes of their meetings, merely stating that her resignation had been accepted. SRO: D339/1/1, p127. Newcastle under Lyme Guardians' Minute Book, April 1838-December 1839. 27 August 1838.
299   Ibid.

idea from neighbouring poor law unions advertising similar posts at the same time. The Stoke upon Trent Union stated that

> ...she will be required to instruct the children in reading, writing and plain sewing and knitting, to assist the Matron in cutting out the women's and children's wearing apparel, to superintend the making up of the same and generally to assist the Matron in the discharge of her duties and in the maintenance of order and due subordination in the house. Salary £15 pa with board and lodging. Not to be under 21 years.[300]

Were the Newcastle guardians penny-pinching? Clearly Sarah's counterpart in the next union had been earning 50% per year more, and even higher salaries were available for schoolmistresses working within existing established educational institutions. For example, the Cheadle National School was offering a salary of £20, their advertisement describing basically the same duties as the Stoke on Trent Union plus arithmetic.[301] But despite low pay and diversity of duties, it should be considered that the government, by way of the local poor law unions, offered employment opportunities to women that provided respectable alternatives to marriage or domestic service.

It was left to individual boards of guardians to decide how, and to what level, to educate the children of the poor in their union. At this time the founding unions were using existing parish buildings whilst making speedy arrangements for new purpose built workhouses. With regard to schooling the children of the poor during those early years the need to educate beyond the practical skills required for the world of manual and domestic work was questioned. Boards of guardians often refused the expense of providing writing equipment, arguing that the ability to write went beyond the necessary requirement

---

300   *Staffordshire Advertiser*, p1. 6 January 1838.
301   *Staffordshire Advertiser*, p1. 27 July 1839.

for the labouring classes. Even with the building of the new workhouses, teaching space was arbitrary, with some unions allocating a separate room for the purpose, others providing a purpose built school block and some sending their children out to existing National or British schools in the area.[302] In the case of Newcastle under Lyme, Sarah Hand's appointment meant that she would be working and lodging in the town's old workhouse in close proximity to the incoming Irish community.

These early appointments of union officials suggest that the intentions of the central authority to send out printed forms for the union clerks to work from, as stated by Stevens, did not materialise for some time. The central authority could not keep up with the urgency with which new unions were forming themselves. Applicants for union posts merely turned up hopefully with, but often without, written testimonials and relied largely on word of mouth acknowledgment of their competencies, skills and suitability. It also seems that the appointment of poor law union officials at this time reflected social and gender traditions. Although the Newcastle under Lyme guardians debated and discussed at length the qualities and skills pertaining to the class of men employed as the (male) clerk they were less specific when it came to the (female) schoolmistress. They merely wanted '...a person to act as a schoolmistress' without, it seems, giving any thought to the notion of class of person and probably even less to the idea of formal qualifications. True, they expected testimonials and rejected Harriet Worth for not providing any. Yet Samuel Harding was appointed clerk despite hurriedly scribbling out his application during the meeting and relying on verbal testimony; and this after Thomas Stevens had pointed out that this was not the accepted manner of appointment.

---

302   Fowler, S. Workhouse: the people, the places, the life beyond doors, 2008, pp 152-156.

A respectable connection

It is quite likely that Sarah Hand's motives for leaving her position as a poor law union schoolmistress were social rather than financial. Six weeks of life in the workhouse – not as a pauper but as the respectable townswoman Doyle tells us that she was – would perhaps have been seen as beneath her. Yet if it had not been for her involvement with Taylor, which led to the Poor Law Board correspondence in 1857, her name would probably be lost to history. So, who was she and how was she respectably connected?

It appears that Sarah's social standing came from her own family's position amongst the town's traders and manufacturers and the 'good' marriages of two of her sisters. She was born in Newcastle under Lyme around 1819/1820,[303] one of probably eight children of Ralph Hand, a hat manufacturer with an established business in the town.[304] The manufacture of felt and hats in Newcastle had its origins in the seventeenth century and was still flourishing at the time of Sarah's birth. In addition to his business, Sarah's father was also active in civic matters, being elected councillor for the town's west ward in 1836,[305] and appointed a rate assessor in 1847.[306]

It is not known what level of education Sarah had received or if she had any experience in teaching when she applied for the position of workhouse schoolmistress in 1838. We do know that her application was supported by testimonials. And there were links to genteel schooling in the town, thereby providing another respectable connection. In 1804 a Mrs Illidge announced to her friends and the public at large the re-

---

303   Based on age quoted in poor law correspondence, 1851 census, death certificate and grave stone. No record of her baptism has been found.
304   TNA: HO/107/1009/4, f 25, p 42. Census. 1841.
305   *Staffordshire Advertiser*, p 3. 2 January 1836.
306   Ibid, p 5. 6 March 1847.

opening of her 'School for Young Ladies'.[307] Sarah's older sister Mary had married William Illidge junior, a third generation tailor. Like the Hands, the Illidge family was long established in Newcastle. Educated and successful, they ran trade and commercial enterprises in the town and further afield. Other family members were engaged in the manufacture and retail of hats and bonnets and the management of a servants' registry office. Another Illidge – John, uncle of Sarah's brother in law William, had been a stockbroker and Mayor of London and Surrey in the 1830s. As a 'native of Newcastle under Lyme' John Illidge's death in 1847 was reported in the local press, not least to say that he left an estate of £60,000.[308] The Mrs Illidge with the school was probably Sarah's sister's mother in law.

The hatting industry benefitted from the Newcastle under Lyme Poor Law Union in two ways. Amongst the tenders for provisions and services came tenders for hats. During the summer of Sarah's brief employment at the workhouse, with changing fashions and decreased trade, the guardians sanctioned the purchase of 'Miss Pass's tender for straw bonnets @ 1/4d each…',[309] and it was resolved that Josiah Fox's tender for '… stout felt hats and caps at 1/8d be accepted'.[310] And whereas the hatters gained business from the new union, those without business received relief. By the mid-1840s what had been the main industry in the town of Newcastle under Lyme was well in decline, with the mayor stating '…our population are only half employed and half starved having nearly lost the hat trade…'.[311] The number of hatters in Newcastle workhouse during the mid-century may reflect this statement if only mildly. In 1841 there

---

307   Ibid, p 1. 14 July 1804.
308   Ibid, p 7. 23 January 1847.
309   SRO: D339/1/1, p 73. Newcastle under Lyme Guardians' Minute Book, April 1838-December 1839. 11 June 1838.
310   Ibid, p 93. 2 July 1838.
311   Stuart, D. 'From Pauper's Badge to Social Security', in Briggs, J. Newcastle under Lyme, 1173-1973, North Staffordshire Polytechnic, 1973, p 38.

were three male hatters aged 65-70 and one 35 year old female hat binder. In 1851 this had risen to eight males, one aged 53 and the rest aged 73-82, and in 1861 a total of six, one aged 41 and the rest aged 65-82.[312] The total number of inmates for these years remained at around 120. As the workhouse was intended for 300 inmates this shows an under capacity by more than half. [313]

Here we are presented with a paradox: the Hand family lived in Fletcher Street around which the hat manufacturing trade seems to have been based. Yet this was one of the least desirable areas of the town, highly populated and situated in the same ward as the workhouse. A long street consisting of all types of houses - beer, lodging, private and of ill repute - Fletcher Street was often represented in the local press. In 1857, just a couple of months before the respectably connected Sarah Hand lay dying at number 62, James Timson, keeper of a registered lodging house, was fined for '...accommodating prostitutes' but pleaded '...a want of a knowledge of the true character of the parties he had let his lodgings to...'.[314] Being named amongst those streets which caused most concern in matters of morality and public health, Fletcher Street was of the sort not generally associated with mid-nineteenth century respectability.[315] Yet the case of Sarah Hand demonstrates that living in a less affluent area was not necessarily an indicator of individual wealth or respectability. Sarah's father died in 1849 and the business was carried on by her mother. In 1851 the manufactory employed ten men and two apprentices. It was a family enterprise, with Sarah herself working as a hat trimmer, her brother John, one

---

312   TNA: HO 107/1009, f 53, p1. Census. 1841; HO 107/2001, f 352, p 54. Census. 1851; and RG 9/1917, f 103, p 48. Census. 1861.
313   SRO: D339/1/1, p 5. Newcastle under Lyme Guardians' Minute Book, April 1838-December 1839. 16 April 1838.
314   *The Newcastle and North Staffordshire Pioneer*, p 1. 27 January 1857.
315   'Newcastle-under-Lyme: Local government and public services', A History of the County of Stafford: Volume 8 (1963), pp. 24-39. URL: http://www.british-history.ac.uk/report.aspx?compid=53358

of the '...two gentlemen of Newcastle...' who was to bring the case against Taylor six years later, as '...foreman over hatters...' and their niece Maria Illidge as an eight year old errand girl.[316]

Disharmony in the house

In many ways the appointment of Ambrose Taylor as a poor law official followed a familiar pattern. Boards of guardians were eager to appoint ex-service men as masters and porters. Being familiar with regimented routines and experienced in maintaining order and discipline, these men were considered ideal candidates.[317] The porter, as the first point of contact with paupers at the workhouse gate, required the skills and attributes that service life instilled. Taylor had been a naval man, having served 21 years in the Royal Marines until his discharge in 1844.[318] In 1846 he was appointed baker and porter at the Stafford Union workhouse where he stayed until 1850,[319] leaving to start in business in his native town of Nantwich, working as a journeyman baker.[320] His time in the ranks of the self employed was short lived. In November 1851 he returned to the reliable rations and salary of workhouse life, being appointed baker at Newcastle under Lyme workhouse at a salary of £20 a year.[321] In addition to unions preferring ex-servicemen those with additional skills were also favoured and in February 1853 Taylor was assigned the dual roles of baker and porter on one month's

316   TNA: HO/107/2001, f 234, p 47. Census. 1851.
317   Crowther, Workhouse System, p 117.
318   TNA: ADM/157/365/246, ff 246-249. Attestation papers. Ambrose Taylor. 1823-1844.
319   TNA: MH 12/11365/114, ff 186-188. Letter from Samuel Harding, Clerk to the Guardians of the Newcastle under Lyme Poor Law Union, to the Poor Law Board (with enclosures). 5 April 18.
320   TNA: HO/107/2169, f 626, p 22. Census. 1851.
321   SRO D339/1/5, p 213. Newcastle under Lyme Guardians' Minute Book, January 1848-March 1856. 10 November 1851.

trial.[322] His permanent appointment was confirmed in April and his salary rose to £26 per year.[323] He was now in the same position at Newcastle Workhouse as he had been at Stafford.

Taylor's elevation to the dual roles of baker and porter in 1853 was due to an internal dispute between George Fox, workhouse master and William Beetinson,[324] the porter, which led to the forced resignation of Beetinson.[325] It was not uncommon for workhouse porters to work their way up the promotional ladder to workhouse master and we may speculate that Taylor had aspirations. That he had left his position at the Stafford Union workhouse to set up in business on his own account certainly shows entrepreneurial ambition. But poor law unions usually appointed married couples as workhouse master and matron. Ex-nurses and schoolmistresses made ideal partners, being able to provide the domestic skills necessary to the female inmates.[326] Were Taylor's proposals to Sarah made as part of his career plan? And did Sarah suspect this? Having already had a taste of workhouse life at the very establishment of the union, she may not, almost 22 later and with her respectable connections seemingly intact, wish to be associated with the town's paupers, despite living in Fletcher Street. At no time throughout the case of immorality brought against Taylor in the spring of 1857 was the standard of his work or his conduct in the workhouse questioned. Andrew Doyle's report confirms

---

322   Ibid, p 259. 7 February 1853.
323   Ibid, p 271. 18 April 1853.
324   The archive variously refers to the spelling of his name as Beetinson or Beetenson.
325   TNA: MH 12/11365/98, ff 151-156, Letter and enclosures from Andrew Doyle, Poor Law Inspector, to the Poor Law Board. 20 January 1853; MH 12/11365/102, ff 163-167, Letter from Samuel Harding, Clerk to the Guardians of the Newcastle under Lyme Poor Law Union, to the Poor Law Board. 9 February 1853; and MH 12/11365/104, ff 170-172. Letter from Joseph Knight, Coroner for the Borough of Newcastle under Lyme, to the Poor Law Board. 18 February 1853. The case involved the death of a workhouse pauper, Samuel Hassell and allegations against Mr and Mrs Fox, workhouse master and matron, other workhouse staff and inmates.
326   Fowler, Workhouse, p 79.

that '...no complaint whatever has been made of the Porter who also acts as the Baker giving in both capacities perfect satisfaction to the Guardians'.[327] Doyle sees the only misconduct by Taylor was that he did not persist in his attempts to wed Sarah once she became pregnant.

Ambrose Taylor's name seems to have stayed out of the poor law correspondence and guardians' minutes books for a couple of years. But in August 1859 the Newcastle under Lyme guardians called on the Poor Law Board for an inspector to attend their next meeting; a complaint had been made against Taylor. Again, Andrew Doyle attended. The charge against Taylor this time was '...of having a number of loaves in his possession unaccounted for...' which, when investigated, was found to be due to '...the defective way in which the bread production account was kept... [the guardians] ...fully acquitted Taylor of any intention to defraud or deceive them...'.[328] The master, still George Fox, then complained that Taylor was '...habitually annoying him by his conduct...'.[329] Taylor and Fox made statements. The guardians concluded that

> ...from this and former disputes the master and porter should never agree together and this being intimated to the porter he tendered his resignation which the guardians accepted.[330]

Ambrose Taylor was, by this time, in his mid to late fifties and unmarried.[331] If he did have ambitions to become a workhouse master they remained unfulfilled.

---

327   TNA MH 12/11366/24, f 38. Report from AD [Andrew Doyle, Poor Law Inspector], to the Poor Law Board. 15 April 1857.
328   SRO D339/1/6, pp 243-244. Newcastle under Lyme Guardians' Minute Book, April 1856-April 1861. 15 August 1859.
329   Ibid. p 245. 29 August 1859.
330   Ibid.
331   The various archive sources used here give a birth year between 1804 and 1807.

Conclusion

In the spring of 1857 the Newcastle under Lyme guardians bowed to pressure from local inhabitants and requested the Poor Law Board to investigate the moral conduct of a workhouse officer. But after an inquiry into '...the truth of such allegations...' against Taylor they decided against dismissal. Their decision was supported by the central authority which felt it unnecessary to overrule the guardians' resolution that severe reprimand was punishment enough. The view taken by the Board was, it seems, that local matters could be locally resolved as long as the issues remained within the law. Taylor had committed no crime, his work ethic was not questioned, no public disorder took place. Whatever bad feeling there had been, his moral conduct was a private matter which did not merit any further intervention from London.

Postscript

Sarah Hand's '...three children at one birth' were born in the early hours of 10 March 1857 at Water Street, Congleton. One died within the first minute of life. The second child to die was Ambrose at three days, and finally Ralph at four days.[332] Astbury parish register confirms that '...three boys were born ill[egitimate] one died soon after birth unbaptized'.[333] Their births and deaths were registered at the same time on 16 March in Congleton. Sarah died of puerperal fever on 22 March at the family home in Fletcher Street, Newcastle.[334] She was aged 38 and still working as

---

332   Birth and death certificates.
333   Diocese of Chester Parish Registers of baptisms and burials 1538-1910 are to be found via www.findmypast.co.uk
334   The family relationship with the Newcastle Union continued. In 1861 her niece Maria Illidge was a pupil teacher in Newcastle under Lyme. TNA: RG 9/1916, f 151, p 34. Census. 1861.

a hat binder. Her brother John was in attendance.[335] She was buried in a family grave in St George's Churchyard, Newcastle on 25 March 1857.[336] Ambrose Taylor returned to his native Nantwich. From 1861 until his death he lived in Weston, with the village schoolmistress Maria Selway. She was ten years his junior, a similar age difference between him and Sarah Hand. In an effort to possibly bow to social

Figure 6/2. Family grave in St George's Churchyard Newcastle under Lyme. Also her sister Rachel, mother Sarah and niece Eliza Stanton. Her father Ralph Hand is buried in Newcastle's other churchyard at St Giles. Copyright Julie Bagnall.

propriety he is variously described as brother or boarder to the schoolmistress. His military career rather than his workhouse role is recorded: '...Royal Marine Pensioner', pensioner, Greenwich pensioner,[337] and when he died, aged 87 in October 1890, it was as Ambrose Taylor, 'late of the Royal Marines'.[338]

---

335   Death certificate of Sarah Hand.
336   St George's Parish Registers accessed via www.freereg.org.uk
337   Census returns Nantwich Cheshire: TNA: RG 9/2615, f 95, p 9. Census. 1861; RG 10/3711, f 111, p 9. Census. 1871; and RG 11/3545, f 41, p 6. Census. 1881.
338   *Cheshire Observer,* p 5, 18 October 1890.

7.

Workhouse Officers in the Wolstanton and Burslem and the Newcastle under Lyme Poor Law Unions in the Early Years of the New Poor Law

David G Jackson

Introduction

Prior to the implementation of the New Poor Law, there was no central authority to supervise the appointment of workhouse officers. This meant that local workhouses were often run by people with no training or experience and this obviously resulted in varying standards between unions and their workhouses. The 1834 New Poor Law, intended to enforce uniform standards across the country, marked the beginning of a period of professionalisation within the poor law service. However, this process was slow to take effect. Crowther describes the lot of workhouse officers between 1834 and 1870.[339] The nature of the workhouse was itself a deterrent to service within it. Social isolation resulted from long hours, with time off and absence allowed only at the master's discretion. The master could absent himself only with the permission of the guardians. Master and matron were usually a married couple, but were not expected to have children. As the main link between guardians and the officers and inmates of the workhouse, the master could often exercise considerable power. Other officers (schoolteacher,

---

339   Crowther, Workhouse System, pp 113-134.

porter, nurse) were normally unmarried, although the schoolmaster and schoolmistress were occasionally a married couple, and duties might be found for a porter's wife. Status of nurse and porter was low, and in the early days these posts were filled by inmates. Teachers fared little better, often being expected to carry out non-teaching duties in addition to teaching and supervising the children at all times. It is therefore unsurprising that early officers under the New Poor Law were often not of the highest calibre. In such a small enclosed community, without recreational facilities, disputes and squabbles were inevitable.[340] Although nurses and teachers could move into and out of the workhouse system, there were fewer opportunities outside the system for masters and matrons. Financial disincentives to poor law service included low salaries, attempts to reduce officers' salaries during times of financial stringency (opposed by the central authority), and the absence of a superannuation scheme for officers until 1864; even at this date payment was entirely at the discretion of the guardians. The consequent reluctance of officers to retire, and the guardians' reluctance to dismiss old and faithful officers, led to a lowering of standards. Despite the control exercised by the central authority, appointments made by the guardians were sometimes influenced by nepotism.

The purpose of this study is to investigate the careers of key workhouse officers, namely master, matron, schoolmaster, schoolmistress, porter, and nurse, who served under the New Poor Law system up to the early/mid 1850s. I will be surveying the age, qualifications, duration of service, former occupations, reasons for resignation/dismissal, and relationships between officers; in a few cases the officers' careers will be followed in other unions. The main sources for this are the poor law union correspondence for the Wolstanton and Burslem and the Newcastle under Lyme poor law unions. Considerable use was also made of the guardians' minutes for these two unions. Other

---

340   See David Finlow's contribution to this volume.

documents used included the poor law union correspondence volumes for other unions where the Wolstanton and Burslem and the Newcastle files indicated that this would be profitable, and the registers of paid officers.

The two poor law unions of Wolstanton and Burslem and of Newcastle under Lyme were situated in North Staffordshire. Wolstanton and Burslem Union comprised part of the Potteries, while industries carried on in Newcastle under Lyme, immediately to the south-west, included hats, silk, cotton, malting, shoes and clocks.[341]

Master and Matron

Master and matron were usually a married couple. The master had overall responsibility for the workhouse; his duties included overseeing admissions, discipline, record-keeping, and registration of births and deaths. The matron was the master's assistant and deputy, had responsibility for children and female inmates, and supervised general domestic matters.[342] The first master and matron to be appointed to the Wolstanton and Burslem Union Workhouse were William and Sophia Welsby, who took up the posts in March 1840,[343] after holding similar posts at Burslem Parish Workhouse since July 1838.[344] In the 1841 census, they were both reported as 50 years of age. [345] Although Welsby was described as well qualified by an assistant commissioner in November 1840,[346] subsequent suggestions of

341   White, W. History, Gazetteer, and Directory of Staffordshire, 1851, pp 300-301.
342   Englander, Poverty and Poor Law Reform, p 35.
343   SSTAS: SD1232/3, ff 364-365. Wolstanton and Burslem Board of Guardians' Minute Book, 1838-1841. 10 March 1840.
344   SSTAS: SD1232/3, f 63. Wolstanton and Burslem Union Board of Guardians' Minute Book, 1838-1841. 26 November 1839.
345   TNA: HO 107/993/23, p 1, f 39. 1841 Census.
346   TNA: MH 12/11196/156, f 289. Letter from W J Gilbert, Assistant Poor Law Commissioner, to the Poor Law Commission. 28 November 1840.

lax management which came to light during the investigation into the conduct of Schoolmaster William Coxon (see below), Welsby's drunkenness, and his consequent absence from his duties, no doubt contributed to the couple's resignation in June, 1842.[347] Their total length of service at both workhouses was four years. Their subsequent activities are unknown.

In the month that William and Sophia Welsby resigned, William Abraham Shore and his wife Hannah, aged 50 and 40 years respectively, took up the appointments.[348] Shore had previously been a mariner, kept a public house, been in the wine and spirit trade, and had been bankrupt and was discharged from Chester Castle under the Insolvent Debtors Act in March 1835,[349] while his wife had kept a boarding school. They had children who would not be living with them in the workhouse. The assistant commissioner did not favour the appointment of Shore, who was constitutionally unfit for the post because of his age, had no knowledge of the workhouse system or of accounts, and needed several attempts to sign his name.[350] As an undischarged bankrupt, he was not eligible for appointment. The assistant commissioner considered that Shore was appointed because he was known to some of the guardians and was 'in want.' Not surprisingly, the Commissioners declined to sanction the Shores' appointments.[351] The couple do not appear

347   TNA: MH 12/11196/290, ff 504-514. Letter from Joseph Lowndes, Clerk to the Guardians of the Wolstanton and Burslem Poor Law Union, to the Poor Law Commission. 13 July 1842. MH 12/11196/254, f 456. Letter from Joseph Lowndes, Clerk to the Guardians of the Wolstanton and Burslem Poor Law Union, to the Poor Law Commission. 1 July 1842. MH 12/11196/271, f 477. Letter from Joseph Lowndes, Clerk to the Guardians of the Wolstanton and Burslem Poor Law Union, to the Poor Law Commission. 17 June 1842.
348   TNA: MH 12/11196/284, ff 494-496. Letter from Joseph Lowndes, Clerk to the Guardians of the Wolstanton and Burslem Poor Law Union, to the Poor Law Commission. 5 July 1842.
349   SSTAS: SD1232/18. Wolstanton and Burslem Union Board of Guardians' Draft Minute Book, 1842-1844. 9 August 1842.
350   TNA: MH 12/11196/276, ff 482-483. Notes and observations from W J Gilbert, Assistant Poor Law Commissioner. 23 June 1842.
351   TNA: MH 12/11196/323, f 558. Letter from Joseph Lowndes, Clerk to the Guardians of the Wolstanton and Burslem Poor Law Union, to the Poor

to have made a career in the poor law service, but are found in Birkenhead in the 1851 census, when William is described as a seaman.[352]

At Christmas 1842 the Shores were replaced by Charles and Emilia Wellum, who, according to their appointment form, were both 30 years of age.[353] They had been schoolmaster and schoolmistress at Northwich Union Workhouse, Cheshire,[354] posts for which they were recommended by Dr Kay.[355] They took up their appointments at Northwich on 3 May 1841.[356] However, their stay there was short and unhappy. On 19 August 1841 Charles Wellum wrote to W J Gilbert, Assistant Poor Law Commissioner, complaining about the guardians' attitude to the education of pauper children, and requesting a testimonial to assist the couple in their search for new posts.[357] Gilbert recommended the couple for the posts of master and matron at Wolstanton and Burslem.[358] Their experience as workhouse schoolteachers may have influenced their handling of an incident (described below) when a schoolboy was ill-treated by William Carr, the schoolmaster. The Wellums were awarded an increase in salary in 1846, in view of the increase in the number

Law Commission. 5 October 1842.

352   TNA: HO 107/2175, p 33, f 50. Census. 1851.

353   TNA: MH 12/11196/335, ff 571-574. Letter from Joseph Lowndes, Clerk to the Guardians of the Wolstanton and Burslem Poor Law Union, to the Poor Law Commission. 17 November 1842.

354   TNA: MH 12/1059, Paper Number: 5875/B/1841. Appointment Form of Charles and Emilia Wellum. 15 May 1841.This gives their ages as 26 for Charles and 28 for Emilia.

355   Later known as James Philips Kay-Shuttleworth, Assistant Poor Law Commissioner, first secretary to the Committee of Council on Education. He devoted much of his life to educational progress.

356   TNA: MH 12/1059, Paper Number: 5875/B/1841. Appointment Form of Charles and Emilia Wellum. 15 May 1841.

357   TNA: MH 12/1059, Paper Number: 9315/B/1841. Letter from Charles Wellum, Schoolmaster to the Northwich Poor Law Union, to W J Gilbert, Assistant Poor Law Commissioner. 19 August 1841.

358   TNA: MH 12/11196/335, ff 571-574. Draft letter from Joseph Lowndes, Clerk to the Guardians of the Wolstanton and Burslem Poor Law Union, to the Poor Law Commission. 6 June 1842.

of inmates and their skilful management of the workhouse,[359] and they held their posts until 1858, when they resigned and Charles was appointed registrar of births and deaths for the Tunstall District.[360] At a guardians' meeting on 9 March 1858, in response to the Wellums' request for a testimonial

> It was unanimously resolved that the clerk prepare a Testimonial expressing the satisfaction of the Guardians of their conduct during the 15 years they had held office, and the regret of the Board at their retirement. That the Testimonial be written on parchment, framed and glazed, and that it be signed by the Chairman and Clerk on behalf of the Board, and the Common Seal affixed thereto.[361]

At the next guardians meeting, Elizabeth Rogers, an orphan, was bound as servant to the Wellums.[362]

In April 1840, the workhouse master at Newcastle under Lyme was Robert Salmon.[363] By December 1840, he had been replaced by George Fox, who was accused in that month of illegally confining a pauper by chaining him. The guardians recorded their disapproval of using restraint that was not permitted by the regulations.[364] The magistrates dismissed the case brought against Fox, on the grounds that the pauper was not sane. During 1841 an investigation was held into the case

---

359   TNA: MH 12/11197/241, f 305. Draft letter from the Poor Law Commission to Joseph Lowndes, Clerk to the Guardians of the Wolstanton and Burslem Poor Law Union. 11 December 1846.

360   SSTAS: SD1230/(125), f 424. Wolstanton and Burslem Board of Guardians Minute Book, 1854-1858. 29 December 1857.

361   SSTAS: SD1230/(125), f 444. Wolstanton and Burslem Board of Guardians' Minute Book, 1854-1858. 9 March 1858.

362   SSTAS: SD1230/(125), f 450. Wolstanton and Burslem Board of Guardians' Minute Book, 1854-1858. 23 March 1858.

363   TNA: MH 12/11363/179, f 296. Copy letters from Henry Ingledew, Chairman of the Newcastle under Lyme Poor Law Guardians, to Sir John Walsham, Assistant Poor Law Commissioner. 24 April 1840.

364   SSTAS: D339/1/2, p.207. Newcastle under Lyme Board of Guardians' Minute Book, 1840-1842. 21 December 1840. *Staffordshire Advertiser*, 9 Dec 1840, p.3, col.6.

of a sick vagrant who had died as a result of shortcomings in the care he received, and the workhouse regime, and officers were criticized; the Commissioners' response was that they thought lessons would be learned from the case.[365] In 1853 the porter, William Beetenson,[366] made a number of allegations against the master and matron; he claimed that they knew about improper behaviour between the former porter and nurse, and between other officers, that the matron did not properly refer cases of illness to the medical officer, and that Mr and Mrs Fox allowed spirituous liquors and food into the house. A special meeting of the guardians, attended by Andrew Doyle, Poor Law Inspector, rejected the complaints and sought the resignation of the porter, whom Doyle clearly regarded as a troublemaker. [367] The introduction of gin into the workhouse, and admission of paupers without examination by the medical officer were, however, considered sufficient to warrant Fox being cautioned.[368] Samuel Hassall, the pauper whose illness was alleged by Beetenson not to have been promptly reported to the medical officer, subsequently died. Although the inquest jury attached blame to the master and matron,[369] the couple were exonerated by a Poor Law Board enquiry. [370] In an earlier case two paupers who were released from the workhouse in 1848 were subsequently deemed incapable of looking after

---

365   TNA: MH 12/11363/218, ff 367 371. Draft letter from the Poor Law Commission to Samuel Harding, Clerk to the Guardians of the Newcastle under Lyme Union. 1 April 1841.
366   The archive variously refers to the spelling of his name as Beetinson or Beetenson.
367   TNA: MH 12/11365/98, ff 151-156. Letter from Andrew Doyle, Poor Law Inspector, to the Poor Law Board. 20 January 1853.
368   TNA: MH 12/11365/99, ff 157-158. Draft letter from the Poor Law Board to Samuel Harding, Clerk to the Guardians of the Newcastle under Lyme Poor Law Union. 29 January 1853.
369   TNA: MH 12/11365/102, ff 163-167. Letter from Samuel Harding, Clerk to the Guardians of the Newcastle under Lyme Poor Law Union, to the Poor Law Board. 9 February 1853.
370   TNA: MH 12/11365/117, f 200. Draft letter from the Poor Law Board to Samuel Harding, Clerk to the Guardians of the Newcastle under Lyme Poor Law Union. 19 April 1853.

themselves.[371] Nevertheless, the master and matron held their posts until November 1867, when George Fox died and his widow resigned.[372] The guardians recorded '...the admirable manner' in which he had discharged his duties over a period of almost 30 years. They were also complimentary about Mrs Fox, but declined to grant her a superannuation allowance on the grounds that '...her pecuniary situation renders such aid superfluous.'[373] In 1849, when the guardians were contemplating reducing officers' salaries, the Commissioners had reminded them that the master and matron were the best of servants.[374]

Schoolteachers

Workhouse schoolteachers have been described as '...a sorry lot who were kept under the master's control.'[375] Their duties extended beyond academic instruction and industrial training, to include supervision of the children at all times, as is illustrated by the draft letter sanctioning the appointment of a schoolmaster at nearby Congleton, prior to the building of the union workhouse

> the Commissioners do not in general approve of the schoolmaster not residing within the walls of the workhouse and they trust that when the new house proposed to be built shall be ready for occupation, the guardians will avail

371   TNA: MH 12/11364/212, ff 272-272. Letter from H Sutcliffe, Poor Law Guardian of the Newcastle under Lyme Poor Law Union, to the Poor Law Board. 29 February 1848.
372   SSTAS: D339/1/7, f 419. Newcastle under Lyme Board of Guardians' Minute Book, 1861-1868. 18 November 1867.
373   SSTAS: D339/1/7, ff 442-443. Newcastle under Lyme Board of Guardians' Minute Book, 1861-1868. 27 January, 1868.
374   TNA: MH 12/11364/279, f 357. Letter from J W Daltry, Vice Chairman of the Newcastle under Lyme Board of Poor Law Guardians, to the Poor Law Board. 9 March 1849.
375   Englander, Poverty and Poor Law Reform, p.37.

themselves of the means it will afford of giving the children the advantage of a schoolmaster being constantly with them.[376]

The Newcastle-under-Lyme guardians took this policy to extreme lengths in August 1847, when they ordered that '...the recess adjoining the Boys sleeping room should be fitted up as a Bed Room for the Schoolmaster with the requisite partition, Bed and Bedding'.[377] Teachers were also expected to carry out duties not related to the children, as we will see in the case of William Carr below who was described as rude, unkind and unfeeling when distributing food in the men's ward.[378] Such working conditions could hardly be expected to attract applicants of the highest calibre, but steps were taken towards improvement in the 1840s, with the introduction of grants to cover schoolteachers' salaries. This was linked to a system of examination and certification of teachers, with the level of the grant determined by their performance.[379] In the 1840s and 1850s training for workhouse schoolteachers was provided at a number of establishments, notably at Norwood and Kneller Hall.[380] The attitude of schoolmasters was an ongoing problem, as shown by the comment of Sir John Walsham, Poor Law Inspector, in his 1853 report on the Lexden and Winstree Union Workhouse, in Essex

The schoolmaster is from Kneller Hall. He appears to make an efficient teacher, and to conduct himself in a very becoming manner, which is not generally the case with young

376 TNA: MH 12/934, Paper Number: 2703/B/1842. Draft letter from the Poor Law Commission to W and J Latham, Clerks to the Guardians of the Congleton Poor Law Union. 16 March 1842.
377 SSTAS: D339/1/4, f 420. Newcastle under Lyme Board of Guardians' Minute Book, 1844-1847. 2 August 1847.
378 TNA: MH 12/11198/296, ff 473-477. Letter from Joseph Lowndes, Clerk to the Guardians of the Wolstanton and Burslem Poor Law Union. 3 February 1851.
379 Crowther, Workhouse System, p 131.
380 Fraser, D. The New Poor Law in the Nineteenth Century, London, 1976, p 70; Fowler, S. Workhouse, The National Archives, 2008, p 155.

schoolmasters, although certainly the Kneller Hall pupils, so far as I have seen of them, are exceptions to that rule.[381]

Schoolmasters

Ten schoolmasters served at Wolstanton and Burslem during the period being studied and these are set out at Appendix 1. Five were single, three were widowed, one was married, and the marital status of another is unknown. None intended to take his wife or children into the workhouse. Of the seven for whom religion was recorded, all except William Carr were members of the Church of England; Carr was a Baptist but conformed to the principles of the Church of England.[382] Let us look at these officers individually. At their meeting on 20 November 1838, when the guardians decided to appoint a schoolmaster, it was decided that he should be single, and in addition to teaching and instilling moral discipline into the boys, would assist the workhouse master generally.[383] Following advertisements in *The Staffordshire Advertiser*, *The North Staffordshire Mercury*, and *The Birmingham Herald*, George Goodwin of Cheadle was appointed on 11 December 1838.[384] He was at the centre of an unpleasant incident in April 1840, when he was assaulted by the mother of a boy he had beaten. Although the magistrate dismissed the case, the guardians considered the case proven, and felt that the schoolmaster's authority was undermined. They did, however, warn him to use only '…proper weapons in

---

381   TNA: MH 12/129, Paper Number: 35004/B/1853. Report on Inspection of the Lexden and Winstree Poor Law Union. 27 September 1853.

382   TNA: MH 12/11198/101, ff 169-171. Letter from Joseph Lowndes, Clerk to the Guardians of the Wolstanton and Burslem Poor Law Union, to the Poor Law Board. 6 March 1849.

383   SSTAS: SD1232/3, f 140. Wolstanton and Burslem Board of Guardians' Minute Book, 1838-1841. 20 November 1838.

384   SSTAS: SD1232/3, f 151. Wolstanton and Burslem Board of Guardians' Minute Book, 1838-1841. 11 December 1838.

correcting the lads'.[385] At the same meeting the guardians noted Goodwin's illness and approved his brother temporarily taking his place, it not being unusual for schoolteachers to be required to provide their own temporary replacements.

The documents relating to John Leigh, particularly a letter from Joseph Lowndes, the Wolstanton and Burslem Union clerk, to W J Gilbert, Assistant Poor Law Commissioner, provide an interesting insight into the politics of the board of guardians, the Poor Law Commissioners, and Joseph Lowndes himself.[386] Lowndes was clearly not happy about the appointment of John Leigh as workhouse schoolmaster which, in his view, had been influenced by the fact that Leigh was a relation of an influential guardian. He commented unfavourably on Leigh's age, previous occupation, lack of training in and experience of teaching, and former irregular habits. He also mentioned Leigh's failure as an earthenware manufacturer. Lowndes also pointed out that there had been nine other applicants for the job of workhouse schoolmaster and singled out three of these as particularly suitable. The Poor Law Commission checked and concurred with Lowndes' allegations. Leigh's appointment was sanctioned provisionally,[387] but within a few months he was dismissed for absenting himself without leave or satisfactory explanation; he was also said to be of unsteady habits, and there was a suspicion that he had been drinking.[388] His appointment form shows nothing adverse, except his former bankruptcy.

William Coxon served as schoolmaster for seven months in 1841-2 before being dismissed for sexual impropriety. The

---

385   SSTAS: SD1232/3, f 392. Wolstanton and Burslem Board of Guardians' Minute Book, 1838-1841. 28 April 1840.
386   TNA: MH 12/11196/206, ff 373-378. Letter from Joseph Lowndes, Clerk to the Guardians of the Wolstanton and Burslem Poor Law Union, to the Poor Law Commission. 22 July 1841.
387   TNA: MH 12/11196/207, f 379. Letter from W J Gilbert, Assistant Poor Law Commissioner, to the Poor Law Commission. 25 July 1841.
388   TNA, MH 12/11196/216, f 390. Letter from Joseph Lowndes, Clerk to the Guardians of the Wolstanton and Burslem Poor Law Union, to the Poor Law Commission. 3 November 1841.

workhouse committee's enquiry into this case found that discipline at the workhouse, under master and matron William and Sophia Welsby, was very lax.[389] Coxon went out of the workhouse one evening, and while in the Brindley Arms public house called to two female inmates who were passing after threatening to climb over the workhouse wall if the master or matron did not allow them to go out. The three were joined by a male inmate who had been sent to get gin for Welsby. They came back only after the master repeatedly sent an inmate and the porter to call them back. There were allegations about female inmates being seen in the male areas of the house and in Coxon's room. Coxon was found in a compromising position with inmate Dinah Belton, but an application for orders in bastardy against him was made in respect of Amelia, daughter of Ann Myatt, another inmate.[390]

George Machin, formerly a National Schoolmaster, succeeded Coxon and resigned after two and a half years, having found another situation. In 1843 the guardians' draft minutes contain the cryptic comment that the guardians approved of the course adopted by the workhouse committee as to the charge preferred against George Machin, the schoolmaster.[391] Early in 1844, the guardians called on Machin to explain his absence from the workhouse for two days and two nights.[392] His explanation was that he had spent longer than intended at a Christmas party in Newcastle. He was reprimanded and undertook not to repeat the offence.[393] In the summer of 1844

389   TNA: MH 12/11196/290, ff 504-514. Letter from Joseph Lowndes, Clerk to the Guardians of the Wolstanton and Burslem Poor Law Union, to the Poor Law Commission. 13 July 1842.
390   SSTAS: SA/CW/3A. Index to Register of Baptisms, Wolstanton and Burslem Workhouse, 1840- 1921. SD1232/18. Wolstanton and Burslem Board of Guardians' Draft Minute Book, 1842-1844. 29 November 1842.
391   SSTAS: SD1232/18. Wolstanton and Burslem Board of Guardians' Draft Minute Book, 1842-1844. 7 February 1843.
392   SSTAS: SD1232/4, not foliated. Wolstanton and Burslem Board of Guardians' Minute Book, 1843-1846. 29 January 1845.
393   SSTAS: SD1232/4, f 36. Wolstanton and Burslem Board of Guardians' Minute Book, 1843-1846. 23 January 1844.

Machin was involved in another breach of discipline, when the master complained that he had neglected his duty and had held an interview at an improper hour with Phoebe Hill, workhouse servant.[394] Despite Machin's claim that Hill was only telling him what she had heard about a report on the school, she was dismissed, but the guardians imposed a suspension on Machin, hoping that this might have a beneficial effect, and allowed him to continue in office, subject to his behaving properly.[395] He resigned with effect from the end of November 1844.[396] His relationship with the guardians can be inferred from an entry in their minutes recording their response to his request for a testimonial – 'Nothing done'.[397] The post was advertised in *The Staffordshire Advertiser* and *The North Staffordshire Mercury*.[398]

Machin was succeeded by William Ward Broadhurst, who, according to his appointment form, had lived in Congleton and helped his father as relieving officer. He had also occasionally managed the Congleton National School, taught regularly on Sundays, and attended a training institution in London (probably Norwood). He did not, however, live up to expectations, and in June 1845 it was recorded that he had been absent for five days without leave, so he was given and took the opportunity to resign, as the guardians considered him an inefficient schoolmaster.[399] This did not, however, mark the end of his career in poor law service. In September 1846 he was appointed relieving officer at Penkridge (subsequently renamed

---

394   SSTAS: SD1232/4, f 119. Wolstanton and Burslem Board of Guardians' Minute Book, 1843-1846. 23 July 1844.

395   SSTAS: SD1232/4, f 127. Wolstanton and Burslem Board of Guardians' Minute Book, 1843-1846. 20 August 1844.

396   SSTAS: SD1232/4, f 160. 6 November 1844. Wolstanton and Burslem Board of Guardians' Minute Book, 1843-1846.

397   SSTAS: SD1232/4, f 169. Wolstanton and Burslem Board of Guardians' Minute Book, 1843-1846. 4 December 1844.

398   SSTAS: SD1232/4, f 161. Wolstanton and Burslem Board of Guardians' Minute Book, 1843-1846. 6 November 1844.

399   SSTAS: SD1232/4, f 241. Wolstanton and Burslem Board of Guardians' Minute Book, 1843-1846. 4 June 1845.

Cannock) Union, Staffordshire,[400] and in 1850 he took on the additional role of rate collector.[401] His books appear to have been satisfactory until 1854 when the district auditor recorded a discrepancy of about £180 which led to his resignation.[402] Nevertheless, the guardians took a very tolerant approach, praising his previous conduct, and allowing him to continue in office until the following Lady Day, with weekly examination of his accounts.[403] They even went so far as to tell the Poor Law Board that

> ...the Guardians have ever found in Mr Broadhurst a valuable and (up to this time) a perfectly trusty officer: and in his private affairs there is much to excite the Guardians to sincere commiseration.[404]

The problems in his private life are unknown. Unsurprisingly, this incident appears to have terminated his career in poor law service. In 1861 he was resident in Penkhull, in the Potteries, as an agent,[405] and in 1871, resident in Macclesfield, he gave his occupation as accountant, obviously making use of some of the skills he developed as a relieving officer.[406] James Taylor, Broadhurst's successor, resigned in January 1846, after having his ability questioned and beating boy about the head. The

---

400   TNA: MH12/11390, Paper Number: 46565/1854. Letter from John Hay, Clerk to the Guardians of the Penkridge Poor Law Union, to the Poor Law Board. 22 December 1854.
401   Ibid.
402   TNA: MH 12/11390, Paper Number: 43813/1854. Audit report form from Richard Stone, District Auditor. 4 December 1854, MH 12/11390, Paper Number: 44307/1854. Letter from Richard Stone, District Auditor, to the Poor Law Board. 8 December 1854.
403   TNA: MH 12/11390, Paper Number: 46565/1865. Letter from John Hay, Clerk to the Guardians of the Penkridge Poor Law Union, to the Poor Law Board. 22 December 1854.
404   TNA: MH 12/11390, Paper Number: 46565/1854. Letter from John Hay, Clerk to the Guardians of the Penkridge Poor Law Union, to the Poor Law Board. 22 December 1854.
405   TNA: RG 9/1938, p 9, f 33. 1861 Census. The type of agent is unclear.
406   TNA: RG 10/3672, p 2, f 80. 1871 Census.

inspector had made unfavourable comments about the state of the school.[407] His successor's appointment form gave deficiency in temper and ability as the reason for the vacancy. James Foden, who was aged 59 years and had spent 35 years in teaching, was the oldest and most experienced of the group. He seems to have made an uncertain start, as there were initial concerns about the cleanliness of the boys,[408] and his age was said to be hampering outdoor training.[409] The reason for his resignation was given on his successor's appointment form as old age and infirmity; he was in fact requested to resign following an inspector's report of declining standards in the boys' school.[410]

William Carr was schoolmaster at Wolstanton and Burslem from November 1848 until the end of 1850. His ability as a teacher was not questioned. In August 1849 he was awarded a certificate of probation second division,[411] and in October 1850 he rose to the first division.[412] However, he had problems controlling his temper, and around the time of his resignation he was the subject of an enquiry by the Poor Law Board in consequence of his excessive punishment of a boy.[413] The master and matron (Charles and Amelia Wellum, former workhouse schoolteachers) defended and supported the boy, to the point where one is forced to wonder if they were coaching him,[414]

407   SSTAS: SD1232/4, f 354. Wolstanton and Burslem Board of Guardians' Minute Book, 1843-1846. 14 January 1846. SD1232/4, f 360. Wolstanton and Burslem Board of Guardians' Minute Book, 1843-1846. 28 January 1846.
408   SSTAS: SD1232/4, f 423. Wolstanton and Burslem Board of Guardians' Minute Book, 1843-1846. 3 June 1846.
409   SSTAS: SD1232/5, f 54. Wolstanton and Burslem Board of Guardians' Minute Book, 1846-1850. 31 June 1847.
410   SSTAS: SD1232/5, f 303. Wolstanton and Burslem Board of Guardians' Minute Book, 1846-1850. 31 October 1848.
411   TNA: MH 12/11198/173, ff 270-271. Teaching Certificate Awarded to William Carr. 20 November 1849.
412   TNA: MH 12/11198/305, ff 492-494. Teaching Certificate Awarded to William Carr. 17 March 1851.
413   P. Anderton, A. Davies, and D. Jackson (2008), 'Living the Poor Life: The Correspondence of two North Staffordshire Poor Law Unions 1834-1854 in the National Archives', Staffordshire Studies, 19, 208, pp101-115.
414   TNA: MH 12/11198/307, ff 499-502. Statement of Peter Lyth. 12

before he gave his evidence to the Poor Law Board's enquiry. Despite the serious nature of the allegations, Carr escaped with a reprimand and obtained another appointment as a workhouse schoolmaster at Oldham,[415] from which he resigned in June, 1851.[416] During the enquiry Carr claimed that he was victimised by the other officers, and that the master and matron were cruel and malicious,[417] while the master claimed that Carr's attitude was offensive and that he disregarded workhouse regulations. Carr had been seen following the workhouse nurse (Catherine Milner), and there was an unproven suggestion (by the boy excessively punished by Carr) of a relationship between the two.[418]

The next schoolmaster, George Lewis Lees was dismissed because of lack of energy and industrial training.[419] The guardians clearly entertained doubts about him from an early stage, as in May 1851 they requested the Poor Law Board to extend his trial period rather than sanction his appointment.[420] In July 1851 he was cautioned over absences from duty,[421] and was given a month's notice in August 1851.[422] He is recorded in

---

March 1851.

415   TNA: MH 12/11198/277, ff 439-440. Letter from Joseph Lowndes, Clerk to the Guardians of the Wolstanton and Burslem Poor Law Union, to the Poor Law Board. 30 December 1850.

416   OLSA: PUO/1/2, f 339. Oldham Board of Guardians' Minute Book, 1850-1852. 25 June 1851.

417   TNA: MH 12/11198/286, ff 455-458. Letter from William Carr, Schoolmaster at the Wolstanton and Burslem Union Workhouse. 10 January 1851.

418   TNA: MH 12/11198/296, ff 473-477. Letter from Joseph Lowndes, Clerk to the Guardians of the Wolstanton and Burslem Poor Law Union, to the Poor Law Board. 3 February 1851.

419   TNA: MH 12/11198/351, f 579. Letter from Joseph Lowndes, Clerk to the Guardians of the Wolstanton and Burslem Poor Law Union, to the Poor Law Board. 6 August 1851.

420   SSTAS: SD1232/6, f 194. Wolstanton and Burslem Board of Guardians' Minute Book, 1850-1853. 27 May 1851.

421   SSTAS: SD1232/6, f 218. Wolstanton and Burslem Board of Guardians' Minute Book, 1850-1853. 22 July 1851.

422   SSTAS: SD1232/6, ff 225-226. Wolstanton and Burslem Board of Guardians' Minute Book, 1850-1853. 6 August 1851.

subsequent censuses as a farmer, landowner, and postmaster.[423]

John Clews was appointed in November 1851, following a difficult period for the guardians, during which there was a shortage of suitable applicants, an appointment was revoked because no testimonials were received, and the guardians contemplated sending the boys aged over eight years to the Stoke upon Trent Union Workhouse.[424] Clews gained a certificate of probation first division in 1853 and he resigned in August 1855 to train as a teacher.[425]

Six schoolmasters served at Newcastle under Lyme during the period under investigation (see Appendix 2). All were Protestants. The first, Edward Steventon, was clearly appointed in a hurry, after the assistant commissioner noted with disapproval the lack of a schoolmaster.[426] Steventon was 46 years old when appointed in 1847 and his previous occupations included merchant's clerk and schoolmaster; immediately prior to his appointment as workhouse schoolmaster he was workhouse porter and had assisted the schoolmistress.[427] He was the only married schoolmaster at Newcastle under Lyme, but had not heard from his wife for ten years. In August 1846 a boy had alleged that Steventon (still officially porter) whipped him in the school, a charge that was dismissed on the evidence of other boys and the schoolmistress.[428] Steventon held the post

423   TNA: RG 9/1911, p 22, f 126. Census. 1861; RG 10/2888, p 7, f 31. Census. 1871; and RG 11/2745, p 2, f 38. Census. 1881.
424   SSTAS: SD1232/6, ff 231, 236, 239, 246. Wolstanton and Burslem Board of Guardians' Minute Book, 1850-1853. August-September 1851.
425   SSTAS: SD1230/(125), f 5. Wolstanton and Burslem Board of Guardians' Minute Book, 1854-1858. 17 January 1854; Ibid, f 158, 3 July 1855; and TNA: MH 12/11199/221, ff 291-293. Letter from Joseph Lowndes, Clerk to the Guardians of the Wolstanton and Burslem Poor Law Union, to the Poor Law Board. 18 July 1855.
426   TNA: MH 12/11364/154, ff 197-198. Draft letter from the Poor Law Board to Samuel Harding, Clerk to the Guardians of the Newcastle under Lyme Poor Law Union, to the Poor Law Commission. 8 March 1847.
427   TNA: MH 12/11364/140, ff 179-180. Letter from Samuel Harding, Clerk to the Guardians of the Newcastle under Lyme Poor Law Union, to the Poor Law Commission. 28 October 1846.
428   SRO: D339/1/4, f 281. Newcastle under Lyme Guardians' Minute

of schoolmaster from March 1847 until mid 1848. He did not make a clean break with the porter's role, and the assistant commissioner noted with disapproval in August 1847 that he was acting as porter.[429] In the same month the chaplain and guardians considered him a satisfactory schoolmaster.[430] However, his abilities were called into question when he failed the examination for degree of permission (the lowest level)[431] and he resigned,[432] subsequently resuming employment as porter.[433]

Steventon's successor, Thomas Eli Bennett, aged 23 years, was appointed in June 1848; he had previously lived at Uttoxeter and taught for a short while in a National School. He fared better in examinations than his predecessor, gaining a certificate of probation, first division in August 1849.[434] In October 1852 he reached the standard of competency, second division,[435] and in 1853 he earned a certificate of efficiency, third division.[436] In 1854, after spending six years at Newcastle, he resigned and returned to working in a National School.

The next schoolmaster was 20 year old Henry Williamson, who had previously been a student at Kneller Hall; after about

Book, 1844-1847. 31 August 1846.

429   TNA: MH 12/11364/181, f 231. Extract from inspection report by Robert Weale, Assistant Poor Law Commissioner. 12 August 1847.

430   TNA: MH 12/11364/175, ff 221-224. Letter from Samuel Harding, Clerk to the Guardians of the Newcastle under Lyme Poor Law Union, to the Poor Law Commission. 10 August 1847.

431   TNA: MH 12/11364/219, f 281. Draft letter from the Poor Law Board to Samuel Harding, Clerk to the Guardians of the Newcastle under Lyme Poor Law Union. 1 May 1848.

432   TNA: MH 12/11364/235, ff 302-304. Appointment form of Thomas Eli Bennett. 31 May 1848.

433   TNA: MH 12/11365/43, f 65. Letter from Samuel Harding, Clerk to the Guardians of the Newcastle under Lyme Poor Law Union, to the Poor Law Board. 1 October 1851.

434   TNA: MH 12/11364/325, f 427. Teaching Certificate awarded to Thomas Eli Bennett. 20 November 1849.

435   TNA: MH 12/11365/89, ff 132-134. Teaching Certificate awarded to Thomas Eli Bennett. 4 December 1852.

436   TNA: MH 12/11365/149, f 240. Letter from Committee of Council on Education to Thomas Eli Bennett. 19 December 1853.

five months at Newcastle under Lyme he resigned through ill-health. Williamson was succeeded by Henry Harrison of Hull, who, for a 22 year old, had impressive teaching credentials. He had been a pupil teacher for five years, had spent 15 months at Kneller Hall, and had been a schoolmaster at Lexden and Winstree Union, Essex, a position to which he was appointed in April 1854.[437] While at Lexden and Winstree he obtained a certificate of efficiency third division,[438] but his record was somewhat marred because shortly before he left the guardians considered that he had punished a boy excessively. However, the Newcastle guardians considered that Harrison had been sufficiently punished, and relied on his good sense not to repeat the offence.[439] In an annotation to the appointment form Doyle recorded that he did not think the circumstances of the offence precluded Harrison's appointment, but he considered that the matter should be reported to the Newcastle guardians. Harrison resigned from Newcastle for a better-paid position at Oldham in Lancashire in July 1856.[440] He held this post only until his resignation in June 1857.[441] Although his stay was short, the Oldham guardians were evidently satisfied with his performance, as they gave him a certificate of good conduct and character.[442] He evidently made a career in teaching, and is recorded in 1861

---

437   TNA: MH 12/3537, Paper Number: 15234/1854. Appointment Form of Henry Harrison as Schoolmaster at Lexden and Winstree. 15 April 1854.

438   TNA: MH 12/3537, Paper Number: 31644/1854. Teaching Certificate awarded to Henry Harrison. 28 August 1854.

439   TNA: MH 12/11365/196, ff 295-296. Appointment Form of Henry Harrison. 23 March 1855. MH 12/11365/198, f 298. Letter from Samuel Harding, Clerk to the Guardians of the Newcastle under Lyme Poor Law Union, to the Poor Law Board. 17 April 1855.

440   TNA: MH 12/11365, Paper Number: 31769/1856. Letter from Samuel Harding, Clerk to the Guardians of the Newcastle under Lyme Poor Law Union, to the Poor Law Board. 5 August 1856.

441   OLSA: PUO/1/5, f 276. Oldham Board of Guardians' Minute Book, 1856-1858. 6 May 1857.

442   OLSA: PUO/1/5, f 295. Oldham Board of Guardians' Minute Book, 1856-1858. 27 May 1857.

as a certificated schoolmaster in Bibury, Gloucestershire.[443]

Harrison's successor was John Slaney, of the Potteries,[444] who had been a warehouseman prior to spending three months under a National Schoolmaster and twelve months teaching at a National School. Slaney's appointment was short-lived, and in September 1856 His request to be immediately discharged on health grounds was granted.[445] According to his successor's appointment form, he was afterwards admitted to an asylum.

Slaney was replaced by Edward Ellison, of Burslem, who, although aged only 20, and entering on his first situation, had apparently received three years training as a teacher. He experienced health problems in June 1858, but received little sympathy from the guardians, being told either to resume his duties or provide a substitute.[446] In June 1859 his supervision of the school was criticised. He was said to have beaten a boy without informing the master, to treat the boys harshly in general, and to neglect industrial training; the boys were not properly washed.[447] He was enjoined to conduct himself better in future. In October of the same year he complained that the master had used threatening language towards him. The response of the guardians was to request Ellison's resignation, on the grounds that he and the master could not live together in harmony.[448] Ellison refused, so the guardians wrote to the Poor Law Board, saying that he should resign because of the disagreements between him and the

---

443   TNA: RG 9/1786, p 7, f 33. Census.1861.

444   TNA: MH 12/11365, Paper Number: 31769/1856. Appointment Form of John Slaney. 5 August 1856.

445   SRO: D339/1/6, f 26. Newcastle under Lyme Guardians' Minute Book, 1856-1861. 1 September 1856.

446   SRO: D339/1/6, f 172. Newcastle under Lyme Guardians' Minute Book, 1856-1861. 21 June 1858.

447   SRO: D339/1/6, f 234. Newcastle under Lyme Guardians' Minute Book, 1856-1861. 6 June 1859.

448   SRO: D339/1/6, f 254. Newcastle under Lyme Guardians' Minute Book, 1856-1861. 24 October 1859.

master, and his inadequate supervision of the boys.[449] On 21 November, Doyle undertook to investigate the matter.[450] He concluded that, although Ellison was a competent teacher, he was weak and conceited, and had no control over the boys. Ellison's unacceptable conduct included excessive beating of boys, neglecting their cleanliness, terrifying the schoolmistress so that she was afraid he would injure her, wasting coal, and throwing the master out of the room when admonished. The allegation of conceit is supported by Ellison's unsuccessful demand for a Queen's scholarship in return for his resignation.[451] The guardians' minutes show that on 19 December 1859 Ellison's resignation was accepted.[452] He was appointed schoolmaster at Wolstanton and Burslem in July 1860,[453] but following correspondence between the Poor Law Board and the guardians he was discharged the following month.[454]

Schoolmistresses

Details of the seven schoolmistresses employed at Wolstanton and Burslem during the period studied are presented in Appendix 3. The letter reporting Margaret Lycett's appointment stated that as well as teaching the girls reading, sewing and knitting, she was to teach the boys to read, to teach writing to

---

449   SRO: D339/1/6, f 256. Newcastle under Lyme Guardians' Minute Book, 1856-1861. 7 November 1859.

450   SRO: D339/1/6, f 259. Newcastle under Lyme Guardians' Minute Book, 1856-1861. 21 November 1859.

451   TNA: MH 12/11366/192, ff 280-283. Letter from Joseph Knight, Clerk to the Guardians of the Newcastle under Lyme Poor Law Union, to the Poor Law Board. 22 November 1859.

452   SRO: D339/1/6, ff 264-265. Newcastle under Lyme Guardians' Minute Book, 1856-1861. 19 December 1859.

453   SSTAS: SD1232/7, f 204. Wolstanton and Burslem Board of Guardians' Minute Book, 1858-1862. 24 July 1860.

454   SSTAS: SD1232/7, ff 209-210. Wolstanton and Burslem Board of Guardians' Minute Book, 1858-1862. 21 August 1860.

any children selected by the guardians, and to perform other duties.[455] She resigned in April 1842.[456]

Joseph Lowndes, the union clerk, was able to exert influence over the appointment of John Leigh as schoolmaster (see above). One must therefore wonder what role he played in the appointment of his sister,[457] Elizabeth Lowndes, as schoolmistress to succeed Margaret Lycett. Elizabeth was 23 years old, resident in Wolstanton, and had formerly been a dressmaker and assistant in a school. When she resigned in 1845, in order to marry, the guardians recorded the following testimonial in their minute book.

> It was ordered that the resignation of Miss Elizabeth Lowndes be received, the Guardians at the same time, express their regret at the loss of her very efficient and valuable services as schoolmistress at the Workhouse, and record their entire approval of the manner in which she has discharged the Duties of the Office for the last three years.[458]

Mary Elizabeth Daniel, Elizabeth Lowndes' replacement, was dismissed after a few weeks. Although she had received a good testimonial as to her ability to teach working class children, her appointment was not sanctioned, on the grounds that she was the daughter of a surgeon and apothecary and within the previous two years had given birth to a bastard child.[459] The reference to her

455   TNA: MH 12/11196/46, ff 120-121. Letter from Joseph Lowndes, Clerk to the Guardians of the Wolstanton and Burslem Poor Law Union, to the Poor Law Commission. 12 May 1838.
456   TNA: MH 12/11196/259, ff 462-464. Letter from Joseph Lowndes, Clerk to the Guardians of the Wolstanton and Burslem Poor Law Union, to the Poor Law Commission. 6 June 1842.
457   SSTAS: Fiche D3534/2/2. Wolstanton and Burslem parish registers show Joseph and Elizabeth, children of Thomas and Margaret Lowndes, baptised in 1809 and 1820 respectively.
458   SSTAS: SD1232/4, f 236 . Wolstanton and Burslem Board of Guardians' Minute Book, 1843-1846. 21 May 1845.
459   TNA: MH 12/11197/122, ff 127-130. Letter from Joseph Lowndes, Clerk to the Guardians of the Wolstanton and Burslem Poor Law Union, to the Poor Law Commission. 13 June 1845.

parentage is puzzling; it may be that as she came from a respectable family, her immorality was all the more culpable. She did not give up teaching, and in the 1851 census she was enumerated, with her seven year old son, in Stoke on Trent, in the house of her brother, a general agent and schoolmaster, when she was described as a private school mistress.[460] The ill-advised appointment of Daniel clearly caused the guardians some embarrassment, as the appointment form for her successor gives the reason for the vacancy as the resignation of Elizabeth Lowndes.[461]

Charlotte Norris was severely criticised by a Poor Law Board inspector in mid-1848, after more than two and a half years of service; she was given help by the chaplain, master, and matron,[462] and attended a training school (possibly the establishment at Norwood) in same year.[463] A slight improvement in the girls' school followed.[464] The reason for her resignation in May 1849 was given as ill-health. Despite her obvious difficulties, Norris seems to have enjoyed an amicable relationship with the guardians, and thanked them for their kindness to her in her letter of resignation.[465] When requested, they gave her a favourable testimonial, albeit one that related entirely to her character.[466] Unlike Daniel, she did not continue teaching, but in 1851 was living with her mother in Uttoxeter, working as a dressmaker.[467]

---

460   TNA: HO 107/2004, p 39, f 123. Census. 1851.

461   TNA: MH 12/11197/131, ff 142-144. Letter from Joseph Lowndes, Clerk to the Guardians of the Wolstanton and Burslem Poor Law Union, to the Poor Law Commission. 11 August 1845.

462   TNA: MH 12/11198/43, ff 69-71. Letter from Joseph Lowndes, Clerk to the Guardians of the Wolstanton and Burslem Poor Law Union, to the Poor Law Board. 13 June 1848.

463   TNA: MH 12/11198/54, ff 87-88. Workhouse Inspection Report from Robert Weale. 1 August 1848.

464   SSTAS: SD1232/5, f 303. Wolstanton and Burslem Board of Guardians' Minute Book, 1846-1850. 31 October 1848.

465   SSTAS: SD1232/5, ff 389-390. Wolstanton and Burslem Board of Guardians' Minute Book, 1846-1850. 1 May 1849.

466   SSTAS: SD1232/5, f 399. Wolstanton and Burslem Board of Guardians' Minute Book, 1846-1850. 29 May 1849.

467   TNA: HO 107/2010, p 23, f 81. Census. 1851.

The next schoolmistress, Elizabeth Jones, despite claiming two years' experience in a private school for girls, resigned after four months; the inspector of schools considered her to be unequal to her duties and wanting in qualifications, declining to grant her a certificate.[468] Jones was succeeded by Fanny Seddon, whose short period in office appears to have been uneventful. She resigned after just over a year's service, to join her parents in Glasgow, after gaining her certificate of probation, third division, in October 1849,[469] a standard she maintained in October 1850.[470]

Seddon's successor was Harriett Gent, who received a very favourable chaplain's report in April 1851,[471] and her certificate of probation, third division, in the same year.[472] In 1853 she gained a certificate of probation third division.[473] In January 1854 she left the workhouse for a period because of illness,[474] and in March of the same year she tendered her resignation on health grounds, at the same time thanking the guardians for their kindness to her.[475]

No appointment forms for schoolmistresses were found for Newcastle under Lyme for the period searched, but the guardians' minutes show the appointment of Sarah Hand in

---

468   TNA: MH 12/11198/182, f 285. Copy Teaching Certificate relating to Elizabeth Jones. 10 December 1849.
469   TNA: MH 12/11198/211, f 325. Copy Teaching Certificate awarded to Fanny Seddon. 28 February 1850.
470   TNA: MH 12/11198/305, ff 492-494. Copy Teaching Certificates awarded to Fanny Seddon and William Carr. 17 March 1851.
471   TNA: MH 12/11198/318, ff 517-519. Letter from Joseph Lowndes, Clerk to the Guardians of the Wolstanton and Burslem Poor Law Union, to the Poor Law Board. 15 April 1851.
472   TNA: MH 12/11198/383, f 634. Copy of a letter from R R W Lingen, Secretary to the Committee of Council on Education, to Harriet Gent. 10 December 1851.
473   SSTAS: SD1230/(125), f 5. Wolstanton and Burslem Board of Guardians' Minute Book, 1854-1858. 17 January 1854.
474   SSTAS: SD1230/(125), f 9. Wolstanton and Burslem Board of Guardians' Minute Book, 1854-1858. 31 January 1854.
475   SSTAS: SD1230/(125), f 19. Wolstanton and Burslem Board of Guardians' Minute Book, 1854-1858. 14 March 1854.

June 1838.[476] She resigned for unspecified reasons in August of the same year,[477] to be replaced the following month by Mary Lodge.[478] In 1846 an increase in Lodge's salary was sanctioned, the Poor Law Commision commenting that she was a good schoolmistress.[479] In August 1849 she was awarded a certificate of permission,[480] the highest level she ever reached.[481] The main incident during her long term of office seems to have occurred in July 1857, when she was taken to Stafford by the Sherriff's Officer for debt, she having stood a security for a Mr Audley.[482] On 11th February 1867 the guardians accepted her resignation, which was tendered because of her age and took effect the following month. She was granted a superannuation payment of £15 12s per annum. [483]

Porters

The porter's main duty was to control who and what entered and left the workhouse.[484] When the guardians at Wolstanton and Burslem advertised for a porter in March 1840, he was required to be single, to be able to read and write well, to have a

---

476   SSTAS: D3391/1, f 86. Newcastle under Lyme Board of Guardians' Minute Book, 1838-1839. 18 June 1838. See also Julie Bagnall's contribution to this volume.
477   SSTAS: D3391/1, f 127. Newcastle under Lyme Board of Guardians' Minute Book, 1838-1839. 27 August 1838.
478   SSTAS: D3391/1, f 137. Newcastle under Lyme Board of Guardians' Minute Book, 1838-1839. 17 September 1838.
479   TNA: MH 12/11364/122, f 157. Draft letter from the Poor Law Commission to Samuel Harding, Clerk to the Guardians of the Newcastle under Lyme Poor Law Union. 10 February 1846.
480   TNA: MH 12/11364/327, f 429. Copy Teaching Certificate awarded to Mary Lodge. 20 November 1849.
481   TNA: MH 12/11365/242, ff 350-352. Teaching Certificate awarded to Mary Lodge. 22 October 1855.
482   SSTAS: D339/1/6, f 103. Newcastle under Lyme Board of Guardians' Minute Book, 1856-1861. 13 July 1857.
483   SSTAS: D339/1/7, ff 342-343. Newcastle under Lyme Board of Guardians' Minute Book, 1861-1868. 11 February 1867.
484   Crowther, Workhouse System, p 132.

knowledge of accounts, and to be able to assist the master and matron generally.[485]

Six porters were appointed at Wolstanton and Burslem between March 1840 and August 1850; their details are summarised in Appendix 4. William Davies was appointed in March 1840,[486] and was employed for over six years, leaving in disgrace after improper behaviour with a female inmate. Although this charge was not proven, being based largely on the evidence of inmates which might easily be rejected, Davies was dismissed in view of his previous conduct.[487] He had come close to dismissal in August 1840 after making serious unjustified allegations about the master,[488] and in July 1846 he was disciplined for allowing ale to be taken into the workhouse and given to inmates.[489]

John Munday, of Burslem, a former corporal in the army, held the post from January to September 1847, and resigned on the grounds of ill-health.[490] Following Munday's short period of office the next porter was Edward Wellum. He was the porter for a few months between 1847 and 1848 and previously lived in Middlesex/London;[491] there can be little doubt that he was a relative of Charles and Amelia Wellum, the master and matron. In common with two of his successors, he had experience

485   SSTAS: SD1232/3, ff 363-364. Wolstanton and Burslem Board of Guardians' Minute Book, 1838-1841. 10 March 1840.
486   TNA: MH 12/11196/123, f 240. Letter from Joseph Lowndes, Clerk to the Guardians of the Wolstanton and Burslem Poor Law Union, to the Poor Law Commission. 25 March 1840.
487   SSTAS: SD1232/5, ff 9-10. Wolstanton and Burslem Board of Guardians' Minute Book, 1846-1850. 18 December 1846.
488   SSTAS: SD1232/3, ff 432-434. 25 August 1840. Wolstanton and Burslem Board of Guardians' Minute Book, 1838-1841.
489   SSTAS: SD1232/4, f 448. Wolstanton and Burslem Board of Guardians' Minute Book, 1843-1846. 29 July 1846.
490   MH 12/11197/250, ff 319-321. Letter from Joseph Lowndes, Clerk to the Guardians of the Wolstanton and Burslem Poor Law Union, to the Poor Law Commission, 22 January 1847.
491   MH 12/11197/309, Folios 419-420. Letter from Joseph Lowndes, Clerk to the Guardians of the Wolstanton and Burslem Poor Law Union, to the Poor Law Commission, 13 September 1847.

of work in a warehouse, which probably gave him useful experience in keeping track of items entering and leaving the establishment. However, neither he nor the other porters had experience of work under the poor law. Thomas Lynn replaced Edward Wellum, but relinquished the post after about two years, when he was appointed assistant overseer, a position he held until June 1862, when he resigned through ill-health.[492] Lynn's successor, John Hammersley, whose testimonials misled the guardians and who admitted to incorrectly stating that he had written his own application, held the post for about a month. Thomas Bruckshaw was cautioned by the poor law inspector shortly after taking up his appointment in 1850, because his lodge was not in high order, but no further action appears to have been taken.[493] He held the office until March 1856, when he was dismissed after being found with a woman of 'questionable character' in the workhouse.[494]

Seven men served as porters at the Newcastle under Lyme Workhouse during the period under consideration (see Appendix 5) with one holding the post for two terms. Clement Styche, the first recorded porter, was appointed in February 1840.[495] He tendered his resignation in February 1841 following his involvement in an incident which led to the death of a pauper. The advertisement for his replacement specified a middle-aged man, either shoemaker or tailor and so it appears that the porter would also be required to provide industrial training to the boys.[496] The successful applicant was Edward Steventon, whose

492   SSTAS: SD1232/7, f 434. Wolstanton and Burslem Board of Guardians' Minute Book, 1858-1862. 10 June 1862.
493   TNA: MH 12/11198/302, ff 486-487. Workhouse Inspection Report Form from H B Farnall. 19 February 1851.
494   SSTAS: SD1230/(125), f 224. Wolstanton and Burslem Board of Guardians' Minute Book, 1854-1858. 11 March 1856.
495   SSTAS: D339/1/2, ff 32-33. Newcastle under Lyme Board of Guardians' Minute Book, 1840-1842. 17 February 1840.
496   SSTAS: D339/1/2, f 230. Newcastle under Lyme Board of Guardians' Minute Book, 1840-1842.15 February 1841.

first period of service as porter began in May 1841[497]. He had previously been admitted as an inmate in November 1840.[498] Whether he was able to instruct the boys in shoemaking or tailoring is not known (it seems doubtful, since none of the documents examined states that he possessed these skills) but in March 1847, he was promoted to schoolmaster. In August 1847 Steventon was succeeded as porter by John Hill,[499] whose incompetence led to his dismissal the same month.[500] The next porter was Edward Bond, who had been a pauper resident in the workhouse in November 1841.[501] He was single, had been a sailor for 18 years and appears to have been appointed in a hurry, when the assistant commissioner noted with disapproval that the school master was also doing porter's work.[502] Bond died in September 1847,[503] and was succeeded the following month by Thomas Barlow, whose resignation took effect from June 1848.[504] He appears to have been replaced by Edward Steventon (there is no appointment form for Steventon's re-appointment as porter) after the latter's dismissal from the post of schoolmaster. Like Bond, Steventon died while serving as porter,[505] and his replacement, William Charles Beetenson, commenced employment in September 1851. Beetenson was 22

497   SSTAS: D339/1/2, f 278. Newcastle under Lyme Board of Guardians' Minute Book, 1840-1842. 10 May 1841.
498   SSTAS: D339/1/2, f 186. Newcastle under Lyme Board of Guardians' Minute Book, 1840-1842. 9 November 1840.
499   SSTAS: D339/1/4, f 421. Newcastle under Lyme Board of Guardians' Minute Book, 1844-1847. 2 August 1847.
500   SSTAS: D339/1/4, f 425. Newcastle under Lyme Board of Guardians' Minute Book, 1844-1847. 16 August 1847.
501   SSTAS: D339/1/2, f 354. Newcastle under Lyme Board of Guardians' Minute Book, 1840-1842. 8 November 1841.
502   TNA: MH 12/11364/182, f 232. Draft letter from the Poor Law Board to Samuel Harding, Clerk to the Guardians of the Newcastle under Lyme Poor Law Union 23 August 1847.
503   SSTAS: D339/1/4, f 437. Newcastle under Lyme Board of Guardians' Minute Book, 1844-1847. 27 September 1847.
504   SSTAS: D339/1/5, f 28. Newcastle under Lyme Board of Guardians' Minute Book, 1848-1856. 15 May 1848.
505   TNA: MH 12/11365/47, ff 70-71. Appintment form of William Beetenson. 8 October 1851.

years old, single, and had been an assistant clerk. He resigned early in 1853, under pressure from the guardians and Poor Law Board, after making unproven allegations about other officers (see above). His replacement, Ambrose Taylor, who, like Edward Bond, had been a sailor, was appointed in February 1853.[506] Taylor had been baker and porter at the Stafford Union workhouse from 1846 to 1850, when he resigned to work as a baker in Nantwich. His appointment form for the Newcastle post indicates that he was already employed as workhouse baker. He was to continue to work as baker at Newcastle Workhouse, in addition to his responsibilities as porter. In August 1859 the master complained that Taylor's conduct habitually annoyed him, and after forming the opinion that Taylor and the master would not agree, the guardians informed Taylor of this and accepted his resignation.[507]

Nurses

The duties of the workhouse nurse were to care for the sick, under the supervision of the medical officer and/or matron. During the period being studied, nurses were untrained. In the early years, nursing in the workhouse was performed by inmates, who could be rewarded with extra food, and the central authority remained resistant to the employment of professional nurses into the 1850s.[508]

Eight nurses served at Wolstanton and Burslem (see Appendix 6) during the period under consideration, with one (Catherine Milner) holding the post for two periods. Little is known about the first two, Elizabeth Goodfellow and Ann

---

506   For further details of Ambrose Taylor see Julie Bagnall's contribution to this volume.
507   SSTAS: D339/1/6, f 245. Newcastle under Lyme Board of Guardians' Minute Book, 1856-1861. 29 August 1859.
508   Crowther, Workhouse System, p 165.

Dennis, who between them held the post from 1840 to 1842. The reasons for their resignations are not known. Dorothy Tirebuck was appointed in 1842, but was dismissed after less than a year because she was unable to discharge her duties. The next nurse, Jane Birks, for whom no appointment form could be found, held the post for almost three years, resigning to take up a similar appointment at Amersham, Buckinghamshire. When the Poor Law Commissioners requested information on her, prior to sanctioning her appointment at Amersham, the Wolstanton and Burslem guardians described her character and conduct as correct and proper, and her discharge of her duties as efficient.[509] However, she resigned from her post at Amersham within three months,[510] the reason being, according to her successor's appointment form, incompetence.[511]

The next nurse was Catherine Milner, who had worked as a servant and nurse at the Cheadle Union workhouse, which she left for a higher salary. Milner was appointed servant and nurse at Wolstanton and Burslem in December 1845. This combined appointment was made after an advertisement for a nurse failed to attract suitable applicants, and reflects the low status of the workhouse nurse. Her appointment at Cheadle, in March 1843, was clearly contentious; the guardians' minutes record that she had been an inmate for three years and was the mother of three illegitimate children, and her appointment was opposed by two of the six guardians present.[512] Her resignation from Wolstanton and Burslem early in 1848 resulted from fever caught during the execution of her duties. Catherine

---

509   TNA: MH 12/383, Paper Number: 14189/B/1845. Letter from Joseph Lowndes, Clerk to the Guardians of the Wolstanton and Burslem Poor Law Union, to the Poor Law Commission. 31 October 1845.
510   TNA: MH 12/383, Paper Number: 248/A/1846. Draft letter from the Poor Law Commission to the Clerk to the Guardians of the Amersham Poor Law Union. 12 January 1846.
511   TNA: MH 12/383, Paper Number: 1872/1846. Appointment form of Maria Woodrow. 17 February 1846.
512   SSTAS: D698/1/5, p.74. Cheadle Board of Guardians' Minute Book, 1842-1844. 24 March 1843.

Milner was succeeded by Ann Mollatt, who, like her successor, Mary Dudley, resigned because she did not feel capable of performing her duties. This period of apparently unsatisfactory nursing was brought to an end in December 1848 by the re-appointment of Catherine Milner, who resigned again in 1850. No reason was given for her second resignation, but there were unsubstantiated allegations of improper conduct involving her and schoolmaster William Carr (see above). Whatever the nature of this episode, it would be hasty to infer that she was the initiating party. Ann Wilson, Milner's successor, had resigned as nurse at Wolverhampton Union Workhouse on grounds of ill-health after almost five years' service. The Poor Law Board's enquiry elicited a favourable reference from the Wolverhampton Union's clerk[513]. Her resignation from the post at Wolstanton and Burslem in 1869 was a result of illness.[514] Her applications for a superannuation payment and gratuity were both refused because her illness was not considered to be a consequence of her employment.[515]

At Newcastle under Lyme only three nurses were recorded during the entire period under consideration. Caroline Tue, for whom no appointment form has been found, was the first, and it is only known that she resigned to be married prior to the appointment in November 1851 of Elizabeth Baylis, a 39 year old widow formerly resident at Clifford Wood, Stafford. She commenced employment in September 1851 but had resigned by February 1853 following disputes involving herself and other officers.[516] Baylis appears to have been a 'career nurse' as prior

513   TNA: MH 12/11198/245, f 372. Letter from Isaac Fellows, Clerk to the Guardians of the Wolverhampton Poor Law Union, to the Poor Law Board. 2 August 1850.
514   SSTAS: SD1232/8, f 20. Wolstanton and Burslem Board of Guardians' Minute Book, 1869-1872. 2 November 1869.
515   SSTAS: SD1232/8, ff 26-27. Wolstanton and Burslem Board of Guardians' Minute Book, 1869-1872, f 56. 11 January 1870.
516   TNA: MH 12/11365/39, f 61. Letter from Samuel Harding, Clerk to the Guardians of the Newcastle under Lyme Poor Law Union, to the Poor Law Board. 1 October 1851. MH 12/11365/92, ff 139-140. Workhouse Inspection

to employment at Wolstanton and Burslem she was a nurse at Gloucester Infirmary, and subsequently worked at North Staffordshire Infirmary.[517] In February 1853, following Baylis' resignation, Caroline Tue was requested to act as nurse until a replacement could be found.[518] In March Harriet Jackson was appointed.[519] In January 1855 and August 1859 Jackson was cautioned for drunkenness.[520] She died on 2 January 1878, after almost 25 years' service, when her sister was requested to fill the post until a replacement could be found.[521]

Analysis

Workhouse masters and matrons could hold the posts for long periods, as is shown by the examples of Charles and Amelia Wellum (16 years) and George and Eliza Fox (27 years). The latter couple's employment was terminated by the death of George Fox in 1867. Not all masters and matrons held the posts for such lengthy periods, however. William and Sophia Welsby left Wolstanton and Burslem after a total of four years' service, when an example of very lax discipline came to light. The role of the central authority in removing unsatisfactory officers is illustrated by the case of William Shore, who was appointed

Report from Andrew Doyle. 15 December 1852. MH 12/11365/102, ff 163-167. Letter from Samuel Harding, Clerk to the Guardians of the Newcastle under Lyme Poor Law Union, to the Poor Law Board. 9 February 1853.

517   TNA: MH 12/11365/45, ff 67-68. Appointment Form of Elizabeth Baylis. 8 October 1851. MH 12/11365/134, ff 218-222. Letter from Samuel Harding, Clerk to the Guardians of the Newcastle under Lyme Poor Law Union, to Andrew Doyle, Poor Law Board Inspector. 9 August 1853.

518   SSTAS: D339/1/5, f 259. Newcastle under Lyme Board of Guardians' Minutes, 1848-1856. 7 February 1853.

519   SSTAS: D339/1/5, f 265. Newcastle under Lyme Board of Guardians' Minutes, 1848-1856. 21 March 1853.

520   SSTAS: D339/1/5, f 341. Newcastle under Lyme Board of Guardians' Minutes, 1848-1856. 22 January 1855. D339/1/6, f 245. Newcastle under Lyme Board of Guardians' Minutes, 1856-1861. 29 August 1859.

521   SSTAS: SD339/1/9, f 492. Newcastle under Lyme Board of Guardians' Minutes, 1873-1879. 14 January 1878.

master at Wolstanton and Burslem despite being totally unsuited to the post. The Poor Law Commission, acting on the advice of William Gilbert, assistant poor law commissioner, did not sanction the appointment. Gilbert's view that Shore was appointed because he was known to some of the guardians suggests that on occasion the interests of the ratepayers and paupers were not the only ones to be considered by the guardians. Correspondence related to this appointment indicates that Joseph Lowndes, union clerk, actively sought the assistant commissioner's recommendations for candidates.[522] The sort of men considered suitable included former Metropolitan Police Officers and non-commissioned army officers.

Charles and Amelia Wellum provide an example of professional career development within the poor law system. They had previously worked as teachers in the Northwich Union in Cheshire, posts in which they were unhappy. They appear to have satisfactorily fulfilled their roles at Wolstanton and Burslem, where they remained until their resignation in 1858, when Charles became registrar of births and deaths. Their recommendation for the posts by an assistant poor law commissioner indicated that these officials took a genuine interest in the officers of the unions under their supervision, and were in a position to assess the suitability of officers for employment in other unions. As we have seen George and Eliza Fox, master and matron of the Newcastle Workhouse, were not blamed for a number of unfortunate incidents that occurred while they held their positions at Newcastle; on the contrary, they were highly regarded by the central poor law officials. Fox appears to have enjoyed the support of the guardians and central authority throughout his employment; whether this is the result of a high level of competence or ability to manipulate those above him is a question that remains unanswered.

---

522   TNA: MH 12/11196/261, ff 466-467. Letter from W J Gilbert, Assistant Poor Law Commissioner, to the Poor Law Commission. 6 June 1842.

Ten schoolmasters served at Wolstanton and Burslem during the period studied. Seven were aged between 21 and 42, while the remaining three were between 50 and 59. Distances from the teachers' former residences varied greatly; in some cases the schoolmasters were local men, while William Carr moved over 50 miles from Sheffield, Yorkshire West Riding. Seven schoolmasters claimed relevant experience or training. Periods of service at Wolstanton and Burslem were in general less than three years, with John Clews proving the exception by resigning after almost four years, in order to undertake training as a teacher. Reasons for dismissal or resignation reveal a sorry state of affairs. Reasons for departure included poor teaching, drinking, sexual improprieties, old age, unauthorised absence and deficiency of temper (including excessive punishment of a boy). Reasons for the departure of George Goodwin are not known. Although William Ward Broadhurst's appointment form gives the reason for George Machin's departure as resignation to take up another appointment, the refusal of the guardians to provide Machin with a testimonial indicates that all was not well. The appointment of John Leigh was clearly ill-advised, and suggests that the guardians did not always have only the interests of the ratepayers and paupers at heart.

Six schoolmasters were employed at Newcastle; five were aged between 20 and 33 years, while Edward Steventon, former porter, was 46 years old. All claimed relevant experience or training. Distances from former residences varied widely; while some men were local, Henry Harrison came from Hull, Yorkshire East Riding, while Henry Williamson had previously been at Kneller Hall in Surrey. Most of the schoolmasters held the post for about three years or less, but Thomas Eli Bennett held the position for over six years. Only one appointment was clearly terminated because of the schoolmaster's poor teaching ability, when Edward Steventon lost the position as a result of failure in the teaching examination. Edward Ellison resigned following a conflict with the master, which appears to have resulted from Ellison's shortcomings, and two resigned through ill-health. Two schoolmasters appear to have gone on to other teaching posts. Thomas Eli Bennett went on to teach in a National School, while Henry Harrison went to the Oldham Union workhouse school and subsequently to a National School.

Six schoolmistresses at Wolstanton and Burslem were aged between 20 and 29 years when appointed. Harriett Gent was 40. Six claimed relevant experience or training. Only two had resided outside of the Potteries. Distances from the previous residences of the schoolmistresses were less than those of schoolmasters, four being from the Potteries, and the other two travelling over 9 and 20 miles. The religious denominations of Margaret Lycett and Elizabeth Lowndes were not stated; of the remainder, three were members of the Church of England and one was described as a Protestant. Wesleyan Fanny Seddon, appointed in 1849, was required to confirm that she was willing to teach the catechism of the Church of England. All the women had been unmarried except widow Elizabeth Jones, whose two children did not go into the workhouse with her but stayed with friends.[523] The reasons for schoolmistresses leaving Wolstanton and Burslem varied, and indicate that good schoolmistresses were not always easy to find. Of the six for whom reasons for departure are known, two had been criticised by the inspector, although the immediate reason in one case was given as ill-health. As the mother of an illegitimate child, a fact concealed from the guardians until after her appointment, Mary Elizabeth Daniel was clearly considered an unsuitable person to look after children.

Mary Lodge, schoolmistress at Newcastle-under-Lyme, was the longest-serving of any of the teachers studied. She served for

---

523   TNA: MH 12/11198/124, ff 203-204. Letter from Joseph Lowndes, Clerk to the Guardians of the Wolstanton and Burslem Poor Law Union, to the Poor Law Board. 4 June 1849.

29 years, having been appointed at the approximate age of 41. Whether she was a dedicated teacher, devoted to her charges, or one of Englander's 'sorry lot', perhaps institutionalised and separated from any surviving family (she was born in West Witton, Yorkshire) cannot be established.[524] However, her failure to gain a teaching certificate beyond the level of permission (the lowest standard) suggests that she was not academically gifted.

Three of the six Wolstanton and Burslem porters are known to have already been resident in the Potteries. Thomas Bruckshaw was resident at Winnington in Staffordshire, Edward Wellum travelled from Marylebone in Middlesex, while the residence of William Davies is unknown. Ages are known for five, and varied from 23 to 42 years. None had experience within the poor law system. Three had worked in warehouses, one of the three also claiming experience as an assistant in a school; one had been an army corporal, and one a farmer. Only Thomas Bruckshaw was married, but he had no dependent children, and his wife was not mentioned, so she presumably did not accompany him into the workhouse. Length of service varied considerably. The shortest tenure was that of John Hammersley, who obtained the position fraudently, while Thomas Bruckshaw and William Davies served for almost six and seven years respectively. Thomas Lynn's resignation came after two years, when he was appointed assistant overseer. Two porters were dismissed for sexual misbehaviour, one left though ill health and Edward Wellum gave no particular reason. His long migration from Marylebone doubtless came about as a result of a family relationship to the master and matron. In 1857, while the Wellums were still in office, the post of porter was filled by James Wellum, aged 35 years and formerly a warehouseman, also from Marylebone and doubtless another

---

524   TNA: HO 107/2001, p 54, f 352. Census. 1851.

relative.[525] He resigned in March 1858,[526] but in April 1860 was appointed deputy registrar to Charles Wellum.[527]

All porters at the Newcastle Union for whom information is available were already resident in the town. Ages at appointment, where known, varied between 22 and 65 years. Edward Bond, a former inmate was appointed in a hurry following Edward Steventon's short-lived promotion to schoolmaster. Ambrose Taylor at Newcastle was the only porter with previous experience within the poor law system, having been baker and porter at Stafford Union and baker at Newcastle, a role he was to continue to fulfil after his appointment as porter at Newcastle. Two porters had previously been in the navy, while one had been an assistant clerk. Reasons for termination of appointments included incompetence, death, promotion, and conflicts with or complaints about the master and other officers.

Prior to the appointment of Ann Wilson in 1850, there was a considerable turnover of nurses at Wolstanton and Burslem. All those for whom information is available were single or widowed. Ages varied between 24 and 37 years. Three had been resident in the Potteries. Of the others, one was previously resident at Cheadle, one at Audley, one at Uttoxeter, and one at Wolverhampton. Catherine Milner and Ann Wilson were the only appointees known to have experience of workhouse nursing. Two others had worked as nurses, although this employment was combined with domestic duties. Other former employments were dressmaking, domestic employment, and shopkeeping. Some women showed a degree of commitment to nursing, and developed careers in the 'profession.' Catherine Milner's progression from inmate to nurse at Cheadle, and subsequent move to Wolstanton and Burslem suggest a degree

525   SSTAS: SD1230/(125), f 340. Wolstanton and Burslem Board of Guardians' Minutes, 1854-1858. 24 March 1857.
526   SSTAS: SD1230/(125), f 443. Wolstanton and Burslem Board of Guardians' Minutes, 1854-1858. 9 March 1858.
527   SSTAS: SD1232/7, f 163. Wolstanton and Burslem Board of Guardians' Minutes, 1858-1862. 3 April 1860.

of commitment, arising either from a genuine concern for the sick or, as is suggested by her wish for an increase in salary, a desire for self-improvement (or perhaps both). Jane Birks resigned from Wolstanton and Burslem to work as nurse at the Amersham Union in Buckinghamshire. Why, after the Wolstanton and Burslem Guardians had expressed a high opinion of her, she was branded incompetent in her next position is unknown, but such lowly employees were no doubt at the mercy of inconsiderate superiors. Although the position of workhouse nurse carried little status, the duties seem to have been too much for some of the nurses. Dorothy Tirebuck was dismissed in April 1843 after less than a year, for general incapacity to discharge her duties, while Ann Mollatt and Mary Dudley both resigned after about five months as they did not feel equal to the work; Dudley attributed this to her health.[528] Most nurses at Wolstanton and Burslem held the post for less than three years, the notable exception being Ann Wilson, whose service spanned 19 years. She provides an example of the value of family connections in obtaining workhouse appointments, for in 1855 her daughter, Emma, began a trial period as infant nurse.[529]

Less information about nurses at Newcastle is available than for those at Wolstanton and Burslem. Elizabeth Baylis held nursing appointments outside the poor law system before and after her appointment at the workhouse. Despite two cautions for drunkenness, Harriet Jackson served for almost 25 years, until her death in 1878. Her sister had been requested to serve as a temporary replacement, providing yet another example of the use family connections.

---

528   SSTAS: SD1232/5, f 304. Wolstanton and Burslem Board of Guardians' Minutes, 1846-1850. 31 October 1848.
529   SSTAS: SD1230/(125), f 132. Wolstanton and Burslem Board of Guardians' Minutes, 1854-1858. 27 March 1855.

Conclusions

Although this study covers only two unions and a short time-period, it is possible make a number of comparisons between the two unions and to draw a few conclusions. It is clear that, in the early days of the New Poor Law, there was wide variation in the competence of workhouse officers, but long-term employment and career progression were options for some.

It was clearly important to have a competent master and matron in charge of the workhouse. Charles and Amelia Wellum provide an example of long and satisfactory service at Wolstanton and Burslem, contrasting strongly with the short tenures resulting from the lax discipline of the Welsbys and the general incompetence of the Shores. No such problems were apparent at Newcastle, where George and Elizabeth Fox were master and matron for more than 27 years. This couple enjoyed the ongoing support of the guardians despite the occurrence of a number of unpleasant incidents.

Finding and retaining competent schoolmasters was a problem in both unions. The great majority of successful applicants claimed experience of or training in teaching, suggesting that the guardians attached importance to the education of the boys, but Wolstanton and Burslem did not in general attract teachers of high calibre. Reasons for departure of the schoolmasters from this union show that good schoolmasters were rare, with most schoolmasters leaving under a cloud. Declining standards in the school in James Foden's time clearly resulted from his age, and one can speculate that this was the reason for his losing his previous teaching position. At Newcastle, although most schoolmasters were also employed for short periods, in only one case (Edward Steventon) was doubt expressed as to the teacher's ability.

Schoolmistresses at Wolstanton and Burslem, like their male counterparts, claimed relevant experience and were employed for short periods, with none achieving more than four years of service. In only two cases was there evidence of lack of ability, and the one case of sexual indiscretion related to an incident some time before the schoolmistress was appointed. Mary Lodge, schoolmistress at Newcastle, was the longest-serving of all the teachers studied, despite never progressing far in teachers' examinations. This may indicate that the Newcastle guardians attached less importance to academic teaching of girls than did the guardians at Wolstanton and Burslem.

The large numbers of schoolteachers who had previous training or experience suggests that the guardians of both unions regarded education of workhouse children as important, but the large number of unsatisfactory appointments could indicate that the applicants had mis-judged the workhouse teaching environment or that workhouse schools attracted mainly the less able teachers. The incident involving William Carr and his ill-treatment of a boy shows that paupers could, in some cases at least, expect help and support from workhouse officers. The guardians and Poor Law Board also supported the boy. Carr's allegation that he victimised by the other officers shows that staff relationships were not always harmonious in what was a very confined environment. Porters were mainly local men, and several had been formerly employed in the army or navy, or as warehousemen, all occupations that would be expected to engender a methodical attitude.

Most nurses served for short periods, of about two years or less. However, Ann Wilson of Wolstanton and Burslem, and Harriett Jackson of Newcastle are notable for serving for almost 18 and 25 years respectively. Nurses at Newcastle served for much longer periods than their counterparts at Wolstanton and Burslem. Several nurses had previous nursing experience, either in workhouses or other environments, or moved on to other nursing appointments.

Charles and Amelia Wellum provide an example of career

progression, from unhappy schoolmaster and schoolmistress at Northwich to successful master and matron at Wolstanton and Burslem, with Charles ultimately becoming registrar of births and deaths. Further examples of career progression are provided by Thomas Lynn, who clearly gave satisfaction as porter at Wolstanton and Burslem, and was appointed assistant overseer after two years, and Edward Steventon, whose capabilities as schoolmaster did not support his early promise. James Wellum, former porter at Wolstanton and Burslem, became deputy registrar to Charles. The most extreme form of promotion was from inmate to salaried officer. Examples are provided by Edward Steventon, who was appointed porter, and Edward Bond, who was hurriedly appointed to replace Steventon as porter following the latter's promotion to schoolmaster. Catherine Milner rose from inmate to nurse at Cheadle before moving to Wolstanton and Burslem.

Movement between unions, with the officer continuing in a similar job, also occurred; two nurses had been similarly employed in other unions, and a third left Wolstanton and Burslem for a similar appointment elsewhere. Nurse Elizabeth Baylis worked in infirmaries before and after her appointment at Newcastle. After leaving their posts as schoolmasters, William Carr and Edward Ellison both worked as workhouse schoolmasters at Oldham. A number of schoolmasters left to take up teaching appointments outside the workhouse system.

Deception of the guardians, as exercised by John Hammersley and Mary Elizabeth Daniel, was uncovered after a short time and the perpetrators' appointments were terminated. In a few cases the guardians must take responsibility for the appointment of unsatisfactory officers. William Abraham Shore was appointed as master by the guardians of Wolstanton and Burslem in the face of serious criticism by the assistant commissioner, and the appointment was not sanctioned. In the same union, Joseph Lowndes, union clerk, wrote to the

Commissioners opposing the appointment of the unsuitable John Leigh as schoolmaster, and gained their support; the Commissioners sanctioned the appointment for one month only, and Leigh was soon dismissed. The Commissioners' response to Lowndes' intervention indicates that they held him in high regard. This had been the case since March 1840, when a request for sanction of an increase to his salary was annotated to the effect that he devoted his whole time to the union, and was well worth the increase.[530]

The Lowndes family provides examples of the value of family connections between union employees when the clerk's sister was appointed workhouse schoolmistress. The Wellum family provides further examples; although the relationships are unclear, Edward and James Wellum, appointed porters at Wolstanton and Burslem, were surely related to Charles and Amelia Wellum, workhouse master and matron. James' involvement did not cease when he relinquished the porter's role, and he later became deputy registrar to Charles. There is no reason to believe that these family appointments were anything but successful, and use of the word 'nepotism' in its pejorative sense is probably not justified. A slightly different use of family influence is provided by an entry in the guardians' minutes for Wolstanton and Burslem in August 1850, when the guardians pointed out to Mr Wellum the desirability of putting his nephew, Thomas Barker, to work and removing him from the workhouse within a month.[531] Thomas, aged 16, was still resident in the workhouse in March, 1851, although he had found employment as a clerk in a warehouse.[532] Family connections also operated at the lowly level of workhouse nurses, with Ann Wilson's daughter being appointed infant

---

530   TNA: MH 12/11196/121, ff 237-238, Letter from Joseph Lowndes, Clerk to the Guardians of the Wolstanton and Burslem Poor Law Union, to the Poor Law Commission. 12 March 1840.
531   SSTAS: SD1232/6, f 88. Wolstanton and Burslem Board of Guardians' Minutes, 1850-1853. 20 August 1850.
532   TNA: HO 107/2002, p 1, f 676. Census. 1851.

nurse at Wolstanton and Burslem, and Harriet Jackson's sister being asked to replace her at Newcastle.

Of the officers studied, William Ward Broadhurst best demonstrates geographical mobility and career progression within the poor law system. His downfall following the auditor's discovery of his dishonesty as relieving officer at Penkridge shows that the bureaucracy of the system, which provides so much information for historians, also informed the central authority on officers' behaviours and thus had a more immediate use during the nineteenth century.

Appendix 1: Wolstanton and Burslem Schoolmasters.

Name	Former residence	Age	Former occupation	Appointment/ start date	Reason for leaving
George Goodwin	Cheadle (12.4 miles)	Approx 50		Dec 1838	Resigned
John Leigh	Burslem	55	Earthenware manufacturer, commission agent	Jul 1841	Dismissed; absent without leave, unsteady habits, suspicion of drinking
William Coxon	Hanley	25	Writing clerk	Nov 1841	Dismissed; drinking, sexual improprieties
George Machin	Wolstanton	21	Teacher in National School	Jun 1842	Resigned – found another situation
William Ward Broadhurst	Congleton, Cheshire (8.6 miles)	24	Helped at National School, Sunday School teacher, assisted father as relieving officer. Has attended the training institution in London.	Dec 1844	Inefficiency.

James Taylor	Newcastle under Lyme (5.6 miles)	39	Schoolmaster	Jul 1845	Resigned; deficient in temper and ability
James Foden	Manchester (36 miles)	59	Schoolmaster (about 35 years)	Mar 1846	Resigned; old age and infirmity; declining standards in school.
William Carr	Sheffield, Yorkshire (51.6 miles)	21	Clerk, was instructed in a British School, taught in a Sunday School	Nov 1848	Resigned; ill treatment of a boy and alleged victimisation by other officers
George Lewis Lees	Blythe Marsh (11.2 miles)	42	National Schoolmaster (8 years, no particular training), farmer	Jan 1851	Dismissed; lack of energy and industrial training
John Clews	Wolstanton	20	Writing clerk, Sunday School teacher	Nov 1851	Resigned August 1855, to enter teacher-training establishment.

Sources: SSTAS: SD1232/3, f.154, 11 Dec 1838; SD1232/4, f.244, 4 June 1845; SD1230/125, f.158, 3 July 1855.

TNA: HO107/993/23, f.39, p 2, 6 June 1841; MH12 11196/206, ff.373–378, 22 July 1841; MH12/11196/216, f.390, 3 Nov 1841; MH12/11196/223, ff.400–402, 3 Dec 1841; MH 12/11196/290, ff.504-524, 13 July 1842; MH12/11196/300, ff.527-529, 28 July 1842; MH12/11197/87, ff. 77–80, 29 Nov 1844; MH/12/11197/127, ff.136-138, 17 July 1845; MH12/11197/195, ff.234-237, 25 Mar 1846; MH/12/11198/74, ff.116-120, 8 Dec 1848; MH 12/11198/286, ff.455-458,

10 Jan 1851; MH/12/11198/288, ff.460-462, 14 Jan 1851; MH/12/11198/373, ff.619-621, 17 Nov 1851; MH12/11199/221, ff.291-293, 18 July 1855.

Appendix 2: Newcastle under Lyme Schoolmasters.

Name	Former residence	Age	Former occupation	Start date	Reason for leaving
Edward Steventon	Newcastle under Lyme	46	Clerk, schoolmaster (kept his own school), workhouse porter	Mar 1847	Failed examination
Thomas Eli Bennett	Uttoxeter (20.5 miles)	23	Teacher in National School	Jun 1848	Resigned to Work in National School
Henry Williamson	Kneller Hall, Twickenham (171.5 miles)	20	Student at Kneller Hall	Oct 1854	Resigned because of ill-health
Henry Harrison	Hull (123 miles)	22	Pupil teacher at National School, Student at Kneller Hall. Workhouse schoolmaster, Lexden and Winstree, Essex.	Mar 1855	Resigned for a better-paid position at Oldham
John Slaney	Hanley/Shelton (2.5 miles)	33	China warehouseman. 3 months training under National Schoolmaster, 12 months schoolmaster in National School	Jul 1856	Ill health. Since gone to the asylum.
Edward Ellison	Long Port, Burslem (5.6 miles)	20	First situation. 3 years training.	Sept 1856	Conflict with master. (Resigned December 1859)

Sources: SSTAS: D339/1/6, f.19, 7 July 1856; D339/1/6, ff.264-265, 19 December 1859. TNA: MH12/11364/161, ff.205-206, 17 Apr 1847; MH12/11364/219, f.281, 1 May 1848; MH12/11364/235, ff.302-304, 31 May 1848; MH12/11365/175, ff.271-272, 7 Nov 1854; MH12/11365/196, ff.295-296, 23 Mar 1855; MH12/11365, Paper Number: 31769/1856, ff.459-460, 5 Aug, 1856; MH12/11365, Paper Number: 49565/1856, ff.485-486, 24 Nov 1856.

Appendix 3: Wolstanton and Burslem Schoolmistresses.

Name	Former residence	Age	Former occupation	Start date	Reason for leaving
Margaret Lycett		Approx 20		May 1838	Resigned
Elizabeth Lowndes	Wolstanton	23	Dress maker, assistant in a school	May 1842	Marriage
Mary Elizabeth Daniel	Tunstall	24	Infant school teacher – two years	Jun 1845	Dismissed. Daughter of surgeon and apothecary, and had given birth to a bastard less than two years previously.
Charlotte Norris	Uttoxeter (20.5 miles)	23	Attended Uttoxeter Union School for instruction for two months	Aug 1845	Ill-health, but had previously been severely criticised by school inspector
Elizabeth Jones	Shelton	29	Had a private girls' school for about two years	May 1849	Resigned following adverse report by school inspector
Fanny Seddon	Burslem	20	Had a private school, but no training as a schoolmistress	Oct 1849	To join parents

Harriett Gent	Betchton, Cheshire (9.3 miles)	40	Experience in a private school	Dec 1850	Ill health (Resigned March 1854)

Sources: SSTAS: SD1232/3, ff.27-28, 1 May 1838. SD1230/(125), ff.19-20, 14 Mar 1854. TNA: HO107/993/23, f.39, 6 June 1841; MH12/11196/259, ff.462-464, 6 June 1842; MH12/11197/122, ff.127-130, 13 June 1845; MH12/11197/131, ff.142-144, 11 Aug 1845;MH12/11198/43, ff.69-71, 13 June 1848; MH12/11198/121, ff.197-200, 21 May 1849;MH12/11198/163, ff.255-258, 2 Oct 1849;MH12/11198/272, ff.431-433, 7 Dec 1850.

Appendix 4: Wolstanton and Burslem Porters.

Name	Former residence	Age	Former occupation	Start date	Reason for leaving
William Davies				Mar 1840	Improper behaviour with a female inmate
John Munday	Burslem	25	Army corporal	Jan 1847	Resigned through ill health
Edward Wellum	Marylebone, Middlesex (162.8 miles)	23	Warehouse assistant, assistant in a day school	Sept 1847	Resigned, no reason given
Thomas Lynn	Longport, Burslem	33	Warehouse at earthenware manufactory	Jul 1848	Appointed assistant overseer
John Hammersley	Shelton	35	Warehouseman	Aug 1850	Left of his own accord. Had incorrectly stated that he wrote his own application. The guardians were misled by his testimonials
Thomas Bruckshaw	Winnington (15.5 miles)	42	Farmer	Aug 1850	Entertaining a woman of 'questionable character'. (Dismissed March 1856)

Sources: SSTAS: SD1230/(125), f.224, 11 Mar 1856. TNA: MH12/11196/123, f.240, 25 Mar 1840; MH12/11197/250, ff.319-321, 22 Jan 1847; MH12/11197/311, ff.422-425, 21 Sept 1847; MH12/11198/52, ff.81-85, 31 July 1848; MH12/11198/248, ff.376-378, 12 Aug 1850; MH12/11198/253, ff.401-403, 16 Aug 1850; MH12/11198/261, ff 414-416, 11 Sept 1850.

Appendix 5: Newcastle under Lyme Porters.

Name	Former residence	Age	Former occupation	Start date	Reason for leaving
Clement Styche			Left shortly after an incident which was followed by the death of a pauper	Feb 1840	
Edward Steventon		40		May 1841	Promoted to schoolmaster
John Hill				Aug 1847	Incompetence
Edward Bond	Union Workhouse, Newcastle	65	Hatter, navy	Aug 1847	Death
Thomas Barlow	Newcastle	23	Hatter	Oct 1847	
Edward Steventon	Union Workhouse, Newcastle		Workhouse schoolmaster		Death
William Charles Beetenson	Newcastle	22	Assistant clerk	Sept 1851	Resigned/dismissed after making unjustified complaints about other officers

Ambrose Taylor	Union Workhouse, Newcastle	46	Navy, baker and porter at Stafford Union, baker at Newcastle under Lyme Union	Feb 1853	Conflict with master. (Resigned August 1859)

Sources: SSTAS: D339/1/2, ff.32-33, 17 Feb 1840; D339/1/2, ff.278, 10 May 1841; D339/1/4, ff.421, 2 Aug 1847; D339/1/4, f.425, 16 Aug 1847; D339/1/4, f.437, 27 Sept 1847; D339/1/5, f.207, 15 Sept 1851; D339/1/6, f.245, 29 Aug 1859. MH12/11364/161, ff.205-206, 17 Apr 1847; MH12/11364/191, ff.245-246, 1 Sept 1847; MH12/11364/197, ff.253-256, 12 Oct 1847; MH12/11365/47, ff.70-71, 8 Oct 1851; MH12/11365/98, ff.151-156, 20 Jan 1853; MH12/11365/114, ff.186-188, 5 Apr 1853.

Appendix 6: Wolstanton and Burslem Nurses.

Name	Former residence	Age	Former occupation	Start date	Reason for leaving
Elizabeth Goodfellow				Apr 1840	Resigned
Ann Dennis	Old Dispensary, Shelton	33	Cook and servant of all work	Midsummer 1841	Resigned
Dorothy Tirebuck	Hanley	26	Cook and nurse	May 1842	Dismissed – incapacity to discharge her duties
Jane Birks		33		Mar 1843	Resigned, to take up similar appointment at Amersham, Bucks
Catherine Milner	Cheadle Union Workhouse (20km)	35	Workhouse nurse	Dec 1845	Resigned through failure of health
Ann Mollatt	Talk o' the hill, Audley (12km)	24	Domestic employment and dressmaking	Feb 1848	Resigned - felt herself incompetent
Mary Dudley	Uttoxeter (33km)	34	Kept a small shop	Jul 1848	Resigned – felt unequal to the task
Ann Wilson	Wolverhampton (65km)	35	Nurse at Wolverhampton Union Workhouse	Aug 1850	Illness (Resigned 1869)

Catherine Milner	Wolstanton	37	Nurse and domestic servant	Dec 1848	Unclear, but a boy inmate had alleged that she had been with the schoolmaster, locked in his sitting room. The schoolmaster had followed her about

Sources: SSTAS: SD1232/3, f.378, 31 Mar 1840; SD1232/8, f.2 Nov 1869. TNA: MH12/383, Paper Number: 12173/1845, 15 Oct 1845; MH12/11196/206, ff.373-378, 22 July 1841; MH12/11196/259, ff.462-464, 6 June 1842; MH12/11197/153, ff.176-177, 28 Nov 1845; MH12/11198/19, ff.30-31, 2 Mar 1848; MH12/11198/46, ff.74, 13 July 1848; MH12/11198/52, ff.81-85, 31 July 1848; MH12/11198/74, ff.116-120, 8 Dec 1848; MH12/11198/238, ff.360-362, 24 July 1850.

8.

Caron Wilkinson: Widow, Mother and Inmate of the Mansfield Workhouse

Fiona Slater

Although this is an unusual 'chapter introduction' I think that it will help to do two things. Firstly, to illustrate my own research motivation - why I chose to write this chapter. Secondly, I wanted to show the human aspect of such historical writing and the connections between the subject matter and the people we write about in undertaking such research. In 2013 there was a three part television series entitled *Secrets From The Workhouse* and by using original records from the poor law archives these programmes followed the fortunes of five well known people's ancestors who had all spent time in the workhouse. Of the case studies followed in the programme Felicity Kendall's past relatives have relevance to this story. The programme showed that Kendall's great-grandmother, Mary Liddell, had nine legitimate children, then a tenth child, Albert Edward, illegitimately, who was born in the workhouse. Albert's birth certificate had no father's name, yet Mary's husband, John, was still alive. She found work enabling her to keep Albert with her, saying she was a widow. Later, in the 1901 census, Mary was listed as still married, she had lost her job and she had returned to the workhouse with Albert. She was separated from him and Albert grew up in the workhouse, left at 15, joined the army, served in World War I, survived the war and went to Australia on a passage supplied by the British government to returning soldiers as he felt his workhouse past would hold him back from employment in this country. The celebrity status of Felicity Kendall is of course irrelevant. It is the history and the life stories of her ancestors which concerned me as I watched the programme which acted as one of those inspirations which can move the historical researcher.

The story resonated with me while I was doing some research into the Victorian poor law in the Mansfield Union in Nottinghamshire. Here I first came across Caron Wilkinson, nee Radford, and her family.[533] Caron was the daughter of Thomas and Elizabeth Radford and she was christened at St Mary Magdalene church in Sutton-in-Ashfield on 7 March 1824. The record of her christening shows that her father was a framework knitter.[534] By the time she was 17 Caron was working as a seamer. At this time she married James Wilkinson, 24, also a framework knitter, on 2 June 1840, again at St Mary Magdalene church.[535] The 1841 census shows James Wilkinson, 25, framework knitter, and Caron Wilkinson, 18, living in Hucknall under Huthwaite.[536] Close by, are Caron's parents, Thomas and Elizabeth Radford, with some of their younger children, including Emma, six and George, four.[537] There is also a possible census entry for Caron's sister, Fanny Radford, at this time a 19 year old seamer living in the same locality.[538] This listing of family members and family relationships reminds us of what the poor laws, poor law authorities and poor law historians were and are dealing with; real people with real family ties and responsibilities.

---

533   Her name is often spelt differently in the archives. She would sign documents with 'X-her mark' so it is likely that poor law officials spelt her name phonetically. I have referred to her as Caron throughout this chapter to avoid needless confusion.

534   NA: P.R. 9799, Parish Baptism Register, St Mary Magdalene, Sutton-in-Ashfield, 1813-1828, fiche 19, page 222, entry 1774.

535   NA: P.R. 9811, Parish Marriage Register, St Mary Magdalene, Sutton-in-Ashfield, 1837-1848, fiche 63, entry 126. GRO: 1840 Quarter 2, Mansfield Registration District, volume 15, page 776.

536   TNA: HO 107/861, f 7, p 11. Census 1841.

537   TNA: HO 107/861, f 7, p 6. Census 1841.

538   TNA: HO 107/861, f 7, p 8. Census 1841.

The New Poor Law was heavily influenced by the publications of political economists from the late eighteenth and through the early nineteenth centuries which criticised the perceived laxity of earlier poor law policies. One of the most influential of these was Thomas Malthus and his *Essay on Population*. First published in 1798 it ran to a sixth edition by 1826. His doctrine stated that human passions tended to augment the number of people at a '...geometric rate of increase, while the best that could be hoped for in the food supply was at an arithmetic rate of increase', thus ensuring the human demand would always outstrip food provision. He also believed that the amount of relief offered under the Old Poor Law, determined by family size, offered inducement to early, improvident marriages and reckless breeding.[539] The nature and extent of families then was very much part of the New Poor Law ethos.

The 1834 report of the Poor Law Commission was really focused on reducing the rates by diminishing resources provided to the able bodied, and usually male, labourer. Thus the report did not focus on women workers.[540] However, for women one of the key concerns of the 1834 Poor Law Amendment Act was that of bastardy. Unmarried mothers had found that they were much blamed from the late eighteenth century onwards for steadily rising local rates. By the time of the 1834 Poor Law Report women were not the victims of seduction but rather the instigators. This was signified in the poor law bill by making bastard children the sole responsibility of the mother and removing the father from any moral or legal accountability. This was altered during the discussions in Parliament and affiliation proceedings were restored, but needed to be sworn before two magistrates rather than one, as had previously been the case. Affiliation actions were made much harder by requiring they be

539   Brundage A. The English Poor Laws, 1700-1930, Palgrave, 2002, p. 32.
540   Thane, P. 'Women and the Poor Law in Victorian and Edwardian England', History Workshop Journal, 6.i, 1978, 29-51.

brought to quarter sessions.[541] It was the guardians and overseers who decided if a man should be charged for maintenance of his illegitimate child. The quarter sessions had to be satisfied that

> ...the person so charged is really and in Truth the Father of such Child.....Provided always, that no such Order shall be made unless the Evidence of the Mother of such Bastard Child shall be corroborated in some material particular by other Testimony to the satisfaction of such Court.[542]

Even in that wording, '...father of such child...' and '...mother of such bastard child...' the moral laxity is attributed to the mother. Furthermore, any money received from the putative father was not given to the mother, but to the parish. Thus the lives of women and children were determined by acts and orders made by wealthy and educated men in London, far removed from the poor in villages and towns. Unmarried mothers were identified by the physical signs of their pregnancy whilst the majority of putative fathers were not pursued for maintenance. The Poor Law Commission and Poor Law Board looked upon unmarried mothers as instigators of their own destitution and deemed they should expect, as a result of their own misconduct or vice, to shoulder the burden. Blame was restricted in this sense and directed at mothers.

The result was an outcry of a dual standard of sexual morality.[543] This was a national debate and we need to cast our nets somewhat geographically wider to capture the flavour. One critic of the bastardy clause was T Simcox Lea, a Kidderminster manufacturer and magistrate who wrote to the Poor Law Commission in 1838 and who stated that '...the punishment of the female is not necessarily connected with the release of

---

541   Brundage A. The English Poor Laws, p 68-69.
542   4 & 5 Will. 4 c. 76 s 72. An Act for the Amendment and better Administration of the Laws relating to the Poor in England and Wales, 1834.
543   Englander, Poverty and Poor Law Reform, p18.

the male delinquent'. He reported two cases of girls becoming pregnant by the head of the households in which they were staying. He also referred to a foreman at a local mill

> ...on whom scores of young women depend for their daily bread, a man giving way to his passions......where is the check or restraint upon him? He further asks "are helpless, exposed girls to be left at the mercy of married men in whose houses they live – overlookers in mills who employ and discharge them at pleasure – and are men who know the force of sexual passions, to legislate as tho, (sic), these girls could protect themselves?"[544]

The reply to his letter has not survived. However, he was still campaigning on behalf of poor unmarried mothers in 1854. He reported the case of a putative father who denied paternity. The woman had no corroborative evidence of the man's paternity and he was excused from making his denial under oath by an alleged misinterpretation of the Evidence Act 1851.[545]

After the passing of the 1834 Act issues surrounding bastardy were fluid. On 12 November 1839 an order was sent to all boards of guardians stating that in charging putative fathers in bastardy cases relative to the Poor Law Amendment Act 1834, these would now revert back to the petty sessions

> ...for the purpose of diminishing the trouble and expense attendant on the application to the Quarter Sessions and of preventing the evil consequences supposed to follow from the publicity given by the examination in that court. [546]

---

544   TNA: MH 12/14016/193, ff 325-328. Letter from T Simcox Lea, Kidderminster, Magistrate for Worcestershire and Staffordshire, to the Poor Law Commission. 24 February 1838.

545   TNA: MH 12/14021/31, ff 41-42. Letter from T Simcox Lea, Magistrate for Worcester, Stafford and Shropshire, to the Poor Law Board. 16 February 1854. This refers to 14 & 15. Vict., c 99 s 3. *Evidence Act*, 1851.

546   *Sixth Annual Report of the Poor Law Commissioners*, Appendix A, no. 5, pp. 57-58. PP., 1840.

From 1844 this changed again and an unmarried mother was able to apply for an affiliation order against the father for maintenance of the mother and child, regardless of whether she was in receipt of poor relief.[547] In March 1840 Edmund Head had produced a report on the 'Law of Bastardy' because '... some of the most violent opposition.....to the amended Poor Law has been directed against its enactments on the subject of Bastardy'. He examined the way in which unmarried mothers and their bastard children were treated historically but found no trace in the many enactments for punishing putative fathers for seduction. He stated that the penalties suffered by the mother alone, were '...not for the sin of *having a bastard child*, but *having a bastard child which may be chargeable to the parish*'. Head wrote that affiliating a child to its putative father '...did practically operate as a check... on seduction, though he also quoted cases of women saying they were pregnant to get a man to marry them.[548] Head also saw that not affiliating a child to a father, could lead to more seduction of the weaker sex. A case demonstrating this was reported in a letter to the Poor Law Commission from the Truro guardians. Hannah Passmore had an illegitimate child, '...the father of the child had for a considerable time been paying his addresses to her and under a promise of marriage at length succeeded in seducing her'. The father was unable to continue maintaining his child, so Hannah, '...who previous to this faux pas bore an irreproachable character and since this time has conducted herself with much propriety...' was in the workhouse, but the guardians '...feel strongly disposed to relax the rule and allow her relief out of the house'.[549] The Poor Law Commission sanctioned the request

547   2 & 3 Vict., c 85. *Bastard Children Act*, 1839.
548   *Sixth Annual Report of the Poor Law Commissioners*, Head, Sir Edmund, Bart., Assistant Poor Law Commissioner. Report on the Law of Bastardy, Appendix B., No. 3, pp. 82-95. PP., 1840.
549   TNA: MH 12/1527/166, f 311-312. Letter from Richard Michell Hodge, Clerk to the Guardians of the Truro Poor Law Union, to the Poor Law Commission. 21 May 1838.

but the annotation advised against referring to the 'promise' (of marriage) in the reply as others would plead the same to avoid going into the workhouse.[550]

Returning to the Wilkinson family we find that by 1842 James and Caron have a son, William, who was baptised on 30 October at St Mary Magdalene church, the scene of his parents' marriage and Caron's own baptism.[551] Their second son, Christopher, followed in 1844 and was baptised at the same church on 23 July.[552] In the same year Fanny Radford, Caron's sister, married John Smith on 18 March in Sutton-in-Ashfield.[553] A major crisis in the family occurred in late November 1847 when James died from typhus fever.[554] James was just 34 and still only a young man and his death left Caron a young widow, she was only 23, and now had sole responsibility for their two little boys. Moreover, a year later we find that Caron was heavily pregnant with her third child and thus Mary Wilkinson was born at Hucknall under Huthwaite on December 31 1848. The registered birth provides no name for the childs father.[555] The crisis took Caron and her children into the working of the bastardy sections of the New Poor Law and into the Mansfield workhouse.[556]

---

550   TNA: MH 12/1527/167, f 313. Draft letter from the Poor Law Commission to Richard Michelle Hodge, Clerk to the Board of Guardians of the Truro Poor Law Union. 28 May 1838.

551   NA: P.R. 9800, Parish Baptism Register, St Mary Magdalene, Sutton-in-Ashfield, 1829-1873, fiche 25, page 260, No entry number.

552   Ibid, page 271, no entry number.

553   NA: P.R. 9811, Parish Marriage Register, St Mary Magdalene, Sutton-in-Ashfield, 1837-1848, fiche 65, page 150, entry 299. GRO; 1844, Quarter 1, Mansfield, volume 15, page 672.

554   Death Certificate: James Wilkinson, 24 November 1847. GRO: 1847 Quarter 4, Mansfield Registration District, volume 15, page 342

555   Birth Certificate: Mary Wilkinson, 31 December 1848. GRO: 1849 Quarter 1, Mansfield Registration District, volume 15, page 561.

556   This story also resonated with me as two years after Caron Wilkinson and her children were in the Mansfield workhouse my three times great-grandmother, Ann Mirfin, was recorded there on the night of the 1851 census with her two illegitimate children, William, 12 and Selina, 4. A third child, Elizabeth, 7, had died in 1848 when her clothes caught fire whilst her mother pawned belongings to buy food. TNA: HO 107/2124, f 74, p 13. Census. 1851.

As the admissions and discharge registers have not survived for the Mansfield union workhouse we do not know exactly when Caron Wilkinson and her children were admitted but as we will see from the correspondence between the Mansfield union and the Poor Law Board, she became a subject of concern in late February 1849. The family must of course have been destitute. Such poverty occurs when material resources are insufficient for a person's needs and can occur at specific times in the life cycle as circumstances change.[557] In Caron's case this came with her husband's death and her subsequent pregnancy with an illegitimate child. The 1834 Poor Law Amendment Act sought the ending of outdoor relief for the able-bodied and their dependants, but it could still be given 'Where such person, being a widow, shall be in the first six months of her widowhood'.[558] Further to this the same exception can be found in more general orders and reports of the Poor Law Commission.[559] It was also included in the 1844 Outdoor Relief Prohibitory Order. Here the commitment to able-bodied persons and their dependent families requiring relief, being relieved wholly in the union workhouse, was reiterated. However, exceptions were listed including the provision that relief other than the workhouse could be offered

> Where such person shall be a widow, and have a legitimate child or legitimate children dependent upon her, and incapable of earning his, her, or their livelihood, and have no illegitimate child born, after the commencement of her widowhood.[560]

---

557   Kidd, A. State, Society and the Poor in Nineteenth-Century England, Macmillan Press Ltd., 1999, p.3.
558   *Poor Law Amendment Act. Order issued to certain unions respecting relief to able-bodied persons*, PP., 1839.
559   See the *Seventh Annual Report of the Poor Law Commissioners*, p 67. PP., 1841.
560   Outdoor Relief Prohibitory Order, 21 December 1844, article 1, fifth exception.

On 26 February 1849 William Goodacre, the clerk to the Mansfield guardians sent a letter to the Poor Law Board. Referring to Caron Wilkinson he stated that

> This woman is a widow, 28 years of age now in this workhouse with her two legitimate children viz; William aged 7 and Christopher aged 4 and an infant of two months, illegitimate. Her sister has requested the Board to let her take out the two elder children and asks for 1 shilling per week each relief with them, <u>leaving the mother in the House</u>. The Board will be obliged by the opinion of the Poor Law Board as to how far they would be justified in giving relief under these circumstances.

On the back of the letter there is an annotation from H B Farnall which illustrates the specific deterrent aspect of the poor laws as they affected women.[561]

> I consider that this widow has just used the workhouse to lie in – as soon as she is strong enough she will go out; in the meantime if her sister is permitted to take out two of her children at 2 shillings a week, she will have the less burden to contend with when she goes out and will in effect be better off than before she had her illegitimate child. I think it would be injudicious to permit the relief because I have no doubt the two children are far better off in the workhouse and if this mother chooses, by and by to leave the workhouse, she can do and take her children with her.

There is a further annotation (unidentified as to the particular official): 'Say that under the circumstances the Board consider that the guardians ought not to grant the proposed relief'.[562] This

561   This is Harry Burrell Farnall, one of the Poor Law Board's poor law inspectors.
562   TNA: MH 12/9364/7, f 578. Letter from W E Goodacre, Clerk to the Guardians of the Mansfield Poor Law Union, to the Poor Law Board. 26 February 1849.

harsh assessment by Farnall reflects one of the main ideological planks of the New Poor Law which shifted responsibility from the parish to the individual to punish moral laxity. This punishment was the mode of relief itself; a refusal of out-relief and entry into the workhouse. The offer of the workhouse to Caron provided her with options set out under the workhouse test. This principle of the New Poor Law questioned the prospective pauper's destitution by their willingness or otherwise to enter the workhouse, when the conditions of the workhouse were deliberately set to be less eligible (worse) than any alternatives outside.[563] Caron would have been deemed to be eligible to receive relief within the workhouse only because she fell in the still commonly used category of 'undeserving poor', as a result of her being considered a moral failure in bearing an illegitimate child,[564] as well as falling into one of the exceptions of the 1844 Outdoor Relief Prohibitory Order.

The annotation by Farnall was used as the template for the draft reply from the Poor Law Board to Goodacre regarding Fanny Smith's offer to take in Caron Wilkinson's sons for two shillings a week. The letter states '...that under the circumstances they [the Poor Law Board] consider that the guardians ought not to grant the proposed relief'.[565] It does appear that the Mansfield Union supported to some degree the proposed measure of providing a small amount of money to the legitimate children's aunt. That much can be determined by the fact that they had thought it worth referring the case to the Poor Law Board at all. Other unions might also have sought similar exceptions. Elizabeth Dodds of Berwick upon Tweed is a useful case for comparison as she appears to have been in

563   Report from His Majesty's Commissioners for Inquiring into the Administration and Practical Operation of the Poor Laws, p 127. PP., 1834.
564   Murray, P. Poverty and Welfare 1830-1914, Hodder and Stoughton, 1999, p.3.
565   TNA: MH 12/9364/7, f 579. Draft letter from the Poor Law Board to W E Goodacre, Clerk to the Guardians of the Mansfield Poor Law Union. 7 March 1849.

a similar situation as Wilkinson. She also had two legitimate children and one illegitimate child and whilst in the Berwick-upon-Tweed workhouse in the early 1840s repeatedly applied for outdoor relief for her two legitimate children. This was always refused as she was not eligible under the fifth exception of article one of the Amended Prohibitory Order, the relevant wording being, '...and have no illegitimate child born, after the commencement of her widowhood'.[566] Dodd's illegitimate child died and she again applied for outdoor relief for her two legitimate children, but was refused and offered the workhouse by a majority vote of the guardians. The chairman, following the split vote, wrote to the Poor Law Commissioners for their comments regarding the minority's grounds for wanting to grant outdoor relief. This was centred on the wording of the fifth exception as she did 'have' only legitimate children as in '...presently existing'.[567] The Poor Law Commission agreed with the minority of the guardians as the illegitimate child had died and thus Elizabeth could have received outdoor relief again as a widow with just dependent legitimate children. This might be regarded by some of the Berwick guardians as a generous interpretation of the fifth exception, although the Poor Law Commission's reply did blame the mother for her destitution by it '...being either wholly or in part the immediate result of her own misconduct...' and they call the outdoor relief, '...the privilege which the exception extends to widows coming within its provisions'.[568]

Caron's two young boys may have been separated from her

---

566   *Seventh Annual Report of the Poor Law Commissioners*, Appendix A, No. 1, p 63. PP., 1841.
567   TNA: MH 12/8977/227, ff 387-397. Letter (with enclosures) from W and E Willoby [William Willoby and Edward Willoby], Clerks to the Guardians of the Berwick-upon-Tweed Poor Law Union, to the Poor Law Commission. 12 December 1842.
568   TNA: MH 12/8977/228, ff 398-402. Draft letter from the Poor Law Commission to W and E Willoby [William Willoby and Edward Willoby], Clerks to the Guardians of the Berwick-upon-Tweed Poor Law Union. 21 December 1842.

when they entered the workhouse and we can only imagine how frightened they must have been as they were only aged seven and four. The central regulations allowed mothers to share beds with their children up to the age of seven and to allow reasonable access to them.[569] However, some unions were less generous than this and separated them so mothers could be put to work even by forcing premature weaning.[570] In general pauper inmates were allowed to receive visitors with the permission of the workhouse master and

> Those who sought assistance from the Poor Law did not in consequence become isolated from their community. Their absence was temporary; they were not shunned and their relatives did not cease to see them in the workhouse.[571]

This is a relevant and instructive assessment in Caron's case. After all, if she gave birth to her daughter Mary on 31 December 1848 and the Mansfield Union was writing to the Poor Law Board asking in late February 1849 whether Fanny Smith, her married sister, might take her two boys, then it is a reasonable conjecture that the two sisters had been finding some way of talking to each other and planning the request. Fanny, who must have been considered respectable enough for the guardians to even entertain the idea of her having the two boys, had to make her offer to them made known somehow to the guardians. Fanny's husband was a framework knitter and it was likely that they would have found it hard to feed the two extra children without this remuneration. Caron perhaps wanted her children to be with her sister to remove the stigma of them living in the workhouse.

It appears that Fanny and John Smith did not take the boys

---

569   *Eighth Annual Report of the Poor Law Commissioners*, p 81. PP., 1842.
570   Crowther, Workhouse System, p 43.
571   Englander, Poverty and Poor Law Reform, p 45.

because further correspondence from the Mansfield Union to the Poor Law Board, dated 20 July 1849, states that, Caron Wilkinson had had an illegitimate child after being widowed

> ...whereby outrelief is rendered illegal. The Board however have found that a man of good and industrious character, a collier and a relative of her late husband will take one of the elder boys.

The wording of this letter is both enlightening and elusive at the same time. It tells us nothing about how the guardians came to know about this collier or whether Caron was the instigator of this step to remove her son from the workhouse. The letter continues by asking the Poor Law Board to sanction 30 shillings to be spent for, '...a certain quantity of clothing by way of outfits...'. Indeed this was a condition made by the collier for taking the boy. The clerk continued that

> The woman, with her family...... had been in the Workhouse till within the last few days - and the Board having made strict inquiry, as to the man's character believe it would be advisable to put this boy under his care...[572]

In their reply the Poor Law Board sanctioned the money with the following direction.

> The Guard[ia]ns should how[eve]r make enquiries from time to time through their Rel[ievin]g Off[icer] or otherwise, as to the future conduct of the boy, and of his relation towards him.[573]

---

572   TNA: MH 12/9364/489, f 691.Letter from W E Goodacre, Clerk to the Guardians of the Mansfield Poor Law Union, to the Poor Law Board, 20 July 1848.
573   TNA: MH 12/9364/490, f 692. Draft letter from the Poor Law Board to W E Goodacre, Clerk to the Guardians of the Mansfield Poor Law Union. 31 July 1848.

This sanctioning of monies payable on paupers, particularly young children, leaving to take up paid employment was common. For example, five months earlier we find the Mansfield Union asking the Poor Law Board to sanction payment for clothing and bedding for Henrietta Jefford and her four illegitimate sons aged between nine and 17. The Mansfield Union wrote on 23 February 1949, stating

> She has procured employment for herself and the children at a factory and this Board has ordered clothing and bedding to the value of £4 to enable her to take up the offer and I am directed to solicit your confirmation thereof under the 6th Article of the Prohibitory Order.[574]

The Poor Law Board replied on 1 March 1849

> ....that if the woman and her children can obtain employment, likely to be permanent and at wages sufficient for their maintenance, the Board will not object to their being furnished with such clothing as may in the judgement of the G[uardia]ns be really necessary, although there are serious objections to such a proceeding. The Board presume that the Guard[ian]s are satisfied with the recent conduct of the woman and it is noticed that the youngest child is nine years old.[575]

Although the Poor Law Board generally sanctioned payment for clothing to help a mother and child who had found work, they would qualify this with comments referring to their entrenched and ideological dislike of the principle of such payments. An example from 1850 shows that the Mansfield Union wrote to

574   TNA: MH 12/9364/397, f 572. Letter from W E Goodacre, Clerk to the Guardians of the Mansfield Poor Law Union, to the Poor Law Board. 23 February1849.
575   TNA: MH 12/9364/398, f 573. Draft letter from the Poor Law Board to W E Goodacre, Clerk to the Guardians of the Mansfield Poor Law Union. 1 March 1849.

the Poor Law Board stating that Elizabeth Keeton, aged 33, who with her two illegitimate children, had been a pauper inmate of the workhouse for over two years, had applied for clothing to enable her to take a place in service. The Poor Law Board eventually decided to '...recommend the clothing be allowed but the danger of giving relief to mothers of illegitimate children out of the workhouse is apparent'.[576] A much later example, taken from 1865, shows the Mansfield Union again writing to the Poor Law Board concerning a female pauper and her illegitimate children. This related to Ann Savage, an inmate of the Mansfield workhouse who resided there with her two illegitimate children, John Savage aged 11 and Sabina Savage aged three. The boy had been found work in a foundry and his mother applied to the guardians for a clothing allowance for him. The union asked the Board to sanction a payment of 30 shillings, which was agreed.[577]

Let us return to the Wilkinson family. It transpires that if one of Caron's boys went to stay with the collier, who had been related to her late husband, it was not a permanent move as both of her sons were with her sister in March 1851.[578] Caron had married Thomas Marriott on 3 August 1850 at St Mary Magdalene church and she was then about six months pregnant with his child.[579] There is a strong possibility that Caron knew Thomas previously because he is recorded as living with his

576   TNA: MH 12/9363/53, f 73. Letter from W E Goodacre, Clerk to the Guardians of the Mansfield Poor Law Union, to the Poor Law Board. 30 April 1850; MH 12/9363/54, f 74. Draft letter from the Poor Law Board to W E Goodacre, Clerk to the Guardians of the Mansfield Poor Law Union. 14 May 1850; and MH 12/9363/81, f 110. Letter from W E Goodacre, Clerk to the Guardians of the Mansfield Poor Law Union, to the Poor Law Board. 5 July 1850.
577   TNA: MH 12/9369/1, ff 3-4. Letter from W E Goodacre, Clerk to the Guardians of the Mansfield Poor Law Union, to the Poor Law Board. 6 January 1865.
578   TNA: HO 107/2123, f 571, p 4. Census. 1851.
579   NA: P.R. 9812, Parish Marriage Register, St Mary Magdalene, Sutton-in-Ashfield, 1848-1855, fiche 68, page 76, entry 152. GRO: 1850, Quarter 3, Mansfield Registration District, volume 15, page 761.

parents, William and Mary Marriott, close to her and James in the 1841 census. [580] Indeed, one of the witnesses at Caron's first marriage was a William Marriott.[581] On their marriage Thomas would have then become responsible for all Caron's children as

> ...every Man who from and after the passing of this Act shall marry a Woman having a Child or Children at the Time of such Marriage, whether such Child or Children be legitimate or illegitimate, shall be liable to maintain such Child or Children as a Part of his Family ...and such Child or Children shall, for the Purposes of this Act, be deemed a Part of such Husband's Family accordingly.[582]

We can set out the full constituents of the family from the 1851 census. The head of the household was Thomas Radford and his wife Elizabeth (Caron's parents), their children George, aged 17, and Benjamin, aged 13; joined now by Caron and Thomas Marriott along with the illegitimate Mary Wilkinson, aged two, and John Marriott, four months. They were all still living in Hucknall under Huthwaite. All working age male members of the family worked as framework knitters.[583] In the same year we find Caron's two older boys are staying in the household of John Smith and Fanny Smith (Caron's sister), also in Hucknall under Huthwaite, and also including Fanny and Caron's sister Emma, 15.[584] Why the family was divided in such a way is difficult to state with full confidence but it is likely that with the eight people making up the Thomas Radford household there was

---

580   HO 107/861, f 6, p 6. Census. 1841.
581   NA: P.R. 9811, Parish Marriage Register, St Mary Magdalene, Sutton-in-Ashfield, 1837-1848, fiche 63, entry 126. GRO: 1840 Quarter 2, Mansfield, volume 15, page 776.
582   4 & 5 Will. 4 c. 76 s 57. *An Act for the Amendment and Better Administration of the Laws relating to the Poor in England and Wales*, 1834.
583   TNA: HO 107/2123, f 584, p 30. Census. 1851. The fact that Mary has the surname Wilkinson suggests that she was not Thomas Marriott's daughter
584   TNA: HO 107/2123, f 571, p 4. Census. 1851.

little room for the two boys who now resided in the five strong John Smith household.

Caron and Thomas Marriott also appear on censuses from 1861 until 1891.[585] A strong sense of family emanates from these entries as various members of their extended household stayed with them on these census nights. Caron's brother, George (listed as deaf, dumb and nearly blind),[586] was part of their household from 1881 following the death of their parents, as he clearly struggled to live by himself.[587] In 1891 the household included their married daughter and her two small children, plus Harold Wilkinson, 15, a grandson, who despite the different Christian name, might have been the son of Christopher and Betsey Wilkinson, both deceased.[588] It appears that Thomas and Caron's son James was living next door with his wife, Harriet. Thomas Marriott, labourer, died on 8 January 1894, aged 72, of debility, and was buried in Hucknall under Huthwaite cemetery.[589] Just over a year later, on 29 March 1895, Caron herself died of cardiac disease aged 71 and was buried in the same cemetery.[590]

As far as can be ascertained Caron's only time in the workhouse was after she had her third child, her illegitimate daughter, Mary. She appears to have lived her whole life in Hucknall under Huthwaite, firstly with her parents, then with

585   TNA: RG 9/2427, f 101, p.29; Census. 1861; RG 10/3470, f 60, p 7; Census. 1871; RG 11/3316, f 129, p 11; Census. 1881; and RG 12/ 2653, f 124, p 13. Census. 1991.
586   TNA: RG 9/2427, f 89, p 6. Census 1861.
587   TNA: RG 11/3316, f 129, p 11. Census. 1881. For some reason Caron, by the 1881 census, has changed her name to Kerrenhappuch
588   TNA: RG 12/2653, f 124, p 13. Census. 1891.
589   www.ashfield-dc.gov.uk/ashfieldcemeteries/intro.php Ashfield Cemetery Records Online, Register Book of Burials in the Hucknall Huthwaite Cemetery Ground, 1888-1903, p.28, entry 271. GRO: 1894 Quarter 1, Mansfield Registration District, volume 7b, page 47. [Accessed 1 March 2016.]
590   www.ashfield-dc.gov.uk/ashfieldcemeteries/intro.php Register Book of Burials in the Hucknall Huthwaite Cemetery Ground, 1888-1903, p 33, entry 329. GRO: 1895 Quarter 1, Mansfield Registration District, volume 7b, page 63. [Accessed 1 March 2016.]

her two husbands, her children and other members of her family. Her 43 year marriage to Thomas Marriott produced a further eight children.[591] One gets a feeling of a close supportive family probably never far above the poverty line as Thomas's jobs were variously recorded on the censuses as framework knitter, farm labourer and road labourer.[592] Mary Wilkinson, Caron's illegitimate daughter and ex-workhouse inmate, was listed as a housekeeper in the 1871 census in Hucknall under Huthwaite, to William Parker, a coal miner and a widower with a six year old daughter. Also in the household were her sons, James aged two years, and John George aged two months.[593] Mary Wilkinson and William Parker later married and in the 1881 census they are listed with their seven children at Auckland St Andrew in Durham. The youngest two are shown to have been born in Shildon, also in Durham. [594] William and Mary lived in Auckland St Andrew, then moved back to Shildon, where William died in 1900 aged 59. In the 1891 census he was no longer a miner, but was a cartman. [595] After William's death Mary became a 'Milk Cow Keeper and General Contractor',[596] which she ran with the help of her five unmarried children still living with her in 1911.[597] Mary Parker died in 1929, aged 81.[598]

The common thread through the Caron Wilkinson narrative is parental love and support. There is no evidence of any attempt at abandonment of any of her children. In fact, in the face of condemnationary legislation, the opposite was true. Caron tried

---

591   One of the children, Thomas Wilkinson, was 'accidently killed in a coal pit in Teversall by the falling upon him of a piece of coal'. Thomas was aged just 13 at the time of the accident in August 1867. GRO: 1867, Quarter 3, Mansfield, volume 7b, p 35.

592   TNA: HO 107/2123, f 584, p 30, Census. 1851; RG 9/2427, f 101, p.29, Census. 1861; RG 10/3470, f 60, p 7, Census. 1871; RG 11/3316, f 129, p 11, Census. 1881; and RG 12/ 2653, f 124, p 13, Census. 1891.

593   TNA: RG 10/3470, f 49, p 5. Census. 1871.

594   TNA: RG 11/4917, f 39, p 21. Census. 1881.

595   TNA: RG 12/4069, f 75, p 24. Census. 1891.

596   TNA: RG 13/4644, f 113, p 16. Census. 1901.

597   TNA: RG 14/29743. Schedule 317, Census 1911.

598   GRO: 1929, Quarter 3, Auckland, volume 10a, p 213.

to have her sons taken in by her sister to get them removed from the workhouse while she stayed with her youngest child in the workhouse. In her middle years Caron opened her home to her disabled brother, her own married daughter and her children and later her orphaned grandson, all in their time of hardships and thus likely saving them from having to experience any part of their life in the workhouse.

9.

Male Able-Bodied Out Relief in Early Victorian Bromsgrove

Anna Kingsley-Curry

The purpose of the Poor Law Amendment Act of 1834 was, as its name implies, to amend the existing law in regard to how poverty and welfare were managed. However, the changes were significant and included the bringing together of parishes, the promotion of a deterrent workhouse system and the creation of a bureaucracy for national oversight. The scale of changes imply something far greater than the use of the word 'amendment'. The new arrangements quickly came to represent a New Poor Law. The pre-1834 Old Poor Law was flexible and had not much changed in principle from the early seventeenth century. The supporters of the New Poor Law claimed the amendments rectified abuses and made it more relevant to an increasingly industrial, urban and commercial society. In particular, its aim was to reduce welfare expenditure through the abolition of any assistance to male able-bodied paupers outside the workhouse.

This study is set in Bromsgrove in Worcestershire in the 1840s. I want to look at the 1834 Act's provisions for poor relief, and to consider how effectively the prohibition against giving out relief to the able-bodied male was implemented. By examining, through detailed case studies, a number of applicants and their varied reasons for asking for relief, I want to show how the Bromsgrove guardians and the central authority differed in their approach. I will argue that the guardians sought to be more pragmatic (helped by their local knowledge), but ultimately submitted to the Commissioners' dictates. In this they were unlike many other unions who happily circumvented instructions from central office.[599] The central authority did take special circumstances into consideration and did at times sanction out relief particularly when extreme hardship meant the workhouse could not house all applicants.

The `hungry forties' were a significant decade for the history of welfare. The dislocation resulting from industrialization was at its height with people flocking into the towns. There was unrest in the countryside as well as in the urban centres as wages and prices became highly politicised through the Chartist cause.[600] Agricultural workers in particular felt the pinch; it has been estimated that a loaf of bread in 1846 cost one-tenth of the agricultural weekly wage as opposed to one-twentieth of that of an industrial worker.[601]

Bromsgrove, described in a Bentley's directory as '...a populous, busy, manufacturing market town' in north Worcestershire, was influenced by the conditions prevailing both in agriculture and industry. A weekly market for corn and other produce, a monthly cattle market, a renowned Midsummer Day Horse Fair and an annual hiring fair in September all served local agriculture.[602] As for industry, in 1841 the manufacture of hand-wrought nails accounted for 31% of employment, with over 3000 men, women and children so engaged.[603] Benjamin Sanders' button factory employed 300 workers (mostly women and children) and was the biggest factory in the area until the

599   Crowther, Workhouse System, pp 46-50.
600   Archer, J.E. 'Under Cover of Night: Arson and Animal Maiming', in Mingay, G.E. ed., The Unquiet Countryside, Routledge, 1989, pp 65-79; Wright, D.G. Popular Radicalism, The Working Class Experience, 1789-1880, pp 112-149; Royle, E. Chartism, Longman Group, 1986, 2nd ed., 1986; Charlton, J. The Chartists: The First National Workers' Movement, Pluto Books, 1997.
601   Bates, S. Penny Loaves & Butter Cheap: Britain in 1846, Head of Zeus Ltd, 2014. p 1.
602   Bentley's Directory of Worcestershire, 1841. p 3.
603   Kings, B. and Cooper, M. Glory Gone: The Story of Nailing in Bromsgrove, Halfshire Books 1989/1999. Appendix D, p 133.

1840s, when the Railway Freight Waggon Factory was built in Aston Fields.[604] In addition, at Stoke Prior there were salt, soap and vitriol works and a rock salt mine, while the neighbouring town of Redditch, part of the Bromsgrove Union, was famous for the manufacture of needles, bodkins, pins, fish hooks and fishing tackle.[605] Although this gives an impression of a thriving area offering a variety of employment, Bromsgrove was vulnerable to industrial slumps and bad harvests, and even in the best times much of the work was low paid.

The 1834 Act sought to prohibit out relief not only to paupers but also to working men whose wages were insufficient to support them and their families. The previous practice of giving relief to

> Persons or their Families who, at the Time of applying for or receiving such Relief were wholly or partially in the Employment of Individuals, and the Relief of the able-bodied and their Families is in many Places administered in Modes productive of Evil...

was to be discontinued.[606]

The evil referred to stemmed from the system of providing allowances to suppliment wages. In practice there were several versions of this but the most well-known has come down to us as the 'Speenhamland system', which was regarded to have been widely used in the south of England for the last 30-odd years of the Old Poor Law. In 1795 magistrates had met at the Pelican Inn at the village of Speenhamland near Newbury to see what arrangements could be made to alleviate the distress of agricultural workers which had been caused largely by the high price of provisions. They agreed to raise weekly wages to match

---

604   Richards, A. The Extraordinary Adventures of Benjamin Sanders, Buttonmaker of Bromsgrove. Bromsgrove Society 1884. p 6.
605   Slater, T. Directory of Worcestershire, 1850, p 6.
606   4 & 5 Will IV, c 76, s 52, *Poor Law Amendment Act*, 1834.

the cost of a three-gallon loaf for each man plus one and a half loaves for a wife and each child. Although not intended, one of the consequences of this was to encourage employers to keep wages low knowing they would be subsidised out of the poor rate.[607]

One of the aims of the 1834 Act was to stop such allowances. However, boards of guardians were credited with a certain amount of discretion and were able to provide such out-relief where people found themselves in 'sudden and urgent' necessity.[608] The table opposite shows the not inconsiderable number of the able-bodied who were in receipt of out relief between 1842 and 1848 '…on account of temporary sickness or accident'.[609]

Stopping outdoor relief entirely to both paupers and underpaid workers was thus clearly impossible. The Marquess of Salisbury had objected so strongly to the clause in the 1834 bill aiming to end all outdoor relief the following summer that it was dropped. As a result the eradication of such relief became '…a piecemeal, drawn-out affair, with everything hinging on the determination of the new central commission and its ability to convince or compel local boards of guardians'.[610] In addition, in spite of attempts such as the 1844 Outdoor Relief Prohibitory Order, outdoor relief for the able-bodied needed to continue in times of bad harvests or industrial slumps since it was often physically impossible for the workhouse to take in large numbers applying for admittance. Thus the subsidising of inadequate wages over a period might cease but occasional outdoor relief, at least half of which was to be in food or clothing, was allowed to those who satisfied the labour test, that is who were willing to work at tasks set by the guardians.[611]

---

607   Brundage, English Poor Laws, pp 27-29, 43.
608   4 & 5 Will IV, c 76, s 52, *Poor Law Amendment Act*, 1834; see also Brundage, English Poor Laws, p 85.
609   *First Report of the Poor Law Board*, Appendix B, p 60, table 5. PP., 1849.
610   Brundage, Making, pp 68-69; Brundage, English Poor Laws, p 68.
611   *Eighth Annual Report of the Poor Law Commissioners, with appendices*, London 1842, p 103, Outdoor Labour Test Order, article 1.

Comparative statement of the number of adult able-bodied paupers relieved in England and Wales during each of the quarters ended Lady-day, 1842 to 1848, distinguishing those relieved on account of temporary sickness or accident.

	In Door			Out Door				
	On account of temporary sickness or accident	All other causes including vagrants	Total in-door	On account of temporary sickness or accident	All other causes including vagrants	Total in-door	Total number of able-bodied relieved. In-door and out-door.
1842	10,922	74,249	85,171	134,641	192,078	326,719	411,890
1843	10,888	88,308	99,196	146,704	220,685	367,389	466,585
1844	11,458	86,327	97,783	158,280	175,419	333,699	431,484
1845	11,407	76,216	87,623	167,277	165,196	332,473	420,096
1846	11,258	74,413	85,671	144,394	152,352	296,746	382,417
1847	13,485	109,739	123,224	202,403	236,728	439,131	562,355
1848	15,084	140,795	155,879	203,373	307,086	510,459	666,338

In general the 1834 Act stated that relief for able-bodied paupers was to be given only inside the workhouse and if a man needed relief he had to be admitted together with all his family. Paupers were to be discouraged from making welfare applications by the harsh conditions attached to relief. This notion of 'less eligibility' was envisaged to produce those conditions worse than those experienced by the poorest labourer not in receipt of relief. If conditions were indeed worse inside than out then they must have been extremely bad. In 1842 a sanitary inspector described the condition of a family of nailers who lived in Bromsgrove in 1842.

> A man and his wife, (and till lately a son 19), a daughter 17, another son 12, another 10, another seven, occupied one room, both for sleeping and eating in, at most not more than 12 feet square; one bedstead and a heap of rubbish *called* a bed, was all the accommodation I could perceive; the roof sadly out of repair and there are large holes in the end of the mud-built hut.[612]

By contrast, the Bromsgrove Union workhouse newly-built in 1838 sounds a veritable 'pauper palace'.

> ...a spacious and convenient brick building situated in an open and pleasant locality, on the Birmingham road, about ¾ mile from the town.[613]

In fact less eligibility under the New Poor Law related not so much to material conditions in the workhouse as to the social discipline which was imposed on inmates and to their loss of independence.[614] So once admitted, families were split up;

---

612   *Sanitary Inquiry: England. Local Reports on the Sanitary Condition of the Labouring Population of England, in Consequence of an Inquiry Directed to be made by the Poor Law Commissioners*, p 104, 1842 (007).
613   Slater's Directory, 1850, p 6.
614   Crowther, Workhouse System, p 40.

mealtimes, the times to go to bed and to rise in the morning were set by the poor law authorities; diets were routine and set low, work was to be hard, boring and sometimes meaningless.[615] Such conditions were set to deter relief applicants.

To be eligible for relief an applicant had to be 'settled', with each parish being responsible for the cost of its settled paupers. The qualification had been defined by the 1662 Settlement Act and this did not change under the New Poor Law.[616] Settlement was granted in several ways, for example by a persons' birth or by a residence of five years (reduced later to three years and then to one) or a wife taking the settlement of her husband. Illegitimate children presented a challenge. In early 1840 the Bromsgrove guardians asked for the Commission's ruling on whether such children under the age of 16 were to take on the settlement of their mother should she subsequently marry; whether, once 16, and not having acquired settlement in their own right, they should revert to their birth settlement; and lastly, if born in a workhouse would the settlement be in that parish.[617] After five years a person became irremovable and therefore a charge on his new parish should he become a pauper; before that he and his family were removable back to their original parish at the expense of his parish of residence.[618]

It was not always easy to determine who was or was not legally removable, and it was made no clearer by the Poor Removal Act of 1846.[619] In December of that year the Bromsgrove guardians set up a committee in response to the '… late Removal Act' which interviewed over 100 people who had

---

615   For 'meaningless work' see the contribution by Carter and Wileman in this volume.
616   14 Chas II, c 12, *Act for the Better Relief of the Poor of this Kingdom*, 1662.
617   WAAS: 251/BA400/1(ii). Bromsgrove Board of Guardians' Minute Book, 1839-1840. 20 January 1840. See also the answer in MH 12/13904/130, folio 178. Draft letter from the Poor Law Commission to Thomas Day, Clerk to the Guardians of the Bromsgrove Poor Law Union. 31 January 1840.
618   Brundage, English Poor Laws, p 103.
619   Lees, Solidarities of Strangers, p 219.

been in receipt of relief and whose place of settlement was different from where they lived. Thomas Day, [620] the union clerk, wrote to the Poor Law Commission giving the committee's report. They considered the Removal Act ambiguous, they talked of '…different constructions of the recent Act', and therefore did not intend to transfer paupers from the lists of parishes where they were settled to parishes '…from which they are supposed to be irremovable;' the parishes all belonging to the Bromsgrove Union. If changes were made, they said, it would result in confusion in the union accounts and cause a great deal of unnecessary trouble. Annotations made by the Commissioners on Day's letter show that they were not swayed by this argument. They conceded that where the committee's recommendations were not in opposition to the law they deserved confirmation, but where the guardians proposed to continue charges simply for the sake of convenience and where the charge would fall on a parish '…not lawfully bound to bear it', they could not sanction it; nor would any auditor pass such an arrangement. [621]

Figure 9/1: Thomas Day, clerk to the guardians of the Bromsgrove Poor Law Union.

As we have already seen, out relief under the New Poor Law was to be given mainly in a combination of two forms, in money

620   The reproduction of Thomas Day's portrait here is by kind permission of the Bromsgrove Council.
621   TNA: MH 12/13907/302, ff 462-463. Letter from Thomas Day, Clerk to the Guardians of the Bromsgrove Poor Law Union, to the Poor Law Commission. 4 December 1846.

and in kind.[622] On the subject of bread and its recipes, the Commissioners took a surprisingly close interest, though this was probably more from a pecuniary angle than a culinary one. In March 1847 Day informed them that the Bromsgrove Union had entered into a contract for a supply of bread made from half seconds wheat flour and half thirds, thus reducing the cost of a 4lb loaf by a halfpenny, to 8¾d, compared to its cost when made entirely of seconds flour. [623] He recommended the Commission accept this practice widely and thus make considerable savings nationally.[624] The Commission acknowledged his letter but did not act upon it and instead they issued a circular advocating a mixture of half seconds wheat flour and half hominy (maize).[625] The Bromsgrove guardians then ordered a series of experiments: with all wheat flour, with wheat flour and hominy, and lastly with wheat flour and rice. They concluded that the last was the most palatable though they were worried it might fall below the nutritional standards required for a healthy person.[626]

I now want to move on to a number of specific Bromsgrove Union cases taken from the 1840s, examining the varied reasons the able-bodied workers gave for applying for out-relief and the reasons given by the guardians to the Poor Law Commission for setting aside the prohibition of such relief. The guardians took a more pragmatic approach than the Commissioners who, perhaps because they did not have the same local knowledge, were on the whole less willing to depart from the letter of the law.

---

622   4 & 5 Will IV, c 76, s 52, *Poor Law Amendment Act*, 1834.
623   Seconds and thirds refer to the quality of the flour used; thirds being inferior to seconds.
624   TNA: MH 12/13908/30, f 41. Letter from Thomas Day, Clerk to the Guardians of the Bromsgrove Poor Law Union, to the Poor Law Commission. 23 March 1847.
625   TNA: MH 12/13908/31, f 42. Draft letter from the Poor Law Commission to Thomas Day, Clerk to the Guardians of the Bromsgrove Poor Law Union. 29 March 1847.
626   TNA: MH 12/13908/70, ff 99-100. Letter from Thomas Day, Clerk to the Guardians of the Bromsgrove Poor Law Union, to the Poor Law Commission. 9 June 1847.

In 1843, James Wall, aged 38, was keen to emigrate to New South Wales in Australia. He was a stonemason by trade and had been struggling for some time to support his family. The family was comprised of James, Dinah, his wife, aged 35, and their seven children aged between 12 months and 13 years. Wall had first applied for relief back in January 1842 when the whole family, then with only six children, had gone into the workhouse. However, he was described as of good character and so perhaps was considered a member of the 'deserving poor'. The guardians offered to help by keeping three children in the workhouse and letting the rest of the family depart to find work. This kind of relief, keeping in some of the children while letting the rest of the family depart (a mix of in-door and out-door relief) was contrary to the 1834 Act's stipulations but was popular with guardians because it saved money. The Commission when asked to approve such actions often agreed to do so but only for a specific length of time. Day asked the Poor Law Commission to sanction this for Wall, which they did.[627] A year later Wall was reduced '...to the last extremity' and emigration seemed the only answer. A private subscription raised just enough funds to pay the charges of £1 each for him and his wife and 10s for each of the children to travel to Liverpool to take a ship sailing on 30 October. Unfortunately the sailing was delayed until 2 November and Wall needed more money to bridge the gap. The guardians had authorised a payment of 20 shillings, preferable to having to support all the family back in the workhouse, and they asked for the Commission's approval. The first official, as shown by annotated remarks on Day's letter, was not too happy and enquired if it were not worth remarking on the disadvantages '...of these irregular transactions'. But William Golden Lumley, Assistant Secretary to the Commission, pointed out that Wall appeared to be a government emigrant, that there

<hr />

627   TNA: MH 12/13905/138, ff 227-228. Letter from Thomas Day, Clerk to the Guardians of the Bromsgrove Poor Law Union, to the Poor Law Commission. 18 January 1842.

had been no call on the poor rate as all the funds had been raised by private subscription and that it appeared to be simply a case of relief being given to a non-resident pauper. [628] Under the circumstances described, the Commission sanctioned the payment.[629]

William Houghton, aged 37, from Alvechurch was also the father of seven children and all under 15 years. However, his circumstances were different from Wall's in that he had recently lost his wife. When employed, he earned 12 shilling a week working on the turnpike and occasionally his two older sons earned between two shillings and six pence and three shillings. He applied to the guardians in February 1844 and they gave him relief, in the same way as they had Wall, by taking some of his children into the workhouse. The two chosen, and they would have been chosen by Houghton himself, were Hannah (seven years) and Joseph (five years). In Houghton's case they sanctioned the arrangement for three months on the assumption that the older children, aged 14 and 12, would soon find permanent work.[630]

In May 1845 Thomas Drinkwater and his family were admitted into the workhouse as his agricultural wages of eight shillings a week were not enough to support them. He was 39, his wife Mary Ann was 27 and they had six children under 11 years. After a month Drinkwater, described as a man of good character who had promised to do his best to keep his family out of the workhouse, was allowed to leave with his wife and four of the children with the parish of Stoke Prior, their place of settlement, paying the costs of the two children left behind.

628   TNA: MH 12/13906/128, ff 230-231. Letter from Thomas Day, Clerk to the Guardians of the Bromsgrove Poor Law Union, to the Poor Law Commission. 3 November 1843.
629   TNA: MH 12/13906/129, f 232. Draft letter from the Poor Law Commission to Thomas Day, Clerk to the Guardians of the Bromsgrove Poor Law Union. 11 November 1843.
630   TNA: MH 12/13906/145, ff 268-269. Letter from Thomas Day, Clerk to the Guardians of the Bromsgrove Poor Law Union, to the Poor Law Commission.6 February 1844.

Meanwhile his wife Mary proposed to go out to work, leaving her older children to look after the younger ones.[631] The Commissioners were not happy with this arrangement citing '...the mischief of it as a precedent,' but they did sanction it for four months.[632]

The precedent, mischievous or not, was, as we have seen, established well before the Drinkwater case. It continued two years later when John Smith left two of his children, though not always the same two, in the workhouse more than once. He also was an agricultural labourer and had recently lost his wife. He lived in Finstall and was the father of six. His wages were 10 shillings a week '...and beer'. His two elder boys, George aged 12 and John aged 11, together earned a further four shillings and six pence weekly, but his other children were too young to contribute. When Smith had first applied for relief in June 1847 the guardians wished to grant him 16lbs of bread weekly for three months and they asked the Commissioners to sanction this. The Commissioners cut the time to one month and stated that if Smith required relief for longer some of his children should be taken into the workhouse for a short time.[633] We next hear of the Smith family in May the following year when Day wrote to the Commission saying that Smith's wages had for several weeks averaged only five shillings, partly because he had had to spend time looking after his children. Then having obtained a situation for his eldest boy where he earned his food, and with the guardians allowing his children Thomas and Emma to stay in the workhouse, he would be able

631   TNA: MH 12/13907/84, ff 132-133. Letter from Thomas Day, Clerk to the Guardians of the Bromsgrove Poor Law Union, to the Poor Law Commission. 6 June 1845.
632   TNA: MH 12/13907/85, f 134. Draft letter from the Poor Law Commission to Thomas Day, Clerk to the Guardians of the Bromsgrove Poor Law Union. 10 June 1845.
633   TNA: MH 12/13908/61, ff 88-89. Letter from Thomas Day, Clerk to the Guardians of the Bromsgrove Poor Law Union, to the Poor Law Commission. 1 June 1847.

to earn ten shillings a week even though he was not strong.[634] That summer he must have been readmitted to the workhouse as once again in September he left leaving two children behind, most probably Thomas and Harriet, as three years later in the 1851 census they are listed as inmates. The same census shows Smith still working as an agricultural labourer and living not far away from the workhouse in the Birmingham Road.[635] He and his two other daughters, Mary Ann and Emma, had been given a home by his younger brother George, a nailer, who was listed as head of a household which also included his 75-year-old father as well as his own family. There is no mention of John Smith's two older boys but as they were aged about 15 and 16 they had possibly left home.[636]

James Lane's case was similar to John Smith's though the outcome was very different. He too was a widowed agricultural worker, living in Pedmore, with five children under 13 years; James, Samuel, Frances, Thomas and Elizabeth, whose mother had died giving birth to her.[637] Lane earned 12 shillings a week, which was above the average wage for an agricultural worker in Worcestershire,[638] while his son James, aged 12, earned his food. Nevertheless, Lane was forced to apply for relief just before Christmas 1846. The guardians wished to grant him two shillings and 16lbs of bread weekly for three months but the Commission would allow it for four weeks only, saying that if further relief were required some children should go into the

634   TNA: MH 12/13908/243, ff 370-371. Letter from Thomas Day, Clerk to the Guardians of the Bromsgrove Poor Law Union, to the Poor Law Board. 1 May1848.
635   TNA: MH 12/13908/320, f 471. Draft letter from the Poor Law Board to Thomas Day, Clerk to the Guardians of the Bromsgrove Poor Law Union. 5 September 1848; and HO 107/2047, f 202, p 28. 1851 Census.
636   TNA: HO 107/2047, f 345, p 2. 1851 Census.
637   TNA: HO 107/2047, f 554, p 17. 1851 Census. `Frances' is listed as son `Frank'.
638   TNA: MH 12/13907/315, ff 478-479. Draft letter from the Poor Law Commission to Thomas Day, Clerk to the Guardians of the Bromsgrove Poor Law Union; annotation by J T Graves. 21 December 1846.

workhouse.[639] Lane appeared again before the guardians in January 1847. They were extremely sympathetic to his plight and Day reported that:

> Lane is a very hardworking, industrious man and bears an excellent character, he is very much attached to his children and is unwilling to part with them and rather than do so the Guardians believe he would enter the Workhouse with all of them. It should be borne in mind that the youngest is only nine months old and the mother died at birth. It is a matter of surprise how this man has continued to support himself this long without relief.... When before the Board, the Guardians felt so sorry for the poor fellow they subscribed a few shillings for him.[640]

This plea of Day's obviously had some effect and the Commission agreed that the relief granted in December should continue for another six weeks. After that they said they could not sanction the pecuniary part of it which presupposes that they would continue to allow bread.[641] So Lane's children were spared the workhouse. Most of the family, according to the 1851 census, were still living in Pedmore. James Lane is listed as head of household living with his mother-in-law Elizabeth Rea, aged 80, and all his children except the eldest, James, who at 16 could well have been in employment away from home, and, more worryingly, Elizabeth, who would by then have been four.[642] All of the examples here show out-relief allowed to the able-bodied working men who were both settled and resident in parishes

---

639   TNA: MH 12/13907/314, ff 477. Letter from Thomas Day, Clerk to the Guardians of the Bromsgrove Poor Law Union, to the Poor Law Commission. 21 December 1846.
640   TNA: MH 12/13908/4, ff 9-10. Letter from Thomas Day, Clerk to the Guardians of the Bromsgrove Poor Law Union, to the Poor Law Commission. 20 January 1847.
641   TNA: MH 12/13908/5, f 11. Draft letter from the Poor Law Commission to Thomas Day, Clerk to the Guardians of the Bromsgrove Poor Law Union. 1 February 1847.
642   TNA: HO 107/2047, f 554, p 17. Census. 1851.

belonging to the Bromsgrove Union. However, a key form of such out-relief was the placing of children in the workhouse which must have often been a heart breaking parental choice.

The next two cases are of men legally settled in Bromsgrove but living elsewhere. The minutes of the meeting of the Bromsgrove guardians held on 31 May 1847 record that Day, the union clerk, was requested to write to the Poor Law Commission regarding Thomas Winscott who lived in Monk Bretton, Yorkshire West Riding, who asked for relief claiming a lack of employment and high price of provisions, as well as having a dependent wife and nine children.[643] Winscott, aged 36, was a linen weaver who, when employed, averaged six shillings a week. This was augmented by two of his children, Sarah, aged 15, and George, 13, who each earned on average two shillings and sixpence a week. His wife Hannah, who was 37, had a month-old baby, Margaret, and was not in employment. The rest of the family were between the ages of two and ten. The guardians wished to allow Winscott ten shillings a week to keep him in Monk Bretton where the family had lived for nearly five years, as if they returned to Bromsgrove there would be no suitable job and the large family would have to be supported in the workhouse.[644] The Commission refused to sanction this, arguing that if the family completed five years' residence in Monk Bretton, they would become irremovable and therefore unfairly a charge on that union.[645] Not deterred by this Day wrote again in February 1848 saying that the Winscott family were still in the north and the Bromsgrove guardians wished to give them relief. The guardians argued that as Winscott was

643   WAAS: 6251/BA400/4. Bromsgrove Board of Guardians' Minute Book, 1847-1850. 31 May 1847.
644   TNA: MH 12/13908/63, ff 91-92. Letter from Thomas Day, Clerk to the Guardians of the Bromsgrove Poor Law Union, to the Poor Law Commission. 1 June 1847.
645   TNA: MH 12/13908/64, f 93. Draft letter from the Poor Law Commission to Thomas Day, Clerk to the Guardians of the Bromsgrove Poor Law Union. 12 June 1847.

a weaver by trade it was unlikely he would get much work in Bromsgrove and that providing a little temporary assistance now would prevent the family becoming a heavy burden on the rates at a later time.[646] The view of the Commission was that as long as the family were resident in Monk Bretton that was the parish which was bound to relieve them; they could not sanction the allowance of non-resident relief. However, it looks as though the family did remain in the north. The 1851 census shows them still living in Monk Bretton, and although there is no mention of three of the children there had been two more additions to the family since 1847. The three eldest children remaining at home were listed as linen handloom weavers like their father, so if they were all in work and with four wages coming in they perhaps no longer needed relief.[647]

Jon (John) O'Neil, although the son of Irish parents, had been born in Bromsgrove and this was therefore his place of settlement, even though he lived in Wigan in Lancashire where he was a handloom weaver in cotton or silk. In August 1841 he had been ordered by two justices to be removed to Bromsgrove but this had been delayed by the sickness of his wife Mary, and of the children, Henry, John and Elizabeth. In April 1842 he and his wife appeared on a Bromsgrove list of 206 '…unemployed and destitute able-bodied…' and were given relief even though they were living in Wigan.[648] By August they had been receiving six shillings and sixpence for many weeks from the Wigan guardians, which was a similar amount to what O'Neil would have earned from full time employment. The Poor Law Commission was worried that this might tempt him to stay out of work and as a result they strongly objected to the

---

646   TNA: MH 12/13908/207, ff 318-319. Letter from Thomas Day, Clerk to the Guardians of the Bromsgrove Poor Law Union, to the Poor Law Commission. 23 February 1848.
647   TNA: HO 107/2332, f 717. p 14. Census. 1851.
648   TNA: MH 12/13905/188, ff 235-237. Letter from Thomas Day, Clerk to the Guardians of the Bromsgrove Poor Law Union, to the Poor Law Commission. 30 April 1842.

continuation of relief unless these concerns were addressed.[649] Wigan finally managed to send the family back to Bromsgrove on 10 July 1843, but later that month O'Neil applied to the Bromsgrove guardians for assistance to move back to Wigan where he had an offer of work. He was asking for six shillings and sixpence a week which was less than the 12 shillings and sixpence weekly cost of keeping the family in the workhouse and so the guardians asked the Commission to sanction this arrangement.[650] The Commission replied that they disapproved of guardians assisting paupers back to parishes from which they had legally been removed as this was at odds with the object of relieving that parish of the burden of supporting them. It would not be expedient for the Bromsgrove guardians to administer relief outside their own union because if O'Neil again became chargeable in Wigan he would be liable to prosecution under the Vagrants Act.[651] There was also an objection to the paying of a direct allowance to an able-bodied man in an area where work was so abundant as to lead to employers offering wages below the level which a man would declare was enough to support himself. To give an allowance in such cases would provide the man with an advantage in respect of the other local weavers and such a practice could lead to an overall reduction in wages.[652]

However, after 1843 O'Neil and his family did manage to return to Wigan as in 1847 they were again under a removal order to Bromsgrove. Once again, in spite of their rebuttal four years earlier, the Bromsgrove guardians wished to support the family

---

649   TNA: MH 12/13905/276, ff 473-474. Letter from Thomas Day, Clerk to the Guardians of the Bromsgrove Poor Law Union, to the Poor Law Commission.10 October 1842
650   TNA: MH 12/13906/108, f 194. Letter from Thomas Day, Clerk to the Guardians of the Bromsgrove Poor Law Union, to the Poor Law Commission. 1 August 1843.
651   5 Geo IV, c. 83, s 3. *An Act for the Punishment of Idle and Disorderly Persons, Rogues and Vagabonds*, 1824.
652   TNA: MH 12/13906/109, ff 195-196. Draft letter from the Poor Law Commission to Thomas Day, Clerk to the Guardians of the Bromsgrove Poor Law Union. 5 August 1843.

in Wigan; they did not want them returning to the Bromsgrove workhouse as there was no hope of their obtaining work in the area.[653] The Commissioners replied, regretfully, that they could not sanction non-resident relief in order to prevent a removal order.[654] By March it appears that the family had returned to Bromsgrove; but were not to the workhouse. There is a note in the minutes of the guardians' meeting of 1 March 1847 ordering relief to be given to John O'Neil because of the infirmity of his wife and including a copy of the medical officer's certificate.

> 24 February 1847 John O'Neil's wife in consequence of Paralysis has for some years partially lost the use of one side which to a certain extent prevents her from performing her domestic and other duties.[655]

However, her illness did not debar an increase in family numbers, and the 1851 census, which shows the family once again living in Wigan, also lists two more children: May who was four and Alice, one. His son Henry at 14 years old was described as a drawer in a coal pit.[656]

Thus far I have discussed individual applicants for relief but in 1848 the workhouse was put under strain as a result of a depression in the nail-making trade caused by strikes at the firms in the Black Country which produced rod iron, the raw material from which nails were made.[657] In Bromsgrove whole families were nailmakers, the forge often being in an outhouse attached

---

653   TNA: MH 12/13908/8, f 15. Letter from Thomas Day, Clerk to the Guardians of the Bromsgrove Poor Law Union, to the Poor Law Commission. 20 January 1847.
654   TNA: MH 12/13908/9, f 16. Draft letter from the Poor Law Commission to Thomas Day, Clerk to the Guardians of the Bromsgrove Poor Law Union. 27 January 1847.
655   WAAS: 6251/BA400/4. Bromsgrove Board of Guardians' Minute Book, 1847-1850. 1 March 1847.
656   TNA: HO 107/2199, f 97, p 49. Census. 1851.
657   The image here is of the interior of a Bromsgrove nailmakers shed. From Sherard, R.H. The White Slaves of England, London, James Bowden, 1896, p 89.

Figure 9/2: Interior of a Bromsgrove nailmaker's shed.

to a nailer's cottage.[658] A large proportion of the population was involved and in 1840 there were 538 heads of households listed in the trade representing over 3000 nailworkers.[659]

In January 1848 Day wrote a long letter to the Poor Law Board about the numbers of paupers in the Bromsgrove Union. The master reported there were 292 paupers in the workhouse (compared with 130 in the same week the previous year) and there was not enough bedding or clothing for them. To make matters worse, accommodation in the workhouse had been reduced from its original quota of 320 to about 270 as one of the rooms had been licensed by the Bishop of Worcester for use as a chapel. Consequently the guardians had had to give out relief and requested the agreement of the Poor Law Board.[660] In reply the Board sanctioned the out relief which had already been given to ten able-bodied men but asked the guardians to adhere to the provisions of the outdoor labour test order in future.[661] This order, published in 1842, allowed

658   Ibid., p 86.
659   Kings and Cooper, Nailing in Bromsgrove, p 20.
660   TNA: MH 12/13908/176, ff 265-266. Letter from Thomas Day, Clerk to the Guardians of the Bromsgrove Poor Law Union, to the Poor Law Board. 24 January 1848.
661   TNA: MH 12/13908/177, f 267. Draft letter from the Poor Law Board to Thomas Day, Clerk to the Guardians of the Bromsgrove Poor Law Union. 29 January 1848.

out relief to able-bodied paupers who satisfied the test by doing physical work, like stone-breaking or oakum-picking.[662] Day sent the Board details of the arrangements which the guardians had made in accordance with this order: male paupers were to be employed at stone breaking and those with wives and children were to be employed at stone picking near the Lickey Hills. The Board was decidedly dismissive of these arrangements annotating Day's letter.

> I do not think the plan proposed a good one in any respect. The employment of men, women and children wandering about the country picking stones would be difficult to implement and it would benefit particular lands of the union.[663]

John Graves, Poor Law Inspector, who had recently visited the workhouse, wrote an internal letter to the Commissioners supporting Day's argument. He said that because of the influx of many able-bodied men, the master had been unable to preserve discipline, the house was overcrowded and there was a need of bedsteads and changes of clothes. The men had refused to break stones in the workhouse yard and as a result the ringleaders had been sent to prison for 21 days. Therefore, it had been necessary to send men out to pick stones and the farmers to whom they had been sent were not guardians. Moreover, the distress of the nailers was not of their own making: the nailmasters who both supplied iron to the nailmakers and then bought the finished nails from them, refused to pay the high price of iron caused by the ironmakers' strike, thus throwing the nailers out of work. Various charities and indeed the guardians themselves had bought iron to supply the nailers, and the nailmasters had been happy to buy the nails thus made. Without such relief the

662   *Eighth Annual Report of the Poor Law Commissioners, with appendices*, London 1842, p 103, Outdoor Labour Test Order, article 1.
663   TNA: MH 12/13908/188, ff 283-287. Letter from Thomas Day, Clerk to the Guardians of the Bromsgrove Poor Law Union, to the Poor Law Board.8 February 1848.

nailers who rented small tenements would have been forced into the workhouse and having sold their tools would have become permanent paupers being unable to take advantage once economic prospects improved. Annotations on the letter show the misgivings of the Board. They were worried that if the nailers had supplied the nailmasters with nails below the natural price, it would be in the interest of the latter for that state of affairs to continue.[664] It is clear the Commission preferred the guardians to use the outdoor labour test order rather than have them interfering in the economics of the nail trade.

Conclusion

The detailed case studies provided here show that both the Bromsgrove guardians and the central authorities accepted some degree of flexibility in applying the law and regulations in regard to out-door relief to able bodied paupers. Overall the Bromsgrove guardians were prepared to be more pragmatic than the Poor Law Commission and more willing to allow individual cases of outdoor relief for longer periods than the Commission would sanction. The guardians were often in favour of providing out relief as it resulted in less expenditure; by 1850 the weekly cost of keeping an indoor pauper was about six shillings compared with out relief at two shillings.[665] These cases also show that although the central authority were willing to allow out relief in special circumstances for paupers who were both settled and resident, they were far less inclined to do so in regard to those living away from their place of settlement.

Much as the Commission might have liked to apply the principles of the 1834 act more rigidly, circumstances invariably

---

664   TNA: MH 12/13908/189, ff 288-292. Letter from J T Graves, Poor Law Inspector, to Poor Law Board. 21 February 1848.
665   Brundage, p 91.

got in the way. In 1844 the Outdoor Relief Prohibitory Order attempted to end out relief for the able-bodied but never achieved its aim as the list of exceptions gave discretion to the guardians to avoid this.[666] Again in 1852 the Poor Law Board tried to tighten restrictions with their Outdoor Labour Test Order but the outcry from boards of guardians and their parliamentary supporters caused them to back pedal and apply the restrictions only to able-bodied males.[667] Actual prohibition of out relief for the able-bodied was a central authority aspiration rather than a fact of the new Poor Law. The guardians proved successful in pushing for discretion in the use of such out-door relief provision. The centre perhaps settled for holding the line where they could rather than seeking to enforce the unenforceable.

---

666   *Appendices to the Eleventh Annual Report of the Poor Law Commissioners*, pp 29-38, Appendix A. PP., 1845.
667   Brundage, p 91.

Index

Page numbers in *italic* refer to tables and those in **bold** denote figures.